NICK

Nick

A Montreal Life

EDITED BY
Dave Bist

INTRODUCTION BY
Mordecai Richler

CARICATURES BY
Aislin

Véhicule Press

EDITORIAL GROUP
Dave Bist, L. Ian MacDonald, Terry Mosher, Stephen Phizicky

The Gazette

So many people made this book possible—Nick's friends,
colleagues, and family, and all the book's contributors.
Véhicule Press would like to thank *The Gazette* for its exceptional
generosity and support, in particular, Michael Goldbloom, publisher,
and Alan Allnutt, editor-in-chief.

Cover design and concept: J.W. Stewart
Front cover photo courtesy of *The Gazette*
Back cover photo courtesy of the Auf der Maur family
Typesetting: Simon Garamond
Printing: AGMV-Marquis Inc.

Copyright © the authors and illustrators 1998
Dépôt légal, Bibliothèque nationale du Québec
and the National Library of Canada, 4th quarter 1998

CANADIAN CATALOGUING IN PUBLICATION DATA
Auf der Maur, Nick, 1942-1998.
Nick : a Montreal life
(Dossier Québec series)
ISBN 1-55065-114-5
1. Montreal (Quebec)—Miscellanea.
2. Auf der Maur, Nick, 1942-1998.
I. Aislin. II. Title. III. Series.
FC2947.35.A84 1998   971.4'2804'092   C98-901039-2
F1054.5.M845A84 1998

PUBLISHED BY
Véhicule Press
P.O.B. 125, Place du Parc Station
Montreal, Quebec H2W 2M9

http://www.cam.org/~vpress

DISTRIBUTED BY
General Distribution Services
325 Humber College Blvd.
Toronto, Ontario M9W 7C3

Printed in Canada on alkaline paper.

Contents

PREFACE
(L. Ian MacDonald) 11

INTRODUCTION
Remembering Nick 15
(Mordecai Richler)

NICK ON BEING NICK
Spokesman to outside world... 23

Tribute: Mark Starowicz 27

ON BEING A DAD
Dear Melissa... 33
Hopelessly old-fashioned dad... 36
Bass guitar indulgence... 38
On tour with my daughter... 41
Melissa loved rock stars long before
she became one 44

Tribute: Josh Freed 47
Tribute: Nathalie Petrowski 49

MONTREALERS
Mayor a figure of hope in golden years of youth 55
When it's beyond tears... 57
Some 'wooden' think joke on Drapeau funny 59
Newspaper job an eye-opener... 62
Friend's death during storm hits hard 65

Tribute: Warren Allmand 69
Tribute: John Lynch-Staunton 71

POLITICS
Voting day hard on the candidate 75
Referendum campaign leaves no hard feelings 77
What's in a name? A word? 79
Paranoia, grovelling and other election joys 82
A little humility is healthy for politicians 85
In Brussels, I lied to Bourassa about his chances 87

Tribute: Allan Fotheringham 91

MEETING THE FAMOUS
Fruit, as in fruitcake…a visit with
Libya's Col. Khadafy 97
The day I fought with Jack Kerouac 100
The evening I drank with Rudolf Nureyev
and felt his behind 103

Tribute: Conrad Black 107
Tribute: Margaret Davidson 109

HISTORY
First "dome" was house of horrors 115
Through the past darkly … 118
Of magpies, chatterboxes, and gazettes 121
Big chunk of our history is wrapped up
in the Angus Shops 124
Do you read this column regularly? … 127
Twin towers of two churches reflect resiliency… 130
In the heyday of taverns, Toe's was biggest and busiest 133

Tribute: Terry Mosher (Aislin) 137

NAPS
Sofa so good: No joy equals afternoon nap 141
It's time to switch the blankets… 143

Tribute: Juan Rodriguez 147
Tribute: Brian Stewart 149

Our City
When Schnozzola played the Point 155
Expo 67: The legend lives in the memories... 157
Anti-anglophone acts should be condemned... 159
Setting the record straight... 162
Without work, without hope... 164
Some say they're pests, but squirrels can
gnaw at your heart 167
Barbecue-chicken debate leaves ex-pats salivating 170
Sight of ravaged trees is heartbreaking 173

Tribute: Leon Harris 177

Peeves
I'm raked over coals over latest hot potato 183
Save us from the foolish rituals of the barbecue 185
I'm just a city boy... 187

Tribute: Benoit Aubin 190

Quebec
Frenglish winners will take a repast 195
Image of tolerance has been scratched 198
Days of Duplessis very like our own 201
A date from our history that can't be forgotten 204
An extraordinary man shaped exciting times 206

Tribute: Oliver Irwin 209

Sports
Rocket Richard riot rocked Montreal 30 years ago 217
Spring can't really be sprung until Canadiens are
out of the playoffs 220
Ball-speed argument has them hopping mad 222
Millionaire hockey players owe a lot to Doug Harvey 225
Speaking of the Stanley Cup... 228

More data about Montreal's role as birthplace of hockey 231
As a leader in sports... 234
Babe Ruth once batted for Ahuntsic...237

PETS
Time for a cat-and-squirrel game 243
Kitty-litter box hits the fan over church-cat controversy 246
Pets take centre stage at my family's holiday dinner 249

Tribute: Brian Mulroney 253

HOLIDAYS
Gift shopping left me 'briefly' embarrassed... 257
A Dutch treat starts the Christmas season 259
Kitchen heresy is in bad taste...262

Tribute: Mark Phillips 265

HATS
We trend-setters don't talk through our hats 269
My hats have turned up but the mystery only deepens 272
In a country built by hats... 274

Tribute: Stephen Phizicky 277

LIFE
Sake warms up the spy business 281
Summer's arrival recalls long-lost days... 284
Beware the red (tie) menace... 287
Today, we ask: Was that really me? 290
Days of the strap and Sabre jets 292
Sex and the gap-toothed woman 294
The inexpressible joy of ridiculing lawyers 297
The toothache that turned a grown man
into a quivering baby 300
How I got my big break on an unsinkable story 303

Tribute: Hubert Bauch 307
Tribute: Jacob Richler 309

HABITS

Almost quitting smoking was a success—sort of 315
Never mind jogging, just munch an onion 318
Stand up for what you believe in, even if it's Donald Duck 321
My recipe for healthy living... 324
Why I steal peanuts from bars to feed the squirrels 327

Tribute: Margo MacGillivray 329
Tribute: Lisa Van Dusen 331

CLAUDE BALOUNE

Disenchantment with foreign affairs... 335
Apocalyptic argument produces a revelation...338
We're fair-weather fans—but who knows why? 341
Of course history repeats itself... 344

Tribute: Anthony Wilson-Smith 347

TRAVELLING

Breaking the sound barrier... 351
We're not unique 354
Sipping from Imelda's teacups 358
Far-flung travellers' tales... 361
Don't make enemas while abroad 364
I could have been in Havana with the Pope 367

Tribute: Brian McKenna 371
Tribute: Robin Siobhan McKenna 375

FAMILY

That first job is a major step toward adulthood... 379
Turkeys Switzerland-bound... 382
City kid goes back in time... 384
A child's dashed hopes live on in recollections 387

A Christmas tradition passes to new hands 389
Lunch comes to a halt when my mother starts to yodel 391
Mama at 89... 394
'Any day now' was my father's mantra 397

Tribute: Dr. Roger Tabah 401

FIGHTING CANCER
Confronting my mortality... 405
Kurt Cobain had a shotgun... 408
It's all a matter of taste... 411
I was Auf der Wall: Hallucinations... 413
Discovery of brain tumour... 416
Brainstorming... 419
From the friends I've never met 423

NICK'S MOTHER
Theresia Auf der Maur 429

AFTERWORD
Melissa Auf der Maur's Eulogy for Her Father 431

Preface

NICK AUF DER MAUR was in journalism and politics. He thought there was honour in both. He also thought both should be fun.

And they were. He had a lot of fun writing his column, first at *The Montreal Star*, then at *The Gazette*, and for a time at *The Montreal Daily News* before returning to *The Gazette* in the 1990s. He was also in broadcasting at CBC television as well as CJAD radio, and he was a gifted documentary film maker and interviewer, who had a way of being in the story without ever getting in the way.

But he was primarily a newspaper columnist, not a crusader, but a storyteller in love with his city, Montreal. When he wrote about other cities, he always used Montreal as his point of reference.

Nick wrote about his city the way Jimmy Breslin wrote about New York. It wouldn't have worked anywhere else, but there were large moments of universal truth. Nick's columns had a beginning, a middle, and an end. And every one had a purpose. They don't teach that in journalism school, though they should.

He also wrote with facility, with the speed of a police reporter knocking out a story on deadline. Much of his legwork was done in bars and many of his notes were written on the backs of napkins.

But when he sat down to write, he was ready to write, and he wrote easily and fast.

Surprisingly, this is the first collection of Nick's columns, though it is his second book. His first book, *The Billion Dollar Game*, a blistering exposé of the scandalous costs incurred by the Montreal Olympic Games in 1976, sparked a commission of inquiry and established Nick as an international authority on what a city shouldn't do in staging the Olympics.

The title "Nick" was a natural. And since he led "A Montreal Life," that became the subtitle. Though its publication is posthumous, the planning for this book began in the final weeks of Nick's life. As it happened, there was a meeting of the editorial group at Ziggy's bar on Crescent Street only a couple of hours before his death in April of 1998.

Dave Bist of *The Gazette* has combed through Nick's columns in three newspapers and assembled the best and most representative pieces from every corner of his varied life. Without Dave's dedication and professional editing skills, not to say his affection for Nick, this book would never have come together. It's all here, though. The people he met, from Jack Kerouac to Rudolf Nureyev. From Melissa growing up, to Nick's abhorrence of baked potatoes in aluminum foil.

Terry Mosher has selected many of the best Aislin drawings of Nick over the years, from the young rake who cut a swath through the city in the '60s, to the world-weary, but still mischievous figure, who could always muster that famous beaver-tooth grin beneath one of his trademark Borsalinos.

Simon Dardick of Véhicule Press agreed immediately and with great enthusiasm to become publisher. This book is appropriately part of Véhicule's 25th anniversary season publishing English-language books in Montreal. Nick would have approved of that.

 Simon's own connection with Nick dated back to the early 1970s, when Simon and Nancy Marrelli, his wife and business partner, had the misfortune to invite him to their country place one weekend with the idea of introducing him to a young lady friend of theirs.

Stephen Phizicky, as executor of Nick's estate, faithfully represented Nick's interests as well as those of his daughter, Melissa.

There are others to be thanked, notably Michael Goldbloom and Alan Allnutt, respectively publisher and editor-in-chief of *The Gazette*, which is both marketing and distributing this book. In his final years, Nick was a freelancer at *The Gazette*, but more to the point, as Michael Goldbloom put it—"He was family."

The Gazette and Véhicule Press are donating their net profits from *Nick: A Montreal Life* to the Nick Auf der Maur Memorial Fund at the Montreal General Hospital. Major booksellers such as Paragraphe Books, through Richard King, are also contributing part of their normal retail markup.

The Fund was the memorial Nick wanted. Income from the principal is to be allocated to underprivileged cancer patients, who wouldn't, for example, have the means to put up a visiting relative or buy a wig after chemotherapy treatments. The Fund is co-chaired by Melissa Auf der Maur, former Prime Minister Brian Mulroney, and former federal cabinet minister Serge Joyal, who once ran for mayor of Montreal at the top of Nick's ticket in the Municipal Action Group.

Nick's own royalties, with Melissa's generous agreement, are also earmarked for the fund. And Nick's friends have all contributed their stories. What friends and what stories.

Mordecai Richler has graciously written the introduction, and his son Jacob, who ran with Nick in his last years, provides the perspective of the next generation. Warren Allmand, Benoit Aubin, Hubert Bauch, Conrad Black, Margaret Davidson, Josh Freed, Allan Fotheringham, Leon Harris, Oliver Irwin, John Lynch-Staunton, Margo MacGillivray, Brian McKenna and his daughter, Robin, Terry Mosher, Brian Mulroney, Nathalie Petrowski, Mark Phillips, Stephen Phizicky, Juan Rodriguez, Mark Starowicz, Brian Stewart, Dr. Roger Tabah, Lisa Van Dusen, and Anthony Wilson-Smith add their tributes.

The last word belongs to Melissa. Nick probably wasn't cut out for married life, but he was a wonderful father, and his daughter was the centre of his life. Nick and Linda Gaboriau were always united as parents, and we are grateful for Linda's generous contribution of family photos.

Nick's readers were also among his friends and contributors to his column. When he wrote about the best barbecue chicken in town, he received hundreds of letters and phone calls, more than any other column he had written until then.

When he became ill over Christmas of 1996, he decided to share the news with his readers. "Why not?" he said at the time. "My whole life has been lived in public." Some of his best work was done in the last year of his life. He faced his illness with courage and good humour, and he touched a deeply responsive chord in his readers.

One of the things I always found amazing about Nick was how much he knew about Montreal. I didn't know where he knew it from, he just knew it. And one of the things I learned from him was that it's okay to write about your daughter, provided you're not exploiting her, and providing it illuminates the story.

My seven-year-old daughter was quite struck by all the coverage of Nick's passing and his funeral on television. "Daddy," she said, "I didn't know Nick had so many friends." She had met him only once, in a radio studio, when he refused to talk down to her, told her some terrible jokes, and engaged her at her own level. It was his magical way with kids.

We were walking down Ste. Catherine Street, the day after Nick's funeral when Gracie asked a very good question: "Why is Ste. Catherine Street called Ste. Catherine Street?"

"I don't know, sweetie," I replied. "We must ask Nick."

L. Ian MacDonald

Author and broadcaster L. Ian MacDonald writes a column in *The Gazette* and *The Globe and Mail*.

Introduction

Remembering Nick

Mordecai Richler

*The next big event was the October Crisis, and many of those same journalists—
sent here because of their previous Montreal experience—sought me out. My status
was enhanced by the fact that I had been one of those arrested under the War
Measures Act and, arguably, I knew as much about the radical movement as anyone,
police included.*
    —Nick Auf der Maur, Gazette, April 27, 1996

ROOTED IN A SPRAWLING HOUSE on Kingston Hill, Surrey, in 1970, one
evening I took a phone call from *Life* magazine in New York. Could I leave
for Montreal immediately? I flew into town two weeks after the funeral of
then Quebec Labour Minister Pierre Laporte, who had been kidnapped
and murdered by the FLQ. Those copycat revolutionaries were still holding
British Trade Commissioner James Cross. The evening of my arrival in
Montreal enthusiastic friends drove me past consulates, public buildings,
and certain rich private mansions, where battle-ready soldiers stood guard.
"There are a lot of people who are insulted," I was told, "because they
aren't considered important enough to have troops posted outside their
door."

Strolling through Westmount it was impossible not to note the plethora
of mountain mansions for sale, seemingly unmovable at fire sale prices.
Everybody knowledgeable, according to the gossip, was going liquid. A
French Canadian novelist I had known for years invited me to lunch at his
house in Outremont. "It is no longer a question," he assured me, "of if we
separate, but when. Our children no longer call themselves Canadian, but
Québécois."

I met Prime Minister Pierre Trudeau for lunch in Ottawa. I ate breakfast
with Claude Ryan at the Ritz-Carlton and the admirable Senator Thérèse
Casgrain gave me an hour of her time. John Scott, who was then editor of

Time Canada, arranged for me to meet René Lévesque for drinks in an East End bar. "I should warn you," said Scott, "that he will be at least an hour late." But Lévesque, who was still running in place on the political periphery in those days, turned up on time—not for me, certainly, but for *Life* magazine.

On first meeting, I took the chain-smoking, obviously high-strung Lévesque to be an authentic people's tribune. As I wrote in *Life*, he struck me as a man effortlessly in touch with the bookkeeper with sour breath, the wasting QLC clerk with dandruff, the abandoned mother of five, the truck driver on welfare, in fact with all the discontented lives. Later I did learn that the man had many sides to him. But, back in 1970, we were hardly into our second drink when Lévesque, determined to dissociate the Parti Québécois from the FLQ, dismissed them as "a bunch of bums." At the time, I had no idea that seven years earlier, when the FLQ was much given to planting bombs in mailboxes that could explode in the faces of children, Lévesque had had said to André Laurendeau, "You've got to hand it to them, they're courageous, those guys."

I read off a list of political notables already interviewed to an old friend. He was unimpressed. "I think you should check things out with Nick Auf der Maur," he said.

"Nick who?"

"Auf der Maur. It means 'Off-the-Wall' in German."

"He's a German?"

"Of Swiss origin, actually."

So I became another one of those reporters, who, taking the Montreal pulse, made sure to consult Dr. Auf der Maur. In those days Nick's surgery was the now defunct basement Le Bistro on Mountain Street, and that's where we first got together. Terry Mosher was also there. At the time Nick and Terry were both involved in producing an irreverent political monthly called *The Last Post*. Nick was both entertaining and informative that evening, but I took him for an unreliable charmer, quick but lightweight, and it never occurred to me that one day we would become good friends.

After I quit England and settled in Montreal with my family in 1972, I did run into Nick from time to time—at Au Cépage, Woody's, Winnie's, or other stations of the imbibers' cross—where I had usually gone to shoot the breeze with other journalists who were already good friends, Ian Mayer or Doris Giller; and I continued to keep my distance from Nick. But slowly, inevitably, I did succumb to his irreverence, his gifts as a raconteur, his sure eye for the absurd, his jaunty manner, what I took to be an unacknowledged inner sadness, as well as his unmatched knowledge of Montreal lore. To come clean, in need of confirming some recherché Montreal factoid, I sent a bucket down Nick's memory well more than once. As he was a compulsive peddler of inane jokes, I also came to rely on him for knee-slappers that would make an intelligent reader wince, if I required one for a novel-in-progress.

Nick was a throwback. An atavism. One of the last of a breed of hard-drinking, honest but cynical reporters, usually divorced and scrabbling to keep up with child support payments, who—when Nick was still a bright-eyed copy boy—used to seek succour from their sorrows in the Montreal Press Club in the old Mount Royal Hotel. If an irate wife or girlfriend phoned the club, asking for somebody called Ian or Sam, Joe Servant, the incomparable bartender, would cover the mouthpiece, look directly at whichever delinquent was wanted, and ask in a loud voice, "Is Ian/or Sam here?" As a rule, Ian or Sam would respond with a throat-cutting gesture, and Joe, uncovering the mouthpiece, would report, "Sorry, he isn't here."

Those, those were the days when the tabloid *Montreal Herald* had already folded, but the *Star* was still with us, as were *Weekend* magazine and *Time* Canada. Reporters from *La Presse* and *Le Devoir* were also Press Club regulars, as were Tim Burke, Bobby Stewart, and many a CBC hack who then laboured downtown in the old Ford Hotel.

By common consent the most respected Press Club regular was Dink Carroll, sports columnist for *The Gazette*. I remember once sailing into the club for a nightcap in the early morning hours, and joining Dink at the bar at a time when airplane hijackings were our daily dread. "Three things worry me," said Dink.

"Terrorism. Inflation … and Peggy," who was his wife.

"Why Peggy?" I asked, concerned.

"I promised her I'd be home by 7 o'clock tonight."

Nick, of course, seldom got home before 4 a.m., if then.

Item: Retired MUC detective Kevin McGarr once told me that, years ago, when he and his patrol car partner wanted to know where the illegal after hours drinking clubs were they relied, in the absence of a bird dog, on Nick. Parked near whichever watering hole Nick favoured in those days, they would wait until he emerged at closing time, usually accompanied, said McGarr, by a fetching young woman. And, inevitably, Nick would lead them to a blind pig.

The unelected spokesman of after dark downtown Montreal, Nick was alert to its pulse, his ear attuned to its voices. He seemed to be on convivial terms with everybody, from the city's movers and shakers, through its nuns, detectives, and professional athletes, to its layabouts, felons, pimps, drug dealers and call girls. All of them, it seemed, responded to his appetite for fun.

Item: Nick once told me that years ago he and Conrad Black, out on the town, inadvertently repaired to a gay bar for drinks. Taken for unwelcome intruders, they were asked to leave, but an irate Black insisted on their democratic right to stay as long as they pleased. And so they did.

Nick had a real gift for writing fluent, anecdotal columns, but too much should not be made of them. He never threatened to become Montreal's Mayhew. So I sometimes scolded him for not working harder at his stuff. For being guilty of clunky sentences. For being satisfied too often by prose that was no more than functional. For accepting the first adjective that came to mind. His laziness irritated me.

Item: Seated on his customary bar stool at Winnie's with his usual stack of newspapers, sporting what had become his signature Borsalino, one day Nick asked me: "How many hours a day do you work?"

"Three," I said.

His eyes lit with glee. Nick said, "I only work three hours a week."

The truth is Nick knocked off his columns on the fly, and I gradually came to accept he put most of his energy and art into being Nick. Endearing prankster. Boulevardier. Bar-room raconteur. Bottom-pincher. But beyond what came to be role-playing of a sort, Nick was also a serious reader and an intelligent observer. A reporter with a forgiving feel for the human comedy.

Florence and I had Nick out to our cottage on Lake Memphremagog more than once, but he seldom ventured outside where there was no asphalt, no intruding traffic, no twitching neon signs. Instead, all those goddamn flower beds. Intimidating trees. A threatening lake. Unlike Crescent or St. Denis Street at 3 a.m., it could be dangerous out there. Hedgehogs and porcupines were not unknown. A guy minding his own business, nursing a vodka and cranberry juice, just might be confronted by a deer.

During the summer months when Florence and I are rooted in the Townships, we spend one day a week in Montreal. We usually drive into town early Thursday morning, and then I would look forward to catching up with Nick at Winnie's late in the afternoon. I could count on finding him seated on his customary bar stool, fielding phone calls. Or pronouncing on our fevers for a reporter from Stockholm or Madrid. Or sifting through his stack of newspapers. Or trading insults with our mutual friend Richard Holden. The two of them hollering. Eventually, in dire need of exercise, we would cross the street to Ziggy's Pub, where we would continue to mull over the day's political idiocies; and I saw no good reason why our enjoyable Thursday afternoon bantering should not go on forever. Then, a week before Christmas 1996, Nick wrote in *The Gazette*, "…while in the shower, I felt a small lump in my neck, near the jawbone." It proved to be a malignant tumour, squamous cell carcinoma, in the back of his left tonsil, near the larynx. So Nick had to be zapped with some heavy duty radiation treatments, which left him with no taste buds and only a 50-50 chance of survival. He gave up his 40-to-60 Gitanes-a-day habit and found it all but impossible to swallow one vodka and cranberry juice, never mind his daily ration. His manner, once boyishly reckless, was now tentative, understandably apprehensive.

Then the carcinoma recurred, and the following autumn Nick was obliged to endure a 14-hour operation in the Montreal General, and he was hardly over that ordeal when he was struck by a brain tumour. And lung cancer.

And a tumour pressing on his spine.

I phoned Nick from our flat In London last spring to say we would be home in a few weeks. "We both hope to see you then, Nick."

"I will no longer be here," he said.

Nick went to an early grave, his departure from this world—for which he had such appetite—protracted, punishing, but managed, on his part, with uncommon grace. Nick was a cherished friend. An original. And the columns collected here are as near as we will ever get to a self-portrait of an endearing, if sometimes exasperating, man, blessed with all the right instincts and prejudices.

When Nick's death was announced our two truculent cultures were in agreement for once: Montreal was diminished.

Nick on Being Nick

Spokesman to the outside world: There's a free lunch in lively anecdotes

[Saturday, April 27, 1996]

LAST FALL, this is how *The Independent* led off a full-page pre-Referendum analysis of "the Canadian situation:"

"A middle-aged man in a pea-green shirt, matching Donald Duck tie and a brown fedora was sitting at a bar in downtown Montreal reading *La Presse*, a newspaper that describes itself as 'the biggest French daily in the Americas.' The man was chuckling. 'They say Canadians are dull and boring,' he said in English. 'Actually we're quite insane.' Nick Auf der Maur, a former city councillor …"

Well, there you have it, an example of how, through a combination of circumstance, I somehow have emerged over the years as a spokesman for Montreal to the outside world.

I write this with all due modesty, because I certainly never planned on this. It's a role I just sort of naturally fell into.

Whenever outside journalists come to town, whether singly, on a feature assignment, or in hordes during big news events, they call on me for two principal reasons:

They know I can usually give them all pertinent background information more or less objectively, plus colourful anecdotes and quotes as required.

Also, I can show them the town.

Whoever said there is no free lunch and dinner doesn't know this fortuitous little sideline I have developed over the past 30 years.

I suppose it started when, as a cub reporter at *The Gazette*, I was assigned to cover Expo 67. Every day and every week, there was a new batch of foreign journalists in town and, like every Montrealer, I took delight in showing them around and sharing any information I could.

And, of course, journalists like to talk to journalists they think they can trust.

The next big event was the October Crisis, and many of these same journalists—sent here because of their previous Montreal experience—

sought me out. My status was enhanced by the fact that I had been one of those arrested under the War Measures Act and, arguably, I knew as much about the radical underground as anyone, police included.

I already had been used to being of service to TV, newspaper and magazine reporters, but during that period I helped writer Brian Moore, who had worked for *The Gazette* in the 1950s, write a novel about separatist radicals. It was called *The Revolution Script* and it wasn't much good.

To get authentic background, Moore would get me to bring radical separatist kids to the Stanley Tavern. He had a peculiar method of working. He'd sit with us for an hour, buying beers, then he'd scurry back to the Mount Royal Hotel and write down his notes from memory for a half-hour, then he'd come back for another hour, and so on. I think I spent a week with him at the Stanley Tavern and he produced a novel from the experience.

My next big era of contact with foreign journalists came in the period leading up to the Olympics. By this time, not only was I a journalist, but I had managed to get elected to city council and become the leading critic of Games construction. Plus, I wrote a book on the subject.

Well, they were practically beating down my door to get to me.

I remember once, when I lived on Esplanade Avenue, opposite Fletcher's Field, Linda, my Boston-born wife woke me up at 11 in the morning to tell me there was an ABC-TV crew at the door wanting to interview me.

"Tell them to wait in the park," I mumbled groggily.

"But it's Pierre Salinger," she said excitedly. Salinger had been John F. Kennedy's speechwriter.

Sometimes, outside journalists reciprocated and helped me.

During the construction of Olympic Stadium, I could never get on site, despite the fact that I was a city councillor, or more likely because of that.

But when Morley Safer and his CBS "60 Minutes" crew came to do an advancer, they insisted on doing their interview with me inside the stadium. That was the first time I got an inside view of the building that was at the heart of the book I was just about finished writing.

The Olympics brought notoriety not only to Montreal, but to me.

When Los Angeles sought the Olympics, their city council brought me down as an expert witness, and a local political booked me on every conceivable radio and TV show during a week of committee hearings.

In a major editorial, the *Los Angeles Times* advised authorities to heed the man from Montreal.

To this day, whenever any city in the world mulls over the idea of bidding for the summer Olympics—Bam! I'm all over the local newspapers and airwaves.

In short, all this activity put my name and phone numbers in an awful lot of address books and Rolodexes around the world.

I think at one time or another, I've entertained journalists from all the leading newspapers in the world, been on TV from Australia to Cuba, from Japan to Finland.

Not a few times, I'd be sitting in a bar like Winnie's, and the barmaid would answer the phone and say: "It's for you. Long distance. The BBC." Or Australia. Or Switzerland. They all seem to know where to find me.

I suspect that in every press club in the world, there's graffiti in the toilets that says: "When in Montreal, call Nick."

It goes without saying, that my expertise in Montreal dining and nightlife is a major factor in all this.

More than once, I've heard from an American reporter that so-and-so was trying to get his foreign Canadian bureau moved from Toronto to Montreal because of a short visit with me here.

A few years back, a *National Geographic* writer came here to do a feature on Montreal. He interviewed me in an earnest manner, one that I took to be *Geographic* detachment.

But before he could finish his assignment, he was recalled to Washington and another sent in his stead.

A little later, I was sitting in Grumpy's one evening when a man walked in with his luggage, direct from the airport. It was the new *Geographic* guy and he had been listening to the tapes made by the previous one, and decided—to heck with formalities!—he'd get right down to where the action was.

He stayed for three months, and I kept thinking: "What a terrific job— he gets paid to spend three months out on the town with me."

A few years ago, Murray Sales, the Japan-based Australian journalist, was in town to do a PBS-British TV documentary on the transcontinental train. They filmed an interview/conversation over dinner with me and a *La Presse* columnist. When it was over and the crew had packed up, I invited Sales out on the town, having noticed during dinner that he liked the grape.

When Jimbo's closed at 3 a.m., I asked him whether he'd like to go to an illegal all-night bar full of lowlife. Love it.

We hustled over to this St. Denis Street place I knew and arrived just in time to catch the end of a police raid and people being led out in handcuffs.

"Terribly sorry," I said to him. "You would have loved it. Weird people."

Just then, a cop came up to me and whispered, "I hear they're opening a new one" at such and such an address.

We jumped in a cab, but when we arrived there, the place looked dead. No sign of any patrons.

We sat down, ordered drinks and when we tried to pay, the waiter said: "Mais non, Monsieur Auf der Maur, you are our very first customer. It's on the house."

"I love this town," Sales exclaimed. "It's not like Toronto. 'City councillor cuts ribbon to open illegal all-night bar.'"

"I'm not here in that capacity," I told him. "I'm here as a fact-finding columnist."

He eventually wrote up that incident in the *New Statesman*.

My international exposure as a Montreal mouthpiece has had some unexpected results.

One day, the Swiss consul-general called me up and, in a pained tone, said: "Every time I pick up a Swiss newspaper and see a story about Quebec and Canada, your name is in it."

Now the Swiss are very concerned about propriety. He said he was distressed because he feared that one day a visiting Swiss journalist would find out there was an arrest warrant out for me in Switzerland.

It's a convoluted story, but I was a Swiss draft-dodger.

"We must do something about it," the consul-general said. "We don't want scandal."

So the next day, I filled in some papers, paid 28 francs, and a couple of weeks later received my Swiss military service book, which noted that I was officially on leave of absence, retroactive 18 years.

[Tribute]

I Met My Older Brother
When I was 17

Mark Starowicz

SAINT PATRICK'S BASILICA, capacity 2,800, was overflowing. I counted six television crews and 11 photographers. A generation was gathering with the solemnity of musketeers burying D'Artagnan.

This was the unbearable day I dreaded through Nick's 16-month fight with cancer. His friends Stephen Phizicky, Brian McKenna, Brian Stewart, and Jake Richler were equally devastated. If Nick Auf der Maur wasn't invincible, then none of us was. Stephen announced that Nick wanted his closest circle to wear a selection of his trademark Donald Duck ties at the service.

To the organ's hymn, we smoothed our new ties and watched the extraordinary procession enter: altar boys, a sacristan, two priests, a Roman Catholic monsignor, the Roman Catholic bishop, the Anglican archbishop of Montreal filed past. Nick Auf der Maur—champion of radical causes, the Don Juan of 1,000 loves and the Falstaff of 10,000 nights—was being buried with the honours of a field marshal.

You don't have to be born with an older brother. You can find him later in your life. In 1965, I was 17, a copy clerk at *The Montreal Gazette*. Nick was 23, a reporter with an unkempt mustache and a grin like a roguish beaver. He was the son of Swiss immigrants who had lived hard times, and his last job was as a waiter.

He undertook my education.

How to survive on $32.50 a week: "Grab the Rotary Club assignments, they serve chicken," and "Listen to old reporters' stories respectfully, they'll pay for your beer." He introduced me to René Lévesque, we met Phil Ochs, Mary McCarthy, John Lennon, activists, and artists. Every night at the bar he would pull an improbable friend out of the haze of his Gitanes smoke: a Ghanaian poet, a disgraced Algerian journalist. He guided me though first loves, first crises and first defeats.

Nick made everything sound possible, even urgent: Africa, China, distant wars, great causes. And he was there for me—for all of us—for the next three decades, a human harbour where you felt a place had been kept, just for you, whenever you chose to return.

"My life has been so good" he said last fall, "and I've had so much fun—it should be illegal." Some of it was.

The young Nick knew every firebrand in Quebec, and kept landing in jail alongside them after sundry demonstrations. He boasted he never paid a phone bill, yet never got cut off because the Mounties needed to tap his line. It also got him imprisoned in the fruitless War Measures Act roundup of 1970.

Only in Montreal can you run for office with a résumé like that. He defeated Jean Drapeau's right-hand man for city councillor and for 20 years reigned as the "Downtown Councillor," although he switched parties more often than people trade in cars. He tried to run provincially, then federally, but failed. One constant was the sisters of the Grey Nuns Convent in his riding, who didn't seem to mind his Rabelaisian lifestyle, and kept voting for him. Finally defeated in 1994, Nick said: "What the Grey Nuns giveth, the Grey Nuns taketh away."

His *Gazette* columns vividly chronicled the life of his beloved city. But he had an even stronger passion. In 1972, Nick and the writer Linda Gaboriau had a daughter, Melissa. He concocted intricate educational voyages with Melissa. One year it was British naval museums, which he admitted turned out more of a tour of pubs near naval installations. Melissa became an accomplished musician, and a rock star with Courtney Love's band, Hole.

His lifelong cause was civility between French and English, and his achievement was to breach a municipal fortress of secrecy and corruption with democracy and openness. If his politics seemed capricious sometimes, he responded: "I've always fought for the underdog. It's the underdog that kept changing."

As the solemn recession began, the ten bells of St. Patrick's began ringing. Outside the bells mingled with a New Orleans band, and police lights flashed. The man arrested under the War Measures Act rated a full police escort, conducting the congregation down René Lévesque

Boulevard, from a basilica to a Crescent Street bar.

The largest non-state funeral in modern Montreal wasn't for a corporate president, or someone who achieved high office or financial wealth. It was for someone who adopted any stray soul and measured his wealth in friends. Three thousand of them stood in the sunlight, under the pealing bells. I turned to my wife, Anne, whose eyes were also moist, and said, "He did it again!"

Mark Starowicz heads CBC Television's documentary unit and the Canadian History Project. He was editor of the *McGill Daily* 1968/69. He began in journalism at *The Gazette* and with Nick and a group of Montreal journalists, he helped set up *The Last Post*, a national magazine. He lives in Toronto, has two daughters, and a collection of Donald Duck comics second only to the one Nick amassed.

On Being a Dad

Nick and Melissa, September 1984.
Photo by Len Sidaway.

Dear Melissa . . . Birthday card was summit's first agreement

[Wednesday, March 20, 1985]

TURNING 13 is one of those epochal birthdays, like the 21st, 30th and 50th. (The older you get, the farther apart the epochs.)

A couple of weeks ago, I was talking to my daughter Melissa about her 13th birthday on St. Patrick's Day.

She said she didn't particularly want a party this year, something I just put down to adolescent whim. I had been invited to the Shamrock Summit gala in Quebec City on her birthday and I asked if she would mind if I went.

Not at all.

Changing the subject, I asked what she wanted for a birthday present.

"A birthday card from the prime minister of Canada and the president of the United States," she said casually.

I thought that a rather presumptuous if not impudent request.

But over the next few days I kept thinking about it.

Her mother, Linda, is an American; part Boston Irish, part French. I'm Canadian. That makes Melissa a dual citizen. In fact, she also has Swiss citizenship.

In addition, she's a St. Patrick's Day baby and has red hair.

In terms of symbolism, at least, it seemed to fit.

I know it seems indulgent, perhaps even a bit excessive, but it struck me as remotely possible that I might be able to carry out her request.

I imagined myself showing up at the gala, clutching a card and pen, trying to get an autograph and saying: "It's not really for me, it's for my daughter."

But what the heck. What are parents for?

I read up on the security arrangements for the summit and realized that the chances of getting close to either leader let alone to both the prime minister and the president would be slim.

So on Friday I did the sensible thing and called Bill Fox, the former newsman who is now Mulroney's press secretary.

"I know this sounds a bit presumptuous, maybe even silly," I said.

"But as you know, my daughter is American and Canadian and, well, you know…"

"Yes," he replied in a puzzled tone.

"Well, she'd like a birthday card … signed by the prime minister."

There was a long pause.

"And the president."

There was another pause.

"You realize this is an important summit meeting," he said.

"Oh, yeah," I answered. "But I said I'd try. We understand."

"I'll bring it up," Fox said.

I went to Quebec City on Saturday with a sense of nothing ventured, nothing gained.

On Sunday, as I stood in line waiting to catch a bus to the gala, a couple of journalist friends came up and said:

"Did you know at the press briefing they said you were Swedish?"

What press briefing? Why was my name brought up?

"A government spokesman explained what the president and the prime minister had discussed this afternoon—acid rain, North American defence and so on," one friend said.

"And as an afterthought, at the end of the briefing, he said something to the effect that during the limousine ride from the airport to the Chateau Frontenac, they reached agreement on a young girl's birthday."

It seems that in the limo, after the airport welcoming ceremony, the two leaders signed the first document of the Shamrock Summit.

I could see Mulroney passing a pair of scissors and some green paper over to Reagan, saying: "You cut out a shamrock. I've got the paste here."

After the gala, an aide delivered the card. It read:

> Dear Melissa
>
> Given your unique Canadian-American heritage (to say nothing of the Swiss!) the President and I wanted to send special greetings and good wishes on your birthday.
>
> With warm regards,
> (signed)
> Brian Mulroney
> Ronald Reagan

Thirteen-year-olds come up with some outrageous ideas, but they often understand the adult mind.

And vice versa.

And that's a cheery thought.

Tories parachute downtowner Auf der Maur into NDG
to run in Federal election. Nick loses.

Hopelessly old-fashioned dad banished from daughter's shopping trip

[Friday, July 11, 1986]

THERE ARE THESE LINES from cartoon strips and movies that are so clichéd one doesn't expect to hear them in real life.

Well, the other day, I informed my 14-year-old daughter she was to be my escort for a Fourth of July reception at the residence of the U.S. consul general.

"But," she said to me, eyes all innocent, "I don't have a thing to wear." Melissa goes in for baggy pants, bulky sweaters, anonymous black togs and running shoes. In other words, she dresses just like your average, fashionable neo-slob teenager.

Getting her to wear a skirt or dress has been, if not impossible, rather difficult. Not that I or her mother didn't try. It's just that discreet encouragement never produced any desired results.

But since I've always dressed the way I've felt like—which happens to be rather conventional—her style of dress never gave me too much thought. Until she said those words: "But I don't have a thing to wear."

It would be an exaggeration to say images of Imelda Marcos's shoe closet flooded into my mind. But it did occur to me that we may be entering a new and expensive phase of life here. Worse, a phase I've been pushing all along with dumb comments like: "Why don't you like to wear pretty dresses?"

I said that one day when I walked into my house and found her in the bathroom dying her hair orange. On her bed was an insane outfit.

I was only mollified when she explained she was entering a Cyndi Lauper look-alike contest. (She came in second.)

It could have been worse. She could have entered a Boy George look-alike contest. How would you feel if your daughter dressed up as a boy who dressed up as a girl?

Even if you're a jock you can't escape from worrisome trends in dress. Wednesday's sports section carried a story that said U.S. sprinter Carl Lewis wore gold-rimmed glasses, a knee-length tiger-skin shirt and white pants at the Moscow Goodwill games, although he didn't have the lip gloss or the Grace Jones haircut he used to sport.

This androgynous fashion can be confusing, although I must confess I approve of the current fashion that has young girls wearing men's boxer shorts with the fly sewn up. I've always been a booster of boxer shorts rather than those ludicrous tight things most people prefer.

But I digress.

As I was explaining, this Fourth of July reception necessitated a shopping excursion. In the past, shopping trips with my daughter have been rather cheap affairs, since they've been limited to sweat shirts and cotton pants. (Although, like all parents, the price of shoes has always outraged me.)

This shopping excursion didn't last long.

I was thinking of something like a Laura Ashley dress. Flowers and hair ribbons and demure little-girl stuff.

Unfortunately, I committed an unpardonable error right off the bat. In the first shop we walked into, accompanied by one of her friend-fashion advisers, I innocently asked the clerk: "Do you have any dresses for young girls?"

That's not the sort of thing you say about a 14-year-old.

"How can you say that?" they shrieked once we were outside the store.

"We're not children. And the dresses you liked, they're so old-fashioned." (I had liked the pretty Laura Ashley sailor dress. Perhaps this androgynous stuff isn't new.)

They banished me to a bar and took off with my credit card.

As I waited, I thought maybe this new phase is going to turn out dreadfully. Maybe she'll buy an insanely expensive outfit.

On the other hand, maybe she'd come back with surgically implanted shoulder pads and an army camouflage outfit. Or maybe a torn punk dress, a tattoo on her arm and a ring in her nose. Who knows what could happen out there while two teenagers were running amok with my credit card?

She came back with a very normal, pretty, demure, sensible blue dress. At $45, half the price of the one I would have chosen.

At the reception, I was complimented on how poised and well-dressed she was.

Why is it that we worry about these things?

Bass guitar indulgence turned out to be great investment

[Wednesday, August 17, 1994]

KINDNESS and consideration pay off, even in a somewhat raunchy business.

About four years ago, my daughter Melissa went to Foufounes Electriques to see an obscure band.

Like a lot of kids, she's into what they call "alternative music"—loud and abrasive rock. That night, only about 20 kids showed up to hear this band from Chicago.

During the show, one of the kids in the audience, apparently displeased with the band's intensity, yelled: "Get rid of that attitude."

To emphasize the point, he threw a beer bottle at the lead singer who promptly jumped off the stage and proceeded to throttle him.

Melissa was horrified. The guy who threw the bottle was her roommate's boyfriend. She was also embarrassed that only 20 people had shown up to see an out-of-town band.

So after the show, she went up to the band and apologized profusely for Montreal and complimented them on their intense style.

This band went on to become a major success.

When Melissa told me the name of this band, Smashing Pumpkins, I giggled and asked: "Really?" And she giggled and we both went into one of those uncontrollable giggle duos that are so much fun.

Anyhow, last year Melissa turned 21 (on St. Patrick's Day) and I asked what she wanted for her birthday.

"A bass guitar," she said.

"Why?" I asked.

Well, she wanted to try to form a band with her friend Steve.

I didn't try too hard to dissuade her with the usual practical nonsense. It was her 21st and a little indulgence was warranted—even $700 worth. Only a few days after her birthday did she inform me it was no good without an amplifier. More indulgence.

So she formed this band, Tinker, and began to play in bars around the Main, and at places like Station 10, building up a small following and earning a bit of praise in the student press, *Hour* and *Mirror*.

Last fall, the Smashing Pumpkins came to Montreal to play at Metropolis. This was a big deal on the local music scene and a guaranteed sellout, unlike their first visit as unknowns.

But Melissa was outraged when she found out the local producers were not hiring a local band to warm up the crowd. Another U.S. band had been lined up.

Melissa thought a local band should be hired, to give them exposure and experience. She complained, along with many others.

So the producers decided to include a local band and to Melissa's delight, two days or so before the show, they chose her band. That, she said, was the biggest day of her life.

A few weeks ago, Lollapalooza—a sort of travelling rock festival—rolled into town with Smashing Pumpkins as headliners.

A day or so before it opened, the Big Pumpkin, lead singer Billy Corgan, called Melissa and invited her out to dinner.

She was telling me this about 10 days ago.

"Billy made me an offer but I turned him down," she said. He told her he had recommended her to another band that was looking for a bass player. And they wanted to audition her.

This band is called Hole and is run by Courtney Love, the widow of Kurt Cobain, whose suicide this year made headlines the world over. Hole needed a bass player because the previous one died of a heroin overdose in June.

Why did Melissa turn down the offer of an audition? Because she didn't really want to play in a band dominated by somebody else and maybe Hole's music was a tad commercial.

What a girl, I thought to myself. Spunk. Her own boss. Her own mind, not swayed easily. Full of artistic integrity.

It wasn't easy, she explained, because bands like that can make a lot of money on album sales and tours. And if they go to the top, the sums can be really big, and Courtney Love has a chance of doing that.

Well, I suggested, artistic integrity is one thing and sometimes we should be flexible. But, she said, you told me you have to be honest with yourself.

Well, yes, I said, but I strongly suggest you get a hold of Mr. Big

39

Pumpkin and tell him you've reconsidered.

Evidently all her friends gave her the same advice, because she reconsidered and Hole flew her out last week to Seattle, where the band is based and where it gave her an audition. Her competition was the bass player from a British band with 12 years' experience.

Melissa came back to Montreal last weekend with the news that she got the job, and two months of touring to promote Love's latest album, Live Through This, an ironic title since it came out at the same time as Cobain's death.

Last night Melissa flew back to Seattle for a few days of rehearsal. After all, she has to learn how to play the songs on the album they're promoting.

Then she flies to England next week, where she'll play on the main stage of the Reading Festival, the biggest annual music deal in Europe.

Then comes two months of touring all the big cities, and a spot on "Saturday Night Live."

Melissa has her head screwed on right and is going to have a great time. That's what bass guitars are for, I'm now fond of saying.

Melissa's mother, Linda Gaboriau, is only worried about how to tell her grandfather.

On tour with my daughter, the rock star from Ca-na-da

[Wednesday, March 15, 1995]

SOUTH MIAMI BEACH — We were barrelling up Interstate 95 in the heavy rain toward Fort Lauderdale on Monday, caught in the mist and spray between two trucks.

"Could you turn on the radio?" Melissa asked the driver. "The metal station, please."

A melodic guitar and cello instrumental filled the car and then a voice sang bittersweet lyrics. "That's Nirvana, Nick," Melissa said. "That's Kurt Cobain singing."

I was surprised. It was a good song. The instrumentals were good, not the heavy pounding wail I assumed all grunge music was about.

I suppose I had heard Cobain and Nirvana before on the radio without knowing it. After all, their Nirvana Unplugged album has been at the top or near the top of the charts all over the world for the year or so since his suicide. But music is not my forte.

But now that my daughter is in this band, Hole, with Cobain's widow, Courtney Love, she thought maybe I should pay a little attention to it.

We were heading for Fort Lauderdale for a 4 o'clock sound check of their instruments and the full truckload of electronic gear they drag around.

There was a cluster of fans and groupies hanging around the stage door when we arrived at The Edge, a funky club housed in a converted 1930s sawmill.

Courtney Love didn't show up for the sound check. She's not into details and spends most of her off time during tours in her hotel room with her two-and-half-year-old daughter. Mostly she chats on the Internet. She has a serious computer habit.

She also has a nanny with her. A guy. It strikes me as a curious resemblance to the Doonesbury comic strip, where Zonker works as a nanny.

She also has a personal assistant and a huge entourage.

"It's weird," Melissa commented. "Everything gets done for you. They have this idea the artist is just there to perform so you don't get to do

41

anything else. Never carry a bag, pay a bill, talk to an airline.

"And sometimes I find myself taking advantage of it. Ask an aide casually to do something. And it gets done immediately."

Do you feel comfortable with that, I asked her.

"No," she answered. "It's a bit soulless. I want to stay independent, be my own person."

When we went back to the club after dinner, the crowd at the stage door had grown. A young man with long blond hair walked up to Melissa and very respectfully held out his hand. Melissa took it and he stammered something like "Good luck tonight."

Soon we were surrounded by young fans, holding out CDs, notepads, paper scraps, dollar bills, anything for Melissa to autograph.

I stood back and watched the worshipful faces of these young girls and boys looking at my daughter.

That's when it really struck me that my daughter was becoming a rock 'n' roll star.

I listened to the fans' chatter. "She's so beautiful." "She's so poised." "She's not stuck up at all."

They even pronounced Auf der Maur right. It felt like I was watching a movie.

A car and driver came up to take Melissa back to the hotel for a change of clothes and a little nap before her 10:15 scheduled stage appearance.

But first she dragged me into the tour bus, which is outfitted much like a sailboat, with bunks and lounge, galley and the latest in home entertainment.

For the show that night the place was jammed with 1,700 people. There were no seats. Everybody stands. The show, I was told, sold out within hours of its announcement a few weeks ago.

The booking company never buys advertising for a Hole show. They usually play in venues of up to about 4,500 places.

They've been keeping up a gruelling pace, playing in about 80 North American cities, plus Japan, Australia and New Zealand in the last few months.

The opening act finished about 10 p.m. Then there was a long wait. Courtney got stuck in her hotel room and didn't show up for another hour. But nobody grumbled. That's Courtney.

She has developed this persona of "kinderwhore" (her word), the outrageous bad girl. To play off that, Melissa is presented as the pure Canadian girl.

On Saturday night in Tampa, Courtney slipped her panties off from under her little girl dress—she's 30—and threw them at the audience.

She tried to get Melissa to do the same. Melissa was embarrassed and refused.

For some reason, Courtney never introduces the other two band members, drummer Patty Schemel and guitarist Eric Erlandson. Just Melissa, who in addition to playing bass sings with Courtney. And it's always along the lines: "She's from Ca-na-da. She's pure. She's polite. She's a virgin. She doesn't do bad things."

A radically different rock'n'roll star.

Yesterday, the tour bus headed for Orlando, then on to Memphis.

I checked the schedule to see where they'd be Friday, St. Patrick's Day, Melissa's 23rd birthday.

It was a travel day, with a midnight stop at a hotel in Wichita en route to Denver and Salt Lake City.

Then a few days off in Montreal before the start of a two-month European tour.

Hey, it's a living.

Melissa (left), and Courtney Love's band, Hole.

Melissa loved rock stars long before
she became one

[Wednesday, January 31, 1996]

NEW YORK—This was a trip many Montreal parents look forward to with great trepidation.

Hell, I guess parents everywhere feel it, but it seems to be one of those peculiar afflictions of English-speaking Montrealers—travelling to some other city to visit a child's new abode. True, this isn't necessarily permanent—perhaps just a temporary career move because my daughter Melissa's rock band is based in the United States and logistics dictate an American address.

Well, that's what I'd like to think. But Melissa's enthusiasm for New York City goes 'way back. Every eight years or so, we go there together.

The first time was when she was eight and I took her there for a vacation at her insistence. We stayed at the Hotel Pierre on Central Park—the manager was Swiss, so we were charged half-price—and did all the tourist things, visited the Statue of Liberty, went to the top of the Empire State Building, saw a Broadway show, and had a good time. I wrote a column about it at the time and *The Gazette* published a picture of Melissa wearing wongy-bonkers, those silly balls at the end of a pair of long bouncy springs that people wore on their heads.

I chuckled to myself on the plane coming down, recalling that visit and the next one eight years later when she turned 16.

We're supposed to do something special for a daughter's 16th birthday, and a friend of mine was the head of Pepsico Canada at the time and he suggested I take her down for the opening of the Michael Jackson tour that Pepsi was sponsoring. He would get me a pair of tickets, he said, and told me to stay at the Helmsley Palace.

Not terribly interested in Jackson myself, I invited Melissa's best friend, Alice, to join us. Going up the hotel elevator, the bellboy asked the girls: "So what brings you to New York?"

"We're going to see Michael Jackson tonight," the girls said breathlessly in unison.

44

"Well, you're staying at the right hotel," the bellboy said. "Jackson is staying a few floors above you and half the people from the Grammy Awards last night are in the hotel."

The girls almost swooned.

In our room they unpacked their Kodaks and announced they had to stake out the lobby.

Fine, I said, you check out the lobby and I'll check out the bar.

I sat in the bar reading my newspapers. After about 15 minutes, the girls came running in to announce they had just seen Whitney Houston get off the elevator.

They were so excited they got only a picture of the back of her head as she walked out the front door to her limo.

The barman and I laughed.

At showtime, I took the girls to Madison Square Garden and then picked them up after the show.

"Our tickets were better than Whitney Houston's," they told me later. "She was in the front row but we were on the stage. On the stage!"

Back at the hotel, they resumed their stakeout in the lobby. I went to the bar, where some ditzy New York woman asked me to pass the peanuts. She was sitting at a table next to the bar with a couple of bored-looking guys.

Boy, she was ditzy but kind of fun to talk to.

After about a hour, I realized I hadn't seen my girls, so I asked the barman to keep an eye on my drink while I went for a look.

"You're going to tell them who you're talking to, aren't you?" the barman asked.

"Who am I talking to?" I whispered back.

"Cyndi Lauper," he answered.

"Oh."

Just a few months previously, I had come home to find what I thought was blood all over the bathroom sink. Turns out it was hair dye.

Melissa had entered a Cyndi Lauper look-alike, lip-sync contest held by CHOM's Terry Di Monte at Alexis Nihon Plaza. Melissa came in second.

The girls in the lobby wouldn't believe me when I told them whom I was talking to. The Lauper trio had just paid their bill and were walking out another door. I managed a hurried introduction and then La Lauper whooshed out to the sidewalk.

"How could you talk to her for an hour and not tell us?" Melissa and Alice whined.

The next day, the girls wanted to see all the sights in Greenwich Village.

I found a Mexican restaurant that served decent margaritas and sat there reading newspapers while they wandered around. Then we caught an evening flight back to Montreal.

Now, again, eight years later—Melissa turns 24 on St. Patrick's Day— I found myself in a taxi from LaGuardia heading to the same Mexican restaurant, the Cactus Café, to meet Melissa, because her new apartment is just a few blocks away.

I'm not sure why I wanted to go to the Cactus Café first, instead of going directly to her place. For old times' sake? Trepidation, more like it. When I did get to her place, I was appalled but had to make complimentary noises.

It's a slightly seedy, fourth-floor walk-up in the East Village and little bigger than a Volkswagen camper van. And she's paying more rent than I ever did in mortgage and taxes in my entire life.

However, she's happy, healthy, and hilarious. What more could a father want?

The Last Call was for 3,000

Josh Freed

NICK'S FUNERAL was a fitting last call, a huge gathering of the clan that was almost as eclectic as the people who had drunk with him. There were out-of-town journalists, actors and rock stars, ex-mayors and politicians, pin-striped lawyers, cabdrivers, plumbers, priests, and panhandlers. They were rich and poor, federalist and separatist, left wing and right wing.

All this was for a man who was just an ordinary citizen, an ex-city councillor and part-time newspaper columnist who spent much of his life on a bar stool. It was an outpouring that said as much about Montreal as it did about Nick—for very few cities could have celebrated him as their local hero.

Toronto is too proper to honour Nick's far-from-proper lifestyle, Ottawa and Calgary are too small-town to throw such a big party, and Vancouver, well, most of the town goes to bed before Nick got up. Nick was a non-judgmental guy and Montreal is a non-judgmental city which suited him as comfortably as his Borsalino hat.

Only here would the city's Anglican bishop join a Catholic monsignor and 3,000 others in prayer, trying to help a loveable rascal slip by St. Peter and through the gates of Heaven before last call. Only here would a police escort lead a Dixie band through downtown after the funeral, then close off Crescent Street so we could toast a man who drank too much.

Nick was our one-man Happy Hour. He was the bad boy in many of us, the part that still wanted to be out carousing till dawn, but stayed home to watch the news instead. For many of us who'd long since left the regular bar scene, he was our representative, our designated drinker. Maybe we couldn't be out drinking and shmoozing till dawn every night, but we knew Nick was doing it for us, his big beaverish grin greeting anyone who walked in.

And if we suddenly decided to go downtown after six months away, we could count on Nick to be there with a barful of friends, as though he'd kept things going all along, just for us.

In a city that takes pride in its reputation for sin, he sinned for all of us—and paid the price.

On Crescent Street, after the funeral, many veterans were talking about launching a job search for a successor: a young recruit willing to sacrifice his life and liver to keep up downtown's reputation; a dashing, witty, bilingual fellow who could pinch bums, entertain foreign journalists, and rant at mayors and cabinet ministers; an Olympic-style athlete ready to dedicate his body to vodka, cigarettes, and car exhaust.

But in an era of health-conscious living, it's an impossible task. They don't make them in Nick's mold anymore, and if City Hall has any class, it will help preserve the old mold by naming Nick's street after him. What exactly is Crescent Street supposed to commemorate anyway—or is it just an English translation of "croissant"?

Obviously Crescent is a ridiculous, absurd, and silly name for a street, a travesty that's positively insane!!, as Nick would have put it. Obviously it's time to change the name to Rue Auf der Maur, or just Rue St. Nick in traditional Montreal style.

Then we could declare every Easter Monday to be Nick's day, and head down to his street to celebrate a true Montreal character who was the incarnation of the city he loved.

Josh Freed is a Montreal author, columnist, and filmmaker who admits he's a little too old to take Nick's place.

Nick's brother, Frank (left), with Josh Freed, May 1977.

Monsieur Montréal

Nathalie Petrowski

UNLIKE the 2,800 people who congregated at packed Saint Patrick's church on Monday to pay a final homage to journalist, city councillor, and "monument" Nick Auf der Maur, I have no anecdotes to relate about him. I've searched long and hard, scouring the innermost depths of my memory, and I find nothing. No anecdote, no incredible adventure that only he could launch, no portents or shadows of the beginning of an argument that we would've had late at night in his headquarters on Crescent Street.

Nevertheless, we bumped into each other dozens, even hundreds, of times. As far as I can remember, for at least 25 years, dating back to when I was young and not a journalist, Nick was already a part of our urban folklore. Nick was Monsieur Montréal down to the tips of his fingers. I ascertained this without knowing him personally. I never even had to engage him in conversation to know what he was thinking. Seated, or sometimes collapsed, at the bar of the *petit bistro* on Mountain Street, he would turn his head ever-so-slightly to the assembled crowd, his lips curled, his mustache undulating and half his face positioned to produce a series of methodical winks at every woman or girl who caught his eye.

I remember Nick's presence was as unchanging as it was irrepressible. Nick was always there. More to the point, Nick just was. Period.

That 2,800 people came together at the church to say *au revoir*, that they marched out to the devilish sounds of a Dixieland band, which then snaked its way through the cordoned-off downtown streets before its final assault on Crescent—all this reflects the marvel that Nick was not only for the mourners-cum-celebrants but also for Montreal as a whole.

Nick Auf der Maur was not only the mayor of downtown, as Mordecai Richler has written, or our genial ambassador next to the Castros of this world, he was, above all, the incarnation of this city's soul when it still had one.

Once, downtown had a real centre and not just a big doughnut hole.

Once, celebrations were more important than politics or the economy. Anglos and francos flew together without dwelling on language or religion. Once, above all, Montreal was a completely effervescent city, untidy, as shambolic as a bordello, and open.

Do not believe that Nick's death signals the end of Montreal's soul. Its calcification has been going on for quite some time. Only Nick never seemed to accept it, obstinately refusing to see it.

The signs were everywhere: Crescent Street was transformed into a giant "MacBar." West-end streets gave their life blood away to St. Denis or St. Laurent. English-language journalist friends exiled to Toronto. And those who didn't have the heart to flee retired with their wives and kids to the faraway West Island.

It was practically all that Nick could do to hold the fort downtown, to continue to open and close the bars, cigarette smoke curling above his fedora, tequilas drained behind his loosened tie, going to sleep at the unseemly hours of the city's gloriously bohemian era, now dead and interred.

It was practically all Nick could do to believe that this city was the most *formidable* in the world, a city that deserved him sacrificing all his energies and ambitions. And just as he was a true believer, he also made believers of us all.

Even if Nick was more "west-end" than "east-end," even if his drinking partners and playmates spoke more like Ralph Klein than Lucien Bouchard, even if he rarely arrived at City Hall come rain or shine, even if his best years as an investigative journalist were behind him, even if he no longer had Jean Drapeau to kick around, even if—with his cancer, his neck brace and his eyepatch—he became a shadow of himself, a diminished, suffering, and unhappy shadow, Nick remained Monsieur Montréal to the bitter end. If for no other reason that the fate of his city concerned him personally— that it lived in his very being, 24 hours a day—Montreal and Nick were one.

As long as I can remember, he was *le plus montréalais* of all Montrealers. And as each year went by, the more he came to resemble the last of the Mohicans. No matter that Pedro and the others were either dead or gone, Nick took it upon himself to preside alone at a pantheon reserved for the originals, the eccentrics, the anarchists, the happy, delirious crazies ... and above all the hopelessly entwined lovers of the only real woman in their lives: Montreal.

Nick loved Montreal like few among us. He proved that every day of his life. In doing nothing and everything at the same time. In insisting on staying with his beloved Montreal when three-quarters of his comrades left her. Why he never left, like the rest of the gang, one may never really know. Maybe it was because of his loyalty for the city that welcomed his immigrant parents. Maybe because of his 95-year-old mother who still lives here. Maybe because of his daughter Melissa, who always dropped by between tours with Courtney Love's band Hole. Maybe because he was more Swiss than he let on, and Montreal was, in its indefatigable routine, more Swiss than him. Maybe simply because he had no other place to go, or wanted to go to, that Montreal was his niche, his lair, his port, his aquarium, the beginning and end of his life on Earth.

To say that Montreal will never be the same without him would be a lie. Montreal hasn't been the same for a long time. But Nick believed in Montreal and that's what counts. Now that he is no longer here, what will it mean for us?

Nathalie Petrowski is a columnist for *La Presse*.

[Adapted by Juan Rodriguez from a *La Presse* column, April 15, 1998—originally published Monday, April 27, 1998]

A moustacheless Nick with Mayor Jean Drapeau during the time
of the 1976 Montreal Olympics.

Montrealers

Both Nick and sports writer Tim Burke leave *The Gazette*
to join the ill-fated *Montreal Daily News*.

Mayor a figure of hope in golden years of youth

[Wednesday, July 2, 1986]

THE EVERLY BROTHERS were singing "All I Have to Do Is Dream," in that mellifluous manner of theirs.

I was sitting in the stands Monday night by the lake in La Ronde, watching the duo that had come into prominence in the 1950s, back in the days when as an adolescent I used to listen to "Le Hit Parade avec Léo Lachance" on CKVL and watch Joyce Hawn play Susie when they sang "Wake Up Little Susie" on Cross Canada Hit Parade on CBC-TV.

It was a beautiful night and La Ronde displayed all its magic as the now aging Everly Brothers moved into "Bye, Bye Love." The Jacques Cartier bridge was all lit up, a counterpoint to the huge steel Ferris wheel illuminated with the logo of Man and His World, while the gondolas moved silently overhead.

Most of the audience seemed to be of my generation, people in their 40s who remember the 1950s as the golden years of youth.

Behind us, kids of another generation were frolicking and enjoying the rides, celebrating their youth, and having a wonderful time. Between songs we could hear their shrieks of delight.

The songs moved me to great nostalgia, transporting me back to when I was a kid. I looked at the city, at the enchanting La Ronde vista, and remembered when I was an adolescent and the Everly Brothers rode high in the hit parade. And I thought of Jean Drapeau and was filled with a sadness.

I was 12 years old when Jean Drapeau was first elected mayor of Montreal in 1954. He was, I guess, my first political hero. When he was defeated in 1957 I remember my father telling me: "They stole it from him, Duplessis and his gang." My father was angry about it because he was enthusiastic about Drapeau's reform movement to clean up a corrupt city hall and police department.

It was odd, because my father, as did everyone else in town, liked Drapeau's predecessor, Camillien Houde, the big, fat, flamboyant politician who had dominated Montreal politics in the '30s and '40s.

But that didn't lessen his desire, and that of most Montrealers, to see Jean Drapeau succeed in reforming our political and social structures. In a great sense, Drapeau's assault on city hall was a forerunner of the Quiet Revolution, the great move to modernize the province that would change both the character of Quebec and the country.

So as a teenager, I looked to Jean Drapeau with great admiration and hope, the same way a few years later I looked at my new political heroes—Jean Lesage, René Lévesque, and Eric Kierans.

And so listening to the Everly Brothers and remembering what my world was like back then, I felt a great pang of sadness as I recalled the TV images I had seen a few days ago, showing Jean Drapeau crying as he announced his decision to leave active political life.

As Lysiane Gagnon pointed out in her *La Presse* column, it was revealing to look at the passage in Drapeau's somewhat convoluted departure speech that moved him to tears.

It was at the point, after having outlined his career and the long days he put in being mayor, when he said: "My reward is the feeling that I have contributed to cleansing public affairs, to have significantly contributed to transforming the city we already loved into a city we love even more."

And so on Tuesday night, while sitting in one of the monuments that Jean Drapeau has left to this city, my emotions were mixed with great sentiment for a man who loved his city and whom we loved in return.

Merci monsieur le mâire pour tous les souvenirs que vous nous laissez.

When it's beyond tears all you can do is laugh

[Wednesday, January 6, 1988]

WE WERE SWAPPING personal horror stories and Sandy Dettman, who operates Expressions, a downtown print shop, came up with a lulu.

One morning he woke up and decided to luxuriate in a hot bath instead of a shower. He started the water running and was puttering around when he noticed the bathroom was a bit dusty. So while the tub was filling he decided to pull out his new super-horsepower vacuum cleaner and tidy up a bit. He was vacuuming merrily away, the way bachelors do, when he knocked his electric hair dryer into the tub water.

"Well, I may be dumb, but not that dumb," Dettman told me. "When I saw the hair dryer go in, I jumped. I know it's not a good thing to have plugged-in electric appliances in the bath.

"So I grabbed the cord of the hair dryer and gingerly pulled it out.

"Now, I realized that the dryer could be ruined if I didn't dry it out. I didn't want it seizing up on me. So I shook it to get all the water out. When I got it as dry as I could, I turned it on so it could dry itself out inside.

"No sparks came out of it. Everything seemed to be in perfect order. I was relieved.

"It was only then I noticed the gurgling noise. I looked down and saw water coming out of the vacuum cleaner. I was so nervous when the hair dryer went into the tub that I had dropped the wand of the vacuum cleaner into the tub. It sucked up the water and the bag burst and was spewing all this dirty water on the floor.

"I put down the hair dryer, which I left running, and went to tend to the vacuum cleaner.

"I took out the filters and the remainder of the bag and dried out the vacuum cleaner as best I could. Like the hair dryer I decided the best thing would be to turn it on to let itself dry out.

"The motor and fan worked perfectly. Everything was under control.

"Satisfied, I left it running and went back to inspect the hair dryer. No

57

damage. Perfect.

"Then I noticed a sort of fog or mist in the room. I looked down at the bath to see if it was boiling or something. The surface of the water looked like a grey pool table.

"What I had done was to jam the back end of the vacuum cleaner against the bottom of a boxed-in radiator. And the fan was blowing 50 years of accumulated dust up into the air. Both the vacuum cleaner and hair dryer were working perfectly in tandem, dispersing the dust evenly all over.

"Well, it was one of those things that was so funny you couldn't really be upset. It was one of those times when things go wrong, everything goes wrong."

Dettman said the whole incident lasted maybe five minutes. But the cleanup took considerably longer.

Dettman gave up on the idea of a luxurious bath, or even a shower for that matter, and went directly to the office. No doubt to chuckle quietly to himself.

Some "wooden" think joke on Drapeau funny

[April 25, 1988]

WE WERE TALKING about what's funny and what's not funny, humour being one of those things that lies in the eye, or more often the ear, of the beholder.

The other day, Brian Stewart, my TV journalist friend and I were having a laugh about the old days, telling our lunch companions about some of the funny things we're been through.

"Well, there's the time I took Stewart to see Drapeau..." I started.

"Oh no," Stewart exclaimed. "That story's not funny. It's just plain stupid. It's terribly embarrassing. The trouble with you, Nick, is you're impervious to embarrassment.

"You never think anything is embarrassing. You just think it's funny."

Well, I suppose Stewart was right in a way. There are some things people think are hilarious, while others think of them as just awful.

So, conceding that to him, I quietly declined to tell our companions about the time I took Stewart to see Mayor Jean Drapeau, despite the fact they pleaded to be told.

But that was last week. Now that Stewart's back in Toronto, where he resides, I can tell it. Just as an example, mind you, of different perspectives on seeing things humorous.

It was about six years ago, at another time when Stewart was in town, visiting from London or Frankfurt or wherever it was he was posted at the time.

We were having lunch and Stewart asked how Drapeau was, remarking he hadn't really spoken to the mayor since he stopped doing a City Hall column for *The Gazette* in the late '60s.

"Heck," I said, grabbing a bar phone. "We'll call him up and arrange a meeting. I'm sure he'd love to see you."

Well, sure enough the mayor remembered Stewart and said he'd be delighted to see him. Next day at 4 o'clock. In his office.

Needless to say, Stewart was also delighted. Now Stewart, although a very good friend of mine and endowed with a sense of humour, is fairly different. He's rather formal and very straight about certain things.

The next day we were having lunch together again, preparing for our meeting later in the afternoon. Stewart was slightly nervous, as if preparing for a meeting with the pope or something.

"What'll I say to the mayor?" he asked. "Maybe we should postpone the meeting."

It's not that Stewart is unused to meeting public figures, its just that he has this keen sense of history and tends to view people like Drapeau as historical figures, serious characters who merit serious and weighty conversation. Say like a Trudeau or a de Gaulle.

"Naw, naw," I insisted, pouring Stewart a generous portion of wine, "He's just a regular guy."

Well, we sat there and finished a couple of bottles of wine, followed by a few cognacs before we headed down to City Hall. The policeman on duty greeted us and led us into this antechamber the mayor has where he meets with visitors.

The policeman left us alone for a few minutes while he went and summoned the mayor from his office.

We stood there looking around at the formal, Louis XIV setting we were in. I noticed in the corner a new addition to the decoration since I had last been there. It was one of those antique, French dressing screens.

"Hey," I said to Stewart, "let's hide behind the screen before the mayor comes in and surprise him."

"No, no," said Stewart. "Don't be silly."

But much to Stewart's chagrin, I insisted and went and hid behind the screen, bending down to peer through a crack where I had a good view of the rest of the room.

Stewart stood in the middle, looking perplexed, whispering loudly to me to get out from behind.

Then Mayor Drapeau walked in, beaming away and murmuring "Ah Monsieur Stewart, quel plaisir."

As the mayor vigorously shook his hand, Stewart nervously kept glancing at the dressing screen in the corner. In fact, Stewart was perspiring.

Drapeau took Stewart over to some Louis XIV chairs and sat him down, the mayor droning on quite effusively, Stewart muttering vaguely comprehensible platitudes. And just at the right moment I jumped up, knocking the dressing screen over, and shouting "Surprise!"

And as the two of them gaped at me strolling across the screen on the floor, I said, "Hey, Monsieur le Maire, did you hear about the wooden horse?"

The mayor nodded dumbly, no, while Stewart muffled a groan.

"Wooden't defecate," I said, although I must admit I used the more vulgar, four-letter S word.

"Hear about the steel horse?" I continued.

Again the mayor nodded no, while Stewart looked positively mortified, like he was so embarrassed he was going to faint.

"Steel wooden't defecate," I answered.

"And there's one about an iron horse, but I don't know what it is."

Well, I laughed, and the mayor laughed politely and Stewart rolled his eyes and made soft, weird noises.

I sat down beside the two of them, ready to resume a normal civilized conversation, although the way Stewart looked, it didn't seem as if he could manage to utter anything meaningful through a mouth that kept opening and closing and letting out air.

Well, before we could get on with our friendly chat, Drapeau pulled out an envelope and a pen from his pocket and said to me: "How did those jokes go again?"

And I had to repeat them while Stewart looked on in astonishment, looking like he would expire right then and there in embarrassment.

We proceeded to chat away merrily for an hour or more. Stewart even managed to recover somewhat and join in after 15 or 20 minutes.

After we left, Stewart was fairly beside himself, screaming at me for being such an idiot and how I managed to make the both of us appear like lunatics and how I'd ruined his first meeting with Drapeau in a dozen years. He really huffed and puffed, really he did.

Now, I still think it was funny, and Stewart still doesn't. Strange how two people can have such a different appreciation of the same event.

Newspaper job an eye-opener for spy-flick director

[Wednesday, April 24, 1996]

GEORGE MIHALKA was sitting in a bar ruminating about his "art."

"Accessibility does not always necessarily exclude intelligence," he explained. "Entertaining does not exclude thought."

There are several Quebec movie directors better known and more celebrated than George Mihalka. But more people pay to see Mihalka's movies. On Friday, his latest film, *Bullet to Beijing*, opens at several theatres in town, a sequel to those great Len Deighton spy movies from the 1960s starring Michael Caine as Harry Palmer, two of which—*The Ipcress File* and *Funeral in Berlin*—are arguably among the best films ever made in this genre.

Bullet to Beijing, shot in St. Petersburg and London, takes place in present-day Russia, in a world where the Cold War is over and cold warriors like Harry Palmer are out of official work and forced to ply their craft as freelancers.

Caine reprises his role as Palmer, while my old friend Michael Sarrazin has a supporting role as a washed-up CIA agent. The film also stars Jason Connery, son of Sean.

Mihalka is a curious cross-cultural creature, an English-speaking Hungarian immigrant, one of Quebec's most prolific directors in film and TV (he did the first 19 episodes of Scoop), capable of making Canadian films that look American, and this time "a sort of black, tongue-in-cheek action thriller that looks British."

His comedy *La Florida* was the top-grossing Canadian film two years ago, while his next one—*L'Homme Idéal*, due to open in September—will likely top it. The comedy features almost everybody in Quebec's entertainment industry.

His easy shift between cultures is obviously a reflection of my old drinking buddy's background.

His parents fled Hungary after the Soviet invasion in 1956, escaping through the countryside and taking refuge in France while George and a sister were left behind with grandparents.

His father, a fervent pacifist architect, spoke French but soon soured on France because of the Algerian troubles in the early '60s. He didn't want his son conscripted into the French army, so the parents came to Canada and sent for the children.

"In those days, however," Mihalka explained, "it was hard to get architects' work if you could not speak English, so he ended up in construction work."

The boy grew up on the South Shore, going to MacDonald-Cartier High School.

Just before he turned 17, he applied for various summer jobs, including one at the *Montreal Star*.

He was offered a job with "the publisher, which I assumed meant working in the printing plant."

To his astonishment, when he showed up for work, he was led into the office of publisher J.G. McConnell, the enormously wealthy, eccentric, hard-drinking, and prolific art collector who owned what once was one of the most profitable newspapers in Canada.

The teenager's duties were vaguely defined but it amounted to the best education one could ever have had.

"I'd arrive in the office at 8:30 in the morning," he explained, "and basically I'd read all the newspapers and periodicals that Mr. McConnell had coming in from all over the world—underground art magazines, political tracts, journals of every description. Basically I had to go through it all and clip out what interested him that week. One week it would be modern art, the next Asian economies, the next European fashion … he was very eclectic.

"Then I'd do anything else he wanted me to do. Sometimes it would be to go to the Waddington art gallery to arrange a private showing by some artist that interested him and then I'd accompany him on his 'shopping trip.' He'd ask me if I liked a particular painting and if I said yes, he'd buy it. He bought dozens of objects at a time."

Shortly after he joined the *Star*, the October Crisis erupted and the elder Mihalka, pacifist worrywart, moved to Toronto while his son elected to stay on. The elder McConnell treated Mihalka as a "sort of protegé, although he kept his family life strictly private."

I knew McConnell's son at the time, and it was obvious father and son didn't get along all that well, the son being a bit hell-bent and mostly interested in cars.

So it would seem to me in retrospect the old man might have viewed his Hungarian immigrant as a surrogate son.

In any case, Mihalka got a nifty education in the two-and-half years he worked for him, not the least due to McConnell's habit of making all visitors wait at least 10 minutes in the outer office. There Mihalka would entertain the waiting dignitaries, cabinet ministers and senators, business tycoons, and other supplicants. It must have been like being aide-de-camp to Citizen Kane.

When the publisher decided to retire, he paid Mihalka's tuition for a year at Concordia and bought him a motorcycle as severance pay.

Originally he wanted to become an English literature teacher—which he did for a time at his old MacDonald-Cartier alma mater—but while working on his masters (throughout he went to night classes at Sir George Williams-Concordia University) he became intrigued with educational video and, by extension, film. Now people are intrigued by this 43-year-old's films.

Bullet to Beijing may be a British-American-Russian-Canadian co-production, but it's got a lot of the Montreal outlook in it.

Friend's death during storm hits hard

[Sunday, January 11, 1998]

FRIDAY EVENING, my friend and neighbour Ron Seltzer came over see if there was anything he could do for me during the ice storm.

The power was out, but my woodstove was keeping me warm. I needed more wood from the back balcony, but the sliding doors were frozen tight and difficult to open.

Seltzer pushed and pulled and finally got them open a little, maybe a foot and a half. He strained through the opening to reach the logs and passed them in one by one.

Then he noticed the batteries in my flashlight had gone, so he phoned around to see if anybody had any for me.

A woman around the corner had some batteries, he said, but she didn't know what kind they were, so he took my flashlight and trudged off.

I watched him through the window as he went off navigating the ice-glazed street on his Good Samaritan mission. I had noticed Seltzer out in front often in the past few days, helping clear tree limbs off of cars, out in the back giving orders and directing the extraction of stuck cars.

He helped people carry groceries and he sheltered people in his home during the time we had power and others didn't. He was what we could call an active neighbour.

When he left Friday evening, I lay down for a nap. I woke up sometime later to find my flashlight, all prepped with new batteries on the side table, ready for use.

Then Seltzer called and said to look in the kitchen; in there was a thermos of hot borscht for me, provided by another neighbour.

Yesterday morning as I lay in bed, our mutual friend Stephen Phizicky came to tell my that during the night Ron Seltzer had died of a heart attack.

How sad, how terribly sad I felt.

I can't say that Seltzer enjoyed the ice-storm crisis, but he certainly put his heart into helping people out.

He was always a neighbour like that, the helping guy, the guy who was au courant with what was happening to whom, why the gas main was being dug up, the waste the city public-works department was going through paving the rear laneway … handy neighbourhood information.

Now, of course, I can't help but feel that the extra exertions he went through on our behalf in the past several days helped bring about his heart attack.

Seltzer is perhaps best remembered as the publisher of the *Downtowner*, the weekly he launched in 1980 and which lasted until 1993 when the recession pummelled downtown business.

He enjoyed his role as newspaper publisher, but if truth be told, it was his wife, Mary Wilson, who managed the business and kept the nuts and bolts together while Seltzer sat around philosophizing much of the time.

One of his great charms was that of the bungling visionary, and I took great fun in writing columns back in the early 1980s about our joint misadventures trying to renovate our newly bought homes and create a back garden. (The work is still in progress.)

We bought our Tupper Street triplexes together, me having gotten to know him through his then-wife, Cynthia Gunn, an editor at the *Montreal Star*.

A couple of years before we bought the houses, he went through a terrible tragedy, one that would have shattered many people.

He used to go to the hospital where his wife lay dying of cancer, and then go up two floors to where his mother lay dying.

The double deaths were too cruel.

Although born in Montreal, Seltzer grew up in Saint-Jean, learning French before English. His father was a haberdasher there.

The family moved back to Montreal, where Seltzer made something of a name for himself as an athlete, playing hockey in different leagues, football at Westmount High, and becoming an expert canoeist while working summers as a counsellor in Algonquin Park.

Later, he was to race MG cars and indulge his passion for sailing.

When I met him, he was a soundman, having worked in film both here and in Toronto.

But it was his career as the *Downtowner*'s publisher that most gratified him, saying his father would have been proud of him because his father respected the world of writing, books, and opinion.

By then, he had met and married Mary Wilson, she giving birth to their daughter, Clare, nine years ago.

The *Downtowner* often more resembled a sitcom than a practical business, as it lurched from one crisis to another, but somehow Mary kept the little paper that could going.

She's the daughter of the late Stuart Wilson, the legendary professor of architecture at McGill University, someone I first met at the Stanley Tavern in about 1960. (Wilson was the architect of the novel '50s art-deco St. Regis Tavern on Ste. Catherine past Phillips Square.)

For many years, they ran the *Downtowner* (with Ron's brother David as advertising manager) out of the downstairs flat next door to me.

We had a lot of laughs, as I routinely skewered Seltzer's foibles and his mournful look in my columns back then. (He loved to barbecue, I hated it. He preferred his steak rare, but never managed to produce anything except extremely well-done.)

He was a good, decent soul. He genuinely cared for people.

His friends can't help but feel it was that caring that contributed to his death. I will remember the ice storm for that.

[Tribute]

Sometimes an Opponent Can Be a Friend

Warren Allmand

NICK WAS SOMEONE SPECIAL. When I go to Ziggy's Pub I am sure he's still there in some corner, pinching bottoms and holding court. Whenever I sight a Borsalino bobbing down crowded Crescent Street, I start to holler out his name.

I can't remember when we first met, but I think it was at Darwin's on Bishop Street. It's hard to tell because I knew him first through his columns, CJAD, *The Last Post* magazine, and his reputation.

Nick and I had some great encounters. The strangest one was the 1984 federal election. At one point in the late summer, Nick called and said he wanted to see me. When we met at Winnie's, he told me that Brian Mulroney wanted him to run for the Conservatives—what did I think? Even though I was a Liberal MP, I told Nick it was a great idea. I thought he would do an excellent job in Ottawa. I could already see him jumping up and down in the House of Commons badgering the opposition. We would have great fun on opposite sides of the House.

I then asked where he would run. Downtown he said, "I would never run in a riding where I had to take a taxi to get there." I then said that maybe they would ask him to run in NDG since no Conservative had yet been nominated. He said he would never run against someone he would vote for. Nick had already written two columns praising my work and the positions I had taken.

About a month later Nick called again and once again said it was critical he see me. When we met downtown he told me how the Conservatives had already named a candidate in St. Jacques, which was the downtown riding where he lived and was elected municipally, and that they wanted him to run in NDG. He said he really didn't want to do it, but he hated the Liberals and Brian was the man to straighten out the country. Again what did I think?

Well, I said that was a tough question. I hated the Conservatives, but I would love to see him elected. Moreover, if we ran against each other, only one could be elected—and that would be no fun. What to do? We talked and talked for over an hour and finally agreed that if they insisted he run in NDG, I wouldn't run against him and he wouldn't run against me, but I would run against the Conservatives and he against the Liberals. It was a deal—but I said it was like hockey, when you're on the ice, even if playing against friends, you play hard and you play to win. But when the game is over you go out and have a beer together. He agreed.

So the campaign started and it was the toughest of my life. Not only was Nick well known but Mulroney and the Conservatives kept climbing higher in the polls. In the last week the press predicted a large Conservative victory. I was working night and day, scraping for every vote I could get.

On election night, the Conservatives won an overwhelming victory. I won by a small margin over Nick in NDG, and was one of only 42 Liberals to survive. Downtown, the unknown Conservative candidate lost by an even smaller margin. Everyone was sure that Nick could have taken it.

A few weeks later, I called Nick and said "the game's over. It's time for a beer." We met for lunch at noon and did post-mortems until late in the afternoon. Then Nick invited me to go with him to Henri Henri on Ste. Catherine to buy himself a new hat. I was so impressed I bought one too.

I had a great respect for Nick. He was a good friend, a genuine person, and a formidable opponent.

Warren Allmand, 66, spent almost half of his life as Member of Parliament for Notre Dame de Grâce and served in many cabinet posts. As an MP he was elected in 1968, 1972, 1974, 1979, 1980, 1984, 1988, and 1993. He resigned in 1997. His plurality in each election exceeded 11,200 votes except for the election of 1984, when he beat Conservative candidate Nick Auf der Maur by just 2,065 votes. Allmand is now president of the International Centre for Human Rights and Democratic Development.

[Tribute]

Thumped by a commie!

John Lynch-Staunton

I AM STILL not too certain who was the more surprised at Nick's election to City Council in 1974, him or me. I think it was only half in jest that he was heard to suggest during the campaign that he would ask for a recount should he win. At the time, I had been on council for 14 years, vice-chairman of the Executive Committee for four, and extolled by such perceptive journalists as Brian Stewart then of *The Gazette* (yet an enthusiastic backer along with most press hacks of my commie opponent) as nothing short of a municipal statesman. Was it possible that such a bright light would be turned out by a scruffy ex-con?

Had the result been as foreordained, my political career would have ended with the demise of the Civic Party of Montreal while Nick's progress at *The Gazette* and his friendship with Conrad Black would no doubt have brought him to the editor's chair. The thought of one leads to indifference, the other to horror!

One thing we did have in common was an enormous admiration for Jean Drapeau. While Nick was his main nemesis on the 1976 Olympic Games controversy, and pursued the issue mercilessly, he always had great respect for the man's tenacity and devotion to Montreal.

Looking back as I often have, Nick was probably the right man at the right time. He did exaggerate and embellish. He did bellow and bluster, but behind all the theatrics was someone who also cared deeply for his city, a characteristic which marked him to his last breath. He was a severe and sometimes unfair critic, he could be as rude as he could charm, he could be as annoying as he could be seductive; behind it all, however, was a great heart and a passionate citizen. I could not have lost to a better person.

Indeed, I am glad he did not ask for a recount!

John Lynch-Staunton, Leader of the Opposition in the Senate, lost the 1974 civic election to Nick.

In front of Montreal City Hall, summer 1980.
Photo by Richard Arless, Jr.

POLITICS

With his mother Theresia at his side, Nick thanks
his supporters, November 9, 1986.
Photo by Arne Glassbourg.

Voting day hard on the candidate

[Monday, February 18, 1980]

ELECTION DAY, and all across the land there are nervous people pacing about—candidates. It's a curious sensation being a candidate on election day, without a doubt the worst day in the whole campaign. Because on this most important date, there is absolutely nothing more a candidate can do.

I can sympathize readily with today's candidates, having been through the electoral process three times. On election day, the candidate feels quite alone, reviewing the whole election campaign in his mind, worrying about having done this, or said that, forgotten something or ignored some group of voters.

There are a few general observations I'd like to make about being a candidate. First of all, most challenging candidates, no matter how forlorn their chances, how hopeless the cause, at one point in the campaign entertain the notion that they will win. It comes as a glimmer, usually after having shaken the hands of three successive people who actually smiled at you and said "good luck." The candidate then tells himself, "just maybe we can pull it off" and as the days go by he becomes convinced he can win. Twice I ran as a challenger, and twice I went through those notions (once successfully).

An incumbent also has a tough time. I went through that experience once. And I doubt it's true for all incumbents, but the most overpowering emotion felt on election day was fear of being beaten. The campaign may be exciting and exhilarating, but election day is no fun.

The candidate's day starts early. The candidate is usually the first one at the polling booth. Only once, the last time, did I actually get to vote for myself. And I must say, it felt odd, collecting the ballot, going behind the screen and seeing your own name printed right there in black and white. And then actually voting for yourself. Most peculiar.

The rest of the day, the candidate feels like a small child, being led around by campaign workers and trying to keep, not so much out of trouble, but out of the way. Because the candidate feels that it is actually he whose neck is on the line, he fidgets and worries about details.

The campaign manager usually assigns somebody to baby-sit the candidate. The baby-sitter takes the candidate around on a tour of the various polling stations. At each station, the candidate, feeling foolish and somewhat awkward, goes around to each poll, shaking hands with the deputy returning officers and the scrutineers representing both himself and his opponent. Generally, everything is polite and civilized. But there is always some bickering among party workers, and inevitably heated arguments occur, involving the district returning officer and opposing camps.

It's usually over some minor matter involving a voter without a poll slip or some such thing: party workers then scuttle about, phoning campaign headquarters, summoning a bevy of lawyers who abound on election day. If the candidate happens to be around when such a rumpus occurs, he immediately gets seized by a fit of paranoia, convinced his opponents are trying to steal the election from him. The babysitter has to drag him out of the polling station, take him to the secret apartment kept for such purposes, and pour him a drink.

The real work on election day is done by the campaign staff, volunteers in most cases. Aside from the campaign manager (in my last election a very competent lady called Diane Chaplin), there is always one person in charge of election day, overseeing operations to get out the vote, making sure all polls are covered by scrutineers. From the door-to-door canvassing, records are kept of where the favourable vote is. If the door-to-door canvass has been done properly, it is possible, with the poll lists, to keep track of how you are doing on election day. In my last municipal election, panic began to spread in our organization by noon. Lots of voters had shown up but, according to our workers, they weren't our voters. Your loyal candidate joined other party workers in hitting the phones, calling up our identified supporters and urging them to go to the polls. By 2 p.m., there wasn't any noticeable improvement, and the election day manager, Peter Daignan, ordered the whole organization, scrutineers and the lot to abandon the polling stations. Two hundred people went door-to-door, pulling the voters out of their homes down to the polls.

By this time Chaplin had assigned a second baby-sitter, John Jones, to calm my first baby-sitter, David Schulman. Everything worked out properly and it had, for our organization, a happy ending.

Referendum campaign leaves
no hard feelings

[Monday, May 26, 1980]

THERE IS NOTHING quite so pleasant as a fine, summery Saturday night in Montreal, when the sun is still up and the crowds are sparse. It seemed like a perfect time to saunter over to St. Denis Street and try to collect referendum bets.

During the referendum campaign, I took to going to St. Denis restaurants for late dinner after an evening of door-to-door slogging. That usually entailed a few vigorous but amiable political arguments, the type that are only resolved with a firm handshake and a bet.

It also seemed like an appropriate time to check the mood of the street people reputed to be 100 percent, staunch Parti Québécois Oui supporters. During the campaign, I found that something of a myth. I discovered a remarkable number of Non voters. But they would reveal their intentions only in guarded tones, somewhat in the manner of a person confiding he had one of those unspeakable social diseases.

The first person I encountered, at La Côte à Baron, was a young Radio-Canada employee. She recently arrived from Sorel and told me she had come to St. Denis Street in search of good conversation. She explained right off that she was of an intellectual bent and didn't smoke, drink, or go to discos.

Moving right along, I joined a young couple for dinner. He was Les Dabrowski, a 29-year-old of Polish origin, a miner's son born in Noranda (which boasts the only Polish Legion hall in all of Abitibi). Dabrowski is trilingual. He was quietly content with the referendum result.

His girlfriend, Florence Grondin, is a 28-year-old dental assistant from Longueuil, five years out of Thetford Mines.

"I voted Non," she said, "because it was important to. I followed the campaign closely, but Lévesque didn't seem too sure, to be convinced himself. He wasn't really positive. But on voting night, watching him on TV, I felt sorry for him. Just his look, his appearance, it touched me. I felt bad for him. But not more than that, not enough to make me sorry I voted

Non."

She added that a girl in her office who voted Oui said the day after she was glad the Non had won, because "the Oui is too romantic, too idealistic."

LATER ON: Standing at the bar were a Radio-Canada reporter, muted in his disappointment, and a young fellow who had worked backstage security for the Oui rally at the Paul Sauvé arena. The latter said he never really had been interested in politics. Having hired on with the Oui committee, he had been swept up in all the enthusiasm and had ardently hoped for a win. But now that it was over, he felt no great letdown.

Another couple, Yves Melançon and his wife from Côte des Neiges, had worked for the local Oui committee. Saturday night they were in general good humour, and bore no trace of disgruntlement. "Of course, we'll carry on," he said. "We're democrats and accept the result."

Louise Latraverse, whose face adorns the cover of the current issue of *TV Plus*, dropped in for a quick bite to eat between acts. She's appearing, along with Gilles Latulippe, in a show called "Filles demandées pour…" at the Théatre des Variétés on Papineau Avenue.

It was a quick lesson in Two Solitudes. I had never heard of the show, which is apparently packing them in. It's an old-fashioned vaudeville-burlesque show, silly gags and all. On the other hand, Louise had never heard of Yuk Yuk's and Stitches, two comedy clubs operating in English Montreal. We agreed English and French should pay more attention to each other's humour, as it is probably a better reflection of one's soul than any *sondage*.

MUCH LATER ON: Without having found a single debtor, found myself back at Darwin's on Bishop, chatting with Steve Sillers, a 32-year-old child-care counsellor. He's on sick leave from Shawbridge, recovering from a broken ankle and numerous torn ligaments from a snowshoe accident (it took a bevy of juvenile delinquents two hours to drag him out of the woods).

Sillers admitted that May 20 was the first time he had voted since he cast a ballot for McGill Carnival Princess in 1966. "I'm not really political. And even for the referendum I really only decided to vote when I heard my ex-wife was going to vote Oui. I had to cancel her ballot out."

What's in a name? A word?

PLENTY.

For example, there's a world of difference between saying so-and-so is "a fat head" and saying "he has an impressive head."

Between saying so-and-so is "an extremist lunatic" and saying he "has the courage of his convictions." One person's "freedom fighter" is another person's "terrorist."

Your "visionary" may appear to me as an "out-to-lunch crackpot."

Somebody's "liberation theology" can be another's "crunchy-granola Marxism with a collar on it."

One city's "lovable old eccentric" is another's "Harold Ballard."

It's all semantics, and it's important.

We need labels and definitions to help us figure out where we stand.

And nowhere is it more important than in politics.

Here in Quebec, for instance, separatism first started making the front pages in the early 1960s with Marcel Chaput the "renegade federal employee" to some, "heroic patriot" to others.

Anyhow, he got fired and published a book called *Pourquoi je suis séparatiste*. Presto, we had a separatist menace on our hands.

But when the separatist movement began to grow, the more astute manipulators within the movement realized the word *séparatiste* had negative connotations, while the term *indépendantiste* had a more positive sound.

So gradually, especially in the French media, we had a phasing out of one word in favour of another. A small but effective point had been made.

This semantic battle has been going on endlessly ever since.

When the Parti Québécois came to power, René Lévesque would take umbrage if this or another newspaper used "PQ" in a headline in reference to the government.

He claimed that it should always be "Quebec" or "government," arguing that sticking a party label on the "legitimately, democratically elected government" was being partisan and racist.

Forget for a moment that PQ can also mean "Province of Quebec," or that in journalism we routinely use Conservative, Liberal, or NDP to label a government.

Lévesque was headed for a referendum and it was important for the PQ to break down partisan loyalties.

To do so, it had to portray the government as the government of all the Quebecers.

One got the impression that the PQ was employing legions of experts in semantics to translate word changes into votes.

For a long while it was wrong, so they said, to use the term "independence," the meaning of which some Péquistes claimed had been distorted by their opponents.

Then there was an argument over the term "sovereignty-association," and whether it contained a hyphen.

This was actually debated in the National Assembly and by Péquistes. The official line then became that "sovereignty-association" has a hyphen.

The semantics of separatism is very important.

A few weeks ago, I pointed out that when the Parti Québécois split came into the open, the two factions were originally labelled "radicals" and "moderates."

Then, somewhere along the line, it became a battle between the "orthodox" and "revisionist" groups.

Claude Charron, in his new column in *Dimanche-Matin*, picked up on that point yesterday.

"(The radicals) didn't like a name that likened them to intransigents," Charron wrote, "and their journalist friends took up the campaign for them, and they managed to get the names changed.

"And to prove by absurdity a thesis of their adversaries that they lacked realism and had lost their tenuous connection with the real world, they chose to give themselves the title 'orthodox' while describing the others as 'revisionists.'

"Now if I'm not mistaken," Charron continued, "these political labels have been in the past almost exclusively reserved for internal battles within parties of the Communist bloc and revolutionary movements in the Third World.

"It was a typical means of losing people with big words, and putting a debate above popular preoccupations, as if they did it on purpose so people would lose (the significance of it)."

Now, of course, you need a PhD in semantics to figure out what the official line is.

Family matters: Nick (centre) campaigns for brother, Frank.

Paranoia, grovelling and other election joys

[Monday, November 10, 1986]

PARANOIA.

One of the wonderful side benefits of being a candidate in an election campaign is that it gives one an interesting perspective on how it feels to be afflicted with a mental disorder, such as paranoia.

One really has to go through the experience of being a candidate in a hotly contested election to appreciate this fact. Going through an election campaign is perhaps the ultimate ego test. After all, when you put your name up, you're asking an awful lot of people, mostly strangers, to judge you in a most public and open way.

If you win, naturally you feel all sorts of gratification. If you lose, well, it can be a fairly painful experience, alleviated only by the knowledge that your mother probably still loves you.

I know a bit about all this, because I've just completed my seventh campaign in 12 years—four municipal, one provincial, one federal and one referendum.

Inescapably, one goes through wild changes of emotion. On even-numbered days I usually get terribly optimistic about my chances, but on odd-numbered days I reach depths of pessimism, usually on no more basis of fact than somebody either smiled or frowned when I stuck out my hand.

This is no way to run a life on a day-to-day basis.

Candidates invariably end up seeing the world in an us vs. them perspective, surrounded by enemies in a hostile sea.

You look at familiar faces, and judging from the way their eyes move, you guess which way they are going to vote. You see deceit and treachery everywhere. (Frankly, this is often not just imaginary.)

Because of the process, everybody lies.

The candidates lie, the voters lie.

The candidates end up saying what they think the voters would like to hear and vice versa. There often isn't a lot of leadership involved in politics, just platitudes and generalities and the venality of getting into office.

That attitude is reinforced when you find out just how little the voters, to say nothing about the journalists covering the whole thing, know about any substantive issue.

You end up wondering why some people follow sports or Joan Collins's diet in such detail and care so little about the expenditure of tax dollars.

Our electoral process is too often a triumph of form over content. A candidate's hairstyle often has as much influence on the voters as his policies.

This time around, I must profess, I didn't get quite as paranoid as I have in the past, if only because I've lived through it before and can recognize the symptoms.

For example, when they took away my sidewalk this time, I wasn't nearly so deranged as the last time.

In 1984, I rented a campaign office on Peel Street near the Montreal Amateur Athletic Association. A couple of days after we moved in, a public-works crew came along and took away the six metres of sidewalk directly in front of our office. The sidewalk to the north and south remained untouched.

Every time I manoeuvred across the wooden planks to get in to the campaign office, it reinforced my conviction that there was some dastardly plot to undermine my campaign's efficiency.

Well, I won that campaign and afterward I laughed at my paranoia.

But last week, when I walked to my latest campaign headquarters on Dorchester Boulevard near the old CBC building, I found the three metres of sidewalk directly in front had been removed. The new sidewalk on either side remained intact.

In the old days, I would have gone berserk and seen a dark plot. This time, I just laughed and told people how I reacted the last time.

However, the suspicion lingered in the mind.

In previous campaigns, I, like a lot of other politicians I've compared notes with, found myself agreeing mindlessly with idiotic complaints. That's part of the desperate grovelling process of attracting votes.

Some voter says something stupid, such as that popcorn should be banned because it sticks in children's teeth. And the candidate mindlessly mumbles something sympathetic, like: "You may have a point there. I will certainly look into it." Anything for a vote.

This time around, I found myself getting irritable when some dimwit voter said something stupid or asked for some inane promise. And several times I told them so.

"Madam," I told one woman who prattled on about fox traps and demanded I take a position on the alleged use of live lemmings for bait, "your bizarre preoccupation is a lot of twaddle. Why don't you take it up with my opponent?"

In the hunt for votes, you're supposed to suffer fools gladly. I think I've lost the knack.

Activist Arnold Bennet takes on Nick in his downtown riding.
Nick wins handily.

A little humility is healthy for politicians
—and journalists

[Wednesday, November 9, 1994]

SUCH IS LIFE.

Thirty years ago, in 1964, I started working here at *The Gazette* as a copy boy, beginning my career in journalism.

Twenty years ago, in 1974, I started my career in politics by getting elected to Montreal city council.

Things have changed over those years. I've changed newspapers, which journalists are allowed to do. I've changed political parties. The reasons were always different, but I always felt I was doing the right thing. Maybe I was wrong, but I believed them to be the right things to do. Most of all, I believe—and this, of course, might seem terribly immodest—that I served both journalism and politics well. In short, I like to believe I did my duty.

I tried not to let the two duties get into conflict. Indeed, the agreement I have always had here at *The Gazette* was that I would refrain from writing about municipal—at least Montreal municipal—politics.

Now that I'm out of city council, having lost in Sunday's election, and I do not belong to a political party, I presume I might now comment on something I know a little about.

Last week, *The Gazette* suggested in an editorial that people should vote for my Montreal Citizens' Movement opponent—for the fourth election in a row—because in the 20 years I've been on council, the city core has declined.

The Gazette might as well have blamed me for the gigantic Olympic debt because I was on council when the cost overruns occurred. (I literally wrote the book on the Montreal Olympics and fought vigorously against the practices and policies that led to those overruns).

Indeed, worry over the Olympics was one of the main reasons I got into city politics. That and the deterioration of the downtown core illustrated by the demolition of the Van Horne mansion.

The Gazette editorial board—which makes decisions on whom to endorse and oppose—might as well saddle me with responsibility for the paper's declining circulation and readership, because that has occurred while I've been a columnist here.

Naturally, *The Gazette* doesn't really think I'm responsible for all those things. They just needed an excuse for arguing against my re-election.

The real reason, I suspect, that the editorial board of this paper has consistently supported my opponents is that they don't approve of Catholics who have fun and laugh a lot. In short, they disapprove of my lifestyle, which involves hanging around bars a lot.

This apparently is something that is OK for journalists, but not for politicians.

No. Journalists are allowed, indeed obligated, to denounce politicians for hypocrisy. To be judgmental.

They can hide behind some argument about the public's right to know, to anoint themselves as the great arbitrators of public morality.

Accuse them of hypocrisy and you find out just how thin-skinned those who daily criticize everybody else can be. Maybe they won't even print an ex-politician's views because of journalistic sensitivities and ethics.

Well, if there is one thing I have learned in my twin careers of journalism and politics, it's that the public isn't really that stupid. It might make mistakes, real doozers sometimes, but the public isn't so stupid that it can always be manipulated by the media or the politicians.

Abraham Lincoln was right when he said you can fool some of the people all of the time, and all of the people some of the time, but you can't fool all of the people all of the time.

This isn't meant as just a personal rant, although I suppose most people might see it that way.

It's just my observation over the years. I've noticed that both politicians and journalists take themselves too seriously. Misjudge the influence and power they have. Get officious and self-important.

Politicians and journalists live a symbiotic existence. That's why the public is suspicious of both.

It's interesting to note that almost every editorial board, editorialist and commentator in *La Presse*, *Le Devoir*, this paper as well as *Hour*, the *Mirror*, and *Voir*—argued, albeit reluctantly, in favour of Jean Doré's re-election.

Well, both politicians and journalists have to eat crow every now and then. Because the public often thinks for itself.

A lesson in humility every now and then can be a salutary experience.

In Brussels, I lied to Bourassa about his chances

[Sunday, October 6, 1996]

ROBERT BOURASSA sat in his office at the Hydro-Québec building on Dorchester Boulevard, watching the red glow from the fires burning in the city.

He could see the flames spreading down a block near Lafontaine Park as he listened to the increasingly hysterical radio reports. The Sûreté du Québec kept him informed with a constant series of reports. The striking Montreal firefighters were suspected of setting the fires themselves. Firefighters in civilian clothes, but carrying fire axes, were reported to be chopping the garden hoses people were using to try and put out the fires in their homes. Some firefighters considered them scabs for trying to save their homes.

It was in the middle of my first election campaign for city council.

This is insane, the premier thought to himself. Sheer madness. How can one possibly govern a province like this? This couldn't happen any place else.

Bourassa described this scene to me as I sat with him in a restaurant in Brussels, some months after he lost the 1976 election to René Lévesque, an election in which Bourassa had been described as the most hated man in Quebec.

His premiership had been marked by almost constant crises of great magnitude, from the October FLQ kidnappings and the War Measures Act, to the common-front strike, in which strikers had taken over the town, and radio stations, following the arrests of the three major Quebec union leaders.

I had had a less than ambivalent relationship with the premier. Basically, I thought of him with contempt.

I had first met him in 1966. Ironically, it was René Lévesque who had introduced me to him during his first election campaign, in a church basement in Mercier riding, a working-class district in central Montreal.

I greatly admired Lévesque, and after he had introduced me to Bourassa,

Lévesque told me: "Watch this young man. He is going to go far."

He seemed totally innocuous to me.

Bourassa and Lévesque won their ridings in that election, but their Liberal Party that launched the Quiet Revolution went down to defeat.

Lévesque would go on to found his own party, and the young Bourassa took over the Liberals and soon afterward won his first general election. And became premier.

Bourassa and I spent two weeks together on a book project in Brussels in the spring of 1977.

I had been very nasty to him as a journalist, even founded a party to run against his party in 1976. Mind, I felt it was mutual because his government had had me arrested in 1970 during the October Crisis.

Yet when I called to see if he would see me, he received me with much grace, even warmth. And as it turned out, much laughter.

He was studying and teaching in Belgium then. He lived alone in a small bachelor apartment, something you'd expect a student to be in, not a former premier of Quebec. Bourassa, as I was to find out, was not what I had assumed him to be. He was utterly unpretentious.

I thoroughly enjoyed my time with him and came away with great respect for the man.

We laughed and exchanged stories about our times on the opposite sides of the barricades, so to speak.

I told him how Gérald Godin, with whom I became very friendly during our time in jail together, would concoct stories of patronage and corruption in his government.

He'd tell me often hilarious stories about his ministers and their travails.

"Leaks," he complained, "my government was always leaking. We'd discuss something confidentially in cabinet, and the next day it would be on the front pages."

After the kidnapping of his labour minister, Pierre Laporte, the Sûreté came to a private meeting of the cabinet. They distributed belts with hidden homing devices in them, in case any other ministers got kidnapped.

"Only two police officers and the members of cabinet knew about the belts," Bourassa told me, "yet the next day it was on the front page of *Le Devoir*. We were trying to protect them, maybe save their lives. But they couldn't keep their mouths shut."

We discussed the Olympic business, in which I was intently involved.

We talked about the bitterness of the 1976 elections, in which he was personally defeated in Mercier by Gérald Godin, my pal.

In Brussels, all that had seemed far away. Bourassa held no rancour, and we managed to laugh at it all.

He was terribly unpopular in Quebec then; people didn't want to be seen with him in public. One of the few people who would, and who tried to cheer him up following his defeat, was Brian Mulroney.

But the personal animosity toward him in Quebec was one of the reasons he had exiled himself.

Yet, even then, he was contemplating a comeback.

He asked me what I thought about the possibilities. I knew, of course, that there was absolutely no way he would ever redeem himself, much less make a political comeback.

But I was so taken with him personally, that I lied and said: Sure, sure, one day Quebecers would look to him again, just as the French had done toward Charles de Gaulle.

In the summer of 1979, I bumped into him on Sherbrooke Street near where he had an office on Peel Street.

"Well," I said, "You'll be looking pretty good to the public in a few months."

"What do you mean?" he asked.

I explained the Parti Québécois government was going to throw a huge party to inaugurate the LG-2 dam in James Bay, the first power-generator of Bourassa's pet project.

"You're invited, aren't you?" I asked.

"I haven't heard anything from them," he said.

I had been feeling guilty about all the nasty things I had written and broadcast about Bourassa in his first two terms in office. So I ran down to the *Montreal Star*, where I then worked, and wrote a column saying the PQ government was so spiteful, they weren't inviting Bourassa, the father of James Bay, to the big party.

When it came out, it occurred to even his most strident critics that this was patently unfair and the French radio hotlines were outraged at the snub to the former premier.

A few days later, Bourassa phoned me to say how delighted he was to hear people say flattering things about him and defending him in public, something he had not heard in years.

At the dam's inauguration, the workers gave him a monster ovation, overshadowing the reception given René Lévesque.

He called me again and said: "I know you lied to me in Brussels about the comeback possibility. But now I think it may just be possible."

It certainly was.

Urban Nights and the Bright Lights

Allan Fotheringham

MICHAEL WILSON, as the bloodless finance minister who secretly wanted to be prime minister (and thought he was more qualified than the incumbent), once complained that "Canada doesn't have enough millionaires." A wonderfully argumentative concept, granted, considering the wowzer of an example the United States has provided with its contrast between its slobbering rich and those who sleep on the New York streets with cardboard in their shoes and dog food in their gullets, but we suspect he was wrong. It is one of the reasons why Wilson, with his truly charismatic speaking style and palpable warmth, is now contemplating resuming his life on Bay Street rather than at 24 Sussex Drive. What Canada actually needs is more genuine characters, the present example being Nick Auf der Maur, known by all who love him and despair over him as Nick Off-the-Wall, boulevardier supreme. We are in Montreal, steeling the blood and the liver for a two-day birthday party, mounted to celebrate the 50th advent of his arrival—an event we are all astonished that he has reached.

Auf der Maur, thanks to his celebrated living style, looks no more than 60—and that's in a bad light. As he confessed at the first-night dinner at a restaurant on Sherbrooke Street, just a martini toss from most of his proudest watering holes, "If I'd known I was going to last this long I would have taken better care of myself."

No city but Montreal could have produced the birthday boy. Over the years, as *Gazette* columnist and radio personality and city politician, he has dictated the shifting currents of the trendiest pub of the moment—along the axis of the Crescent Street eating-and-drinking enclaves down the slope where Mount Royal subsides into the St. Lawrence.

Where Nick drinks—having been tossed out of his previous haunt—is where the scribes, the gossips, the over-age athletes, the conspirators drink. Montreal is a tribal town and Nick's tribe follows him.

Auf der Maur, through bloodlines, is Swiss. His father arrived in

Montreal two months before the 1929 crash, therefore being, in his son's words: "The only Swiss in the world without timing." Nick, who sports a moustache approximately the size of Luxembourg, is a freak in that he is essentially a journalist who is impatient with the minuscule power of a columnist (you got it right, babe) and discerned that the only route to change society is to grasp power yourself (i.e. get into politics).

He has been running for office so long that half the voters in Montreal think he's a joke and half think he's a legend. He tried to unseat Jean Drapeau as mayor (detailing in a book before anyone else the scandalous truth of the boondoggles involved in the building of the Big Owe and the Olympic Games that were supposed to be Drapeau's proud legacy).

He has now been on city council for 20 years in a variety of parties that would astonish Italian parliaments—is presently leader of the opposition forces at city hall—and there are those, considering the sad view of present Mayor Jean Doré, who think Auf der Maur could actually inherit the office next time around.

This, if truth be told, would probably not astound (if amuse) the present resident of 24 Sussex Drive, who was a drinking companion of Auf der Maur when the present resident was still drinking, which he does no more, and who checks in at the birthday dinner via a fond and amusing telegram. As does Robert Bourassa, current custodian of a part of Canada that sulks and flirts with becoming a non-part.

Both these shrewd politicians know enough to pay obeisance to Nicholas Off-the-Wall, since a previous PM, one P. Trudeau, thanks to the War Measures Act had the moustache kid thrown in the slammer for two weeks, his sins never documented, before shamefacedly releasing him, his martyrdom assured.

There are some 120 supplicants unleashing their wallets for the birthday tribute, countless others shivering out on Sherbrooke since the restaurant ran out of tables and waiters. Among those inside is Pierre Sévigny, the famed one-legged friend of Gerda Munsinger—the German doxy who provided one of Ottawa's few scandals—and who looks hale and hearty at 70-something. Nick tends to attract friends who are indestructible.

Mark Starowicz, the CBC whiz who invented "As It Happens" and "The Journal" and the beloved Barbara Frum, flew in to recall his early days as a revolutionary with this reprobate, now a half a century old. Nick's 89-year-old mother gets up and, to demonstrate her lungs, treats us with a high-decibel Swiss yodel. His daughter Melissa sits and cries.

Next night, the remnants and the survivors crawl to Nick's current redoubt. It is called Grumpy's, one floor below the street, a fireplace that never works. On the wall are original cartoons from Terry (Aislin) Mosher, the *Gazette* artiste.

Best one is a sketch of a Montreal cop—after councillor Nick had been arrested for more-than-usual-obstreperous behaviour in a saloon—marching to the police station along with a limp body on his shoulder: "How's Melissa these days, Nick?"

As the MPs and the other politicos stumble out of Grumpy's near dawn, a snowfall grumples down, the worst April blizzard since the very day of the birthday boy's birth, that being the era when New York Rangers last won the Stanley Cup and goalie Davey Kerr won the Vezina Trophy. It figures.

Allan Fotheringham is a columnist for *Maclean's* magazine and *The Financial Post*.

[Originally published Monday, April 27, 1992]

Nick kept office hours in his bar of choice, always sitting
close to the telephone.

MEETING THE FAMOUS

Fruit, as in fruitcake: remembrances of a visit with Libya's Col. Khadafy

[Friday, January 10, 1986]

Col. Moammar Khadafy only comes out in the gun-black night with a Russian Kalashnikov rifle slung over his shoulder and a bandolier around his waist.

The colonel has been known to prowl the streets of his capital, shooting slugs from his AK-47 through the brain of any prostitutes or nightclub performers he can find.

The mad Libyan who outlawed booze, dice, and adultery and cuts off the hands of thieves is also a published author.

—New York Post

WELL, THE AUDIENCE watching the world stage seems to be emitting blood-curdling shouts of "Author! Author!"

Mention the name Khadafy these days, and the average person's eyes kind of take on a Rambo-like glow.

"They should bomb the bastard," is the type of comment one hears in conversations when the Libyan leader is mentioned.

That's the type of thing even little old pacifist spinsters seem to be thinking.

On talk shows, in editorials, on TV, over lunch, people actually splutter trying to verbalize the vehement feelings Khadafy elicits. Everybody is trying to out-vitriol everyone else, thinking up epithets to call him: maniac, lunatic, murderer, barbarian, twisted madman, crazed czar of terrorism.

No question about it, Khadafy has managed to strike a visceral nerve as he has moved to the top of the list of despots everybody loves to hate, now that his old friend, Idi Amin, has moved to obscurity.

Truly he is one of the stranger characters strutting about the international stage.

The bizarre thing is that just about everything said about him appears to be true. The man is crazed.

He's done weird things like giving student councils in Libya the right to impose capital punishment (scores of students were hanged from campus lamp posts) and a list of other things that, gathered together, would make an improbable scenario for a very bad and outlandish spy thriller.

My interest in the colonel goes back to 1973 when I was invited to meet him in Tripoli.

The reasons for the invitation were kind of fuzzy. It had something to do with my editorship of *Last Post* magazine at the time.

The embassy in Ottawa didn't explain much. But I decided, what the heck, it should be interesting.

In Tripoli, I was put up at a hotel (I forget the name since I've misplaced the bath towel) that contained the most peculiar collection of guests I've ever run across.

I kept bumping into people in the lobby and coffee shop who thrust tattered old press clippings and communiqués concerning bombings, guerrilla attacks, sabotage and such.

Frankly, I felt I was in the middle of a pyromaniacs' convention.

It took me a few days to figure it out. The people at the hotel represented a variety of guerrilla and left-wing terrorist or liberation groups from around the world.

It seems it was the end of the fiscal year and they were there to apply for their annual grants. I suppose the Libyan terrorist grants program is a muddled bureaucracy like every other government grants program in the world, so most of the representatives had little to do except mill around the hotel lobby trying to impress everybody else with how much mayhem they had caused in the previous fiscal year.

This was no mean task, because they had to do it while maintaining an air of secrecy and mystery. But basically, they were as discreet as the Marx Brothers.

However, to say the nature of their business made it somewhat chilling would be an understatement.

I met the colonel twice at receptions, but never had much conversation with him beyond "How do you do? Come here often?"

Toward the end of my 10-day stay, I and the rest of the hotel guests were summoned to a press conference held by the colonel in a theatre ringed by machine-gun-toting soldiers.

In the audience of about 300, I think there were only about six Westerners, including yours truly. Most of the journalists were from Arab and Third World countries.

After a long preamble, Khadafy got to the point: His government, he claimed, had proof positive that certain U.S. oil companies were using their position in Libya to bring in "Zionist, imperialist agents." And he was going to bring the proof onstage.

This provoked consternation and shouts about the perfidy of the Israelis. From the way he put it, I thought they were going to drag some poor, shackled Israeli onstage.

After haranguing the audience about this and that, Khadafy then ordered "the proof" brought out.

A Libyan army officer walked on, holding aloft—a grapefruit. A Jaffa grapefruit, to be precise.

They had found this thing at a drilling station in the desert.

Now, everybody knows "Zionist imperialist agents" don't carry K-rations when they are parachuted in. They carry knapsacks full of grapefruit.

I sat there shrinking in my seat while most of the audience hissed and booed. I kept thinking: "A head of state is waving a grapefruit at me."

Now, whenever I see him on TV or read about him in the paper, the image of a fruitcake, raving away with a grapefruit, flashes in my mind.

The grapefruit of wrath.

The day I fought with Jack Kerouac

[Friday, Aug. 14, 1987]

BACK IN THE 1950s and '60s, Jack Kerouac was a major big deal. Still is, as a matter of fact. At least for those who remember the Beat Generation and all that.

OK, so forget *Espresso Bongo* and such films.

But beatniks and poetry and Kerouac's novels, especially *On the Road*, were the stuff that stuffed the dreams of my generation. So needless to say, I was thrilled to death in the mid-'60s when some Radio-Canada TV producer phoned me up to invite me to dinner with Jack Kerouac.

Kerouac, who by this time had been doing much publicized soul-searching about his French-Canadian roots, was in town to do a lengthy interview for a show called "Sel de la semaine."

Kerouac, a Franco-American from Lowell, Massachusetts, spoke poor French and the producers thought that it would be nice to have somebody he could relate to after the show.

At the time, I had a minor reputation as having been a beatnik poet. When I was about 19 or so, I used to read my poetry at a dive called La Poubelle on Bishop Street.

They paid me $5 a night plus five free beers, which wasn't bad considering that my first job at *The Gazette* paid just $35 a week.

So one evening about 10 o'clock, I toddled over to the basement restaurant of Castle du Roy on Drummond Street to have dinner with Kerouac and about six or seven Radio-Canada types.

Introductions were made and we all sat down to a pleasant evening of dinner conversation.

Right off the bat, Kerouac and I got along famously, because essentially we were speaking the same language.

I recited some of my poetry and he poured great big glasses of wine. We talked of this and that, he telling me about Allen Ginsberg and Lawrence Ferlinghetti and all the other big figures of the day.

I regaled him with a story about how I got arrested at the corner of Stanley and Sherbrooke streets once when I was nude and holding a copy of Ferlinghetti's *Coney Island of the Mind* in one hand and a glass of gin in the other.

It turned out we had a mutual friend, Graham, and he wrote a note for him and we sat there like bosom buddies, laughing and drinking.

In short, we were getting along famously.

Now, Kerouac had obviously had a jump on us as far as the consumption of wine and other alcoholic beverages was concerned that day. Fact is, he was drunk as a newt.

However, when one is in the presence of a genius and visionary and all that, one tends to overlook minor flaws.

The evening proceeded smoothly until the subject of politics intruded in the conversation. Kerouac made some anti-Semitic remark. I was a bit astounded, because it was very crude, and said: "I beg your pardon?"

Kerouac proceeded to expound on this anti-Semitic remark and launch into a harangue about Kremlin-Zionist-Communist conspiracies and insidious infiltrations and all.

Now this was before *Dr. Strangelove*, but Kerouac sounded like a character out of that movie. He was insane.

I didn't know it at the time, but apparently in his later years— he finally drank himself to death in 1969—this was one of the major preoccupations of his addled brain.

Well, no one at the table reacted much. They sat there looking serious and earnest, trying not to be embarrassed and nodding the way you do when somebody important and famous says anything, even if it is totally idiotic.

I looked at Kerouac and said: "You're putting us on, right?"

He continued his diatribe, sprinkled with racist epithets and foul language.

"You're out of your mind," I shouted at him. "I'm not going to sit here and listen to a lunatic. You're a raving maniac."

Mind, I was into the wine a bit, and my voice was near the shriek level.

So we sat there shrieking away at each other while everybody in the restaurant got alarmed. Suddenly, Kerouac reached across the table and grabbed the shoulder of my jacket. He balled his other fist, and I pulled back.

He hung on to my jacket and as I pulled back he fell across the table, knocking over two wine bottles and breaking glasses.

He was still clutching my jacket when I stood up and pushed him off. He fell on to the lap of one of the Radio-Canada ladies.

I moved off my seat and stepped into the aisle.

I noticed that everyone was suitably horrified.

Waiters and the maître d' were running around and the various guests were trying to calm things down.

Kerouac lurched over to me and threw a punch.

I deflected his arm with my forearm and shoved.

He crashed back on to the table, knocking over more glasses.

What to do? Management must have wondered. Here was a literary lion. And there was me.

So two waiters grabbed me and threw me out the door.

I guess I lost the fight.

The evening I drank with Rudolf Nureyev
and felt his behind

[Wednesday, January 13, 1993]

IT WAS SAD these past few months hearing about the declining health and, last week, the death of Rudolf Nureyev.

But it brought back memories of the best summer of my youth, the year of Expo 67, a year many of us lived with incredible bravado and maybe just a little bit of hubris. One warm summer evening, I was sitting in the Mountain Street sidewalk café of the Bistro (Chez Loulou les Bacchantes), the best bar I remember in Montreal. It was a place where you could see anyone, from Pierre Trudeau to Leonard Cohen, from Jeanne Moreau to Gilda.

I was sitting there regaling the patrons with a story about Ethiopian Emperor Haile Selassie's visit to Expo earlier in the week.

I was 25 years old and had what I thought to be the world's best job, covering Expo for *The Gazette*.

There had been a been a fairly large crowd waiting at the Ethiopian pavilion, a round, red affair with a tall peaked roof, sort of a stylized tent. It had been cordoned off for the emperor's visit. He was accompanied by a mangy-looking dog, while a couple of imperial lions, looking forlorn and flea-bitten, lolled, loosely chained, outside.

After the emperor finished inspecting the exhibits, he was seated on a replica of his throne, part of the show. Then they put a cordon in front of him and opened the doors to the pavilion, letting the visitors in. The emperor sat there stiffly with his dog at his feet, scratching.

The whole thing appeared ludicrous to me. I described the scene with great relish to those sitting around me in the café, embellishing the tale, eliciting lots of laughs.

When I had finished, I noticed that a man who had been leaning against a car, smiling at my story, was meandering off up the street.

I jumped up, ran after him and asked: "Excuse, but aren't you Rudolf Nureyev?"

He had a very striking face, a Tatar face that shone when he grinned.

"Yes," he said in a heavy Russian accent. "Is funny. You are first person to recognize me on street. Not like Paris."

He was about 28 then, a few years after he had become a major international celebrity following his defection from the Kirov ballet by leaping over a customs barrier at Le Bourget airport in Paris.

"We must go and drink together," I told him. This evidently struck him as a capital idea.

We jumped on my little motorcycle, the first and only vehicle I ever owned. I had bought the Honda 90 that spring after seeing it for sale in a window, $7.95 a week financed by HFC (Household Finance). I got a licence good for driving scooters, farm tractors and snowmobiles and was always falling off the bike.

Nureyev and I drove over to the Swiss Hut, a fine seedy bar on Sherbrooke near Bleury where a lot of the colourful riffraff of town hung around.

We sat with a bunch of my friends and ordered quarts of beer and shots of vodka and proceeded to have a great time laughing, telling stories and drinking up a storm.

I was fairly left-wing in those days, but his conversation was pretty apolitical, except for his descriptions of daily life in the Soviet Union told matter-of-factly when I pressed him.

Because he was who he was, I couldn't readily dismiss his descriptions. In a way, he sowed doubt in my left-wing enthusiasms.

We sat there for hours having a great time. I even asked whether I could feel his legs and calves and bum, just to see what they felt like (hard as a rock).

There was one guy there, Ivy was his name, who took a real shine to Nureyev and invited him over to his place for dinner sometime, giving him his phone number.

When they threw us out of the Swiss Hut, around 3:30 a.m., I offered him a lift home on my little Honda. But I fell over while trying to kickstart it. He lifted it right off me, straight up, with one arm. And refused the lift.

"It's OK," I tried to assure him. "If we have an accident and you break your leg, I'll be famous."

At his request, I gave him the address of a gay bar on Peel Street and he went on his way.

I ran into him a couple of afternoons later and he told me he had phoned Ivy about that dinner invitation.

"Hello, Ivy," he had said, "iz Rudy here."

"Bug off, Auf der Maur," Ivy responded, thinking it was me imitating Nureyev, and hung up.

We laughed at that.

A critic once said of his dancing: "He had the untouchable arrogance of the gods."

My brief encounter with him indicated he also had a genuine common touch.

Les Nirenberg, Nick, and a "Quelque Show" co-worker, horse around
in the middle of what was then Dorchester Boulevard.
Photo by Jean-Pierre Karsenty.

Maybe a Bounder, Never a Cad

Conrad Black

OVER THE 30 YEARS that Nick and I were friends, his political views gradually evolved from '60s hard left to the beleaguered conservatism of the diehard English Montrealer. None of this altered our cordial relations even when he and Brian Stewart lived on Prince Arthur Street and Nick, ascertaining that Brian was on the telephone with me, marched around the telephone bellowing "Ho, Ho, Ho Chi-Minh! The FLN is going to win!"

There were minor irritations, as when he promised to send me voluminous Marxist texts supporting his positions in our endless, nocturnal, rather bibulous arguments. He faithfully put his material in the mail in large *Gazette* envelopes but boycotted the postal code in sympathy with the perpetually disaffected postal workers, delaying their arrival for up to 10 days.

We had several chess tournaments, at the Sir Winston Churchill Pub, which Nick initially represented as ideological struggles such as he claimed took place at the Olympic games. The intensity of the competition kindled his thirst and his play deteriorated as we progressed. Since I always felt that he was naturally at least as competent a player as I was, I never made much out of it when I won, as I would have had great difficulty replicating the feat without drink as an ally.

Our political differences also had their amusing aspects, as when he was called upon by his friends in organized labour to mediate with me a labour dispute our newspaper in Sept-Iles, *l'Avenir*, was having with the CNTU. Nick came to Sept-Iles when I was there. His mediation talks with the union spokesmen were so tedious and interminable, while his discussions with me degenerated into such a monumental pub-crawl, that he resigned his commission, claiming the union side was too inflexible.

When he and Les Nirenberg were putting on the local television program "Quelque Show," they occasionally invited me on as their caricature of a young fogey, a sort of civilian Colonel Blimp. (Nick would insist that I wear a tab collar and tried to persuade me to sport a Duplessis political button as well. I declined.)

This was the sort of innocuous self-amusement many people in their 20s get up to, but some of this spirit always stayed with Nick and it was one of the reasons Nick always made me feel young. Later, when he was city councillor and a columnist of greater influence, he became a determined and effective, if idiosyncratic, spokesman for the middle and lower income non-French communities. He did this without losing any of his sense of humour, without ever grating on his French friends, and while maintaining and building an immense circle of people who never ceased to regard him with affection.

He became a legend and if he had lived longer would have assumed a fabled status like some of the picturesque municipal journalists prominent in the lore of New York and Chicago. In his intuitive and very sociable way, he was a connoisseur of urban life.

He was also, as far as I could discern, virtually irresistible to women, the more so, no doubt, for never being boastful, indiscreet, raunchy, or even ungentlemanly. It is conceivable to me that he was sometimes a bounder, but not that he was ever a cad.

Above all, in all seasons and circumstances, he was an absolutely reliable friend. He taught all who knew him something of how to live, and in the majestic and good-natured courage of his last days, much about how to die.

The thought of not seeing him again imposes a very great sadness, made bearable only by the wealth of happy and humorous memories he left all who knew him.

Conrad Black is chairman and CEO of Hollinger Inc. and Southam Inc.

The Fall of 1970

Margaret Davidson

IF YOU WENT TO VISIT Nick Auf der Maur at the Stanley Street offices of CBC TV's "Hourglass" in the fall of 1970, the first person you met would be Frank, the elevator operator. Even by the standards of the day the building was old-fashioned. Upstairs you would find a long fluorescent-lit room replete with government-issue office furniture. This was the story editors' office. Nick's colleague Ken Seymour had the most impressive desk. The surface was always covered by a two-foot barricade of newspapers and other research material. Ken could not be seen behind it. By contrast, Nick's desk near the windows was unremarkable. But it was clear that Nick was the sparkplug of the group.

Nick was funny and bright and he laughed as much as he argued. He and Les Nirenberg bantered constantly. Nick never tired of telling a series of corny but endearing jokes to unsuspecting visitors. Then it would be time to go across the street to the Pam Pam for lunch or to the Seven Steps for a beer.

Nick's office visitors often included his dad's friend Harold, a 70-something gentleman in a navy blue overcoat and gray flannels. Harold was quite content to sit and watch us at our telephones and typewriters. Perhaps he phoned Mr. Auf der Maur later on in the day to say he had stopped by the Stanley Street office. Even then, calling on Nick was considered to be an event in Montreal.

People who admired Nick for his individual flair might not have guessed at his strength as a team player. He was a key member of the Hourglass team of journalists, producers and script assistants responsible for a half hour of current affairs programming following the six o'clock news. Each weekday morning we met to put together a lineup for that evening's program and to plan future items. If you were a newcomer to the CBC in the fall of 1970, as I was, Nick was always ready to share his knowledge and resources. He went out of his way to introduce you to the kaleidoscope of people he knew in the city.

"Hourglass" meetings were run by Executive Producer Paul Wright, who started by reviewing the program of the previous evening. Examples of Paul's epigrammatic wit about our efforts had been written out and taped to the walls. "The credits rolled on like an Icelandic saga." Nick, given to late nights, was not always on time for these 10 o'clock meetings.

One fall day in 1970, Nick arrived at the meeting late but without his customary apologies. At that time internal communications at the CBC were labyrinthine. Our news department was located in the old Ford Building on (what was then called) Dorchester Boulevard, five blocks away, and our studio was in Verdun. An elaborate system of taxi rides enabled us to stitch the program together each evening. We were not in constant contact with our own news department. So as the "Hourglass" group was in the midst of its daily meeting that October day, Nick was listening to a breaking story on a radio news report on his way into the office. When he arrived somewhat breathlessly with the news of the kidnapping of British trade envoy James Cross by the FLQ, other items we were working on fell immediately by the wayside. It was the first day of the October Crisis.

After the War Measures Act was proclaimed on October 16, it became known that the RCMP was going to arrest Nick to question him about his knowledge of the FLQ. Hundreds of other citizens would also he arrested. Paul Wright arranged for legal representation for Nick. Following a week or so of cat-and-mouse, the Mounties called Nick at the office to offer him an odd choice: he could be arrested inside the office or they would meet him on a nearby street corner and be taken into custody. Nick decided on the latter. Barbara Black and I walked down the street with him to meet the two Mounties and to record the licence plate of the car he was taken away in. They would not give us their destination. When we found out in the next day or so, Sandra Clementson and I took some clothes to Nick at the Parthenais detention centre. Of course we were not allowed to see him. He was released without charge after three or four days.

I don't know what effect the arrest had on Nick's political thinking. It hadn't been a lark for him but he was able to laugh at the absurdity of the situation. For his friends and colleagues, he provided a ringside seat at a historic event—or at least one a good tale could be told about. The October Crisis also brought its share of the world's press to Montreal, and a lot of journalists sought out Nick at the Stanley Street office. He had become an unlikely hero. He understood the story and he had become part of the story. And that was a pattern that would continue for the rest of his career.

Margaret Davidson worked with Nick for four years at "Hourglass."

At Nick and Linda's wedding reception, May 14, 1977.
From left to right: Brian Stewart, Irwin Block, Nick,
Patrick Brown, and Oliver Irwin.

NICK'S FATHER
NOV 29th. 1988.
(LAST DAY A
TCE BLAKE'S
TAVERN).
86th BIRTHDAY.

HISTORY

First "dome" was house of horrors

[June 28, 1984]

CANADA has the only two retractable roof stadiums in the world. But neither Montreal's Olympic Stadium nor Toronto's SkyDome was the first big stadium with a retractable roof.

Which was the first? It was a stadium that seated 55,000 spectators, and it was, believe it or not, the Colosseum in Rome, built in the first century A.D. Construction started under Emperor Vespesian (after whom public lavatories are named) and completed under his successors, Titus and Domitian.

To protect the crowd from the sun, the Colosseum was equipped with a very elaborate and intricate covering called the velarium, or velum.

The velarium was composed of triangular sheets of linen that were affixed to masts. These strips opened and closed like the iris of a camera.

Although there was a hole in the middle, so the Colosseum centre was open to the sky, all the 55,000 spectators could be shaded.

It wasn't a fixed awning. The whole thing had to be adjusted and manipulated at intervals as the sun angle changed. It was accomplished by a complicated system of pulleys and ropes manned by sailors who stood on the top of the building, along the edges.

And, while the hot Roman sun beat down on the velarium, the spectators underneath were treated to an early air-cooling system.

The air under the velarium was stuffy and dusty. But at intervals, the spectators were revived with a fine spray of perfumed water supplied to the upper tiers by a system of pipes.

Cicero and other writers report it was quite effective.

The trumpets would sound, then the water droplets would spray out and freshen spectators, and then the orchestra that accompanied the combats would start up.

So, while we may think of the Olympic Stadium and the Skydome as modern engineering marvels, the 2,000-year-old Colosseum was equally impressive.

The amazing thing is that if it hadn't been for vandalism—the habit of later Romans of tearing out chunks of the structure for construction materials—over the centuries it would still be usable today.

As it is, a good part of it still stands in downtown Rome. A contemporary structure, the Colosseum in Nimes, France, is still in use today.

But the Roman Colosseum had features that nobody has matched, even today.

Aside from gladiatorial fights and "hunts"—a game in which animals were loosed on captives—and other gory spectacles, the Roman engineers could flood the Colosseum so that naval battles could be staged.

The Colosseum could be filled or emptied with water about six feet deep in about a half-hour, roughly the time it takes to raise or lower the roof at the Olympic Stadium.

The Colosseum was actually not the major structure used in the Roman Games. The biggie was the Circus Maximus, an oblong racetrack where the big chariot races were staged. It is estimated the tiers along both sides could seat between 200,000 and 250,000 spectators.

But while that construction illustrates how Rome was an advanced civilization in many ways, what went on during the Roman Games was perhaps the greatest depravity in human civilization.

The Games are described as the first pornography as a spectator sport, the first and only true theatre of cruelty, where the inescapable conclusion is that the whole population of Rome had been turned into sadists.

The Games would go on for several days, and thousands of people would be killed in the course of the events.

The bloodshed was often highly imaginative.

For example, one account tells of how, after the Colosseum was flooded, a group of young girls would be sent out on rafts to serenade the crowd with voice and instruments.

After a song or two, hungry hippoptamuses and crocodiles would then be sent in to devour the girls. And the crowd would laugh hysterically.

They would do hideous things, like stick a prisoner in a hollow bronze statue of a bull and then set fire underneath it. The hollow statue would act as a sort of loudspeaker so that the victim's howls and screams could be heard throughout the stadium.

It became such a major part of life that even the civilized intellectuals admitted they couldn't stay away from the Games, which often featured such things as baboons and bulls raping women to death, or an actual re-enactment of the capture of some town in battle.

They even had such things as the equivalent of the seventh-inning stretch, and door prizes, boxes which would be catapulted into the crowd.

The lucky spectator would open it and find prizes like the modern equivalent of a $5-million villa.

Sometimes Caligula, in his madness, would have a poisonous snake put in the box. And everybody would laugh when the poor recipient got bit.

The fickle crowd used to get annoyed and boo Augustus when he was seen to have brought office work to his box in the Colosseum.

The Games got so gigantic, so out of hand, that they often moved them to lakes outside of Rome.

And thus, the biggest naval battle in Mediterranean history, in which 20,000 prisoners died, was not in fact a battle. It was a game witnessed by hundreds of thousands.

Madness then, madness now.

Through the past darkly: remembering the explosions that shook Quebec

[Friday, March 6, 1987]

IN EARLY MARCH 1963, then prime minister John Diefenbaker was battling Lester Pearson in the federal election campaign. Voting day was set for April 8.

Late on the evening of March 7, someone threw Molotov cocktails—they failed to explode because they were made of fuel oil instead of gasoline—at three armouries in the Montreal area: the Victoria Rifles and the Royal Montreal Regiment armouries on Ste. Catherine Street and the 4th Battalion of the Royal 22nd Regiment in Châteauguay. The next day, Montreal newspapers and radio stations received copies of the first communiqué from a group nobody had ever heard of: Le Front de Libération du Québec.

The communiqué was brash and florid, in the form of a "notice to the population of the State of Quebec."

"The FLQ," it said, "is a revolutionary movement made up of volunteers who are ready to die for the political and economic independence of Quebec."

It concluded melodramatically: "We demand that our wounded and those taken prisoner be treated as political prisoners and according to the Geneva convention."'

The police and the media didn't take it terribly seriously, although *The Gazette* did make it its top story on Page 3.

Most of those who bothered to pay any attention to it all laughed it off as some kind of a joke.

But in the coming weeks of that spring, Montrealers were destined to take the FLQ very seriously indeed.

Those original March 7 attacks were treated more as juvenile vandalism than anything else. The next time the FLQ popped up was a few weeks later, on March 29, when the monument to General Wolfe on the Plains of Abraham was pulled down. The FLQ claimed responsibility.

Two days later, railway workers discovered that a section of track just outside Montreal had been dynamited a few hours before Diefenbaker's train was due.

A week later, a powerful bomb was discovered on the Canadian Broadcasting Corp. transmitter atop Mount Royal. The device failed to explode because wind caused one of the wires to disconnect.

Two days later, Pearson was elected prime minister.

Two weeks after that, a bomb went off in the garbage container behind the army recruiting centre on Sherbrooke Street, near McGill University. The blast claimed the FLQ's first victim—Wilfred Vincent O'Neill, a 65-year-old watchman who either tried to pick up the 10-stick dynamite bomb or else had just opened the container and the explosive went off.

Terrorism, something that seemed until then only to afflict Europe and the Middle East, had come to Montreal.

The killing of O'Neill was almost accidental, as it turned out. The two teenagers who delivered the bomb had been told to place the device, timed to go off at 10 p.m., at the Sir John A. Macdonald monument in Dominion Square. But there were too many people around, so they stuck it in the garbage container.

They sat in Ben's Delicatessen waiting for it to go off. It didn't explode as planned, so they went back to check it.

They didn't know how to dismantle it, so they just left it.

An hour later, O'Neill found it.

But it was the events of May 17, 1963, that changed the city's mood into one of great apprehension.

Shortly after midnight, two groups of félquistes went about Westmount depositing bombs in mailboxes.

Shortly before dawn, five of these went off almost simultaneously.

All morning long the drama was played out, as police and army experts searched for more bombs. They discovered seven more.

Several were detonated under explosive-covering mats.

Walter (Rocky) Leja, a sergeant-major with the Third Field Engineers Regiment on Hillside Ave. in Westmount, had tackled two of those bombs, removing them from mailboxes.

A fair-size crowd stood off in the distance behind police barricades and watched him approach his third bomb of the morning.

Horrified onlookers, including police, reporters and cameramen, saw the bomb go off in his hands.

Leja survived. But the horrible injuries keep him confined to a hospital, 24 years later.

His near-fatal injuries caused me considerable anguish because I knew Leja when I was a member of the Third Field. On weekend training exercises at Farnham, Rocky taught me demolition work.

For lack of better targets, we used to blow up trees.

In a series of raids in early June, police broke up the original FLQ, arresting about 20 members, all but one teenagers or people in their early 20s.

Sixteen went to jail for terms of up to 12 years, while one skipped bail and went to Algeria.

What shocked me was that one of those arrested and sent to jail was François (Mario) Bachand who was a friend of mine. He was one of those who planted the bombs in Westmount.

By bizarre coincidence I knew both the victim and the criminal.

Bachand got out of jail a few years later.

He got into another scrap with the police and fled to France.

In January 1971, he was found dead in a Paris apartment, killed by a single bullet in the back of the head. The murder was never solved.

All this seems like so long ago. Yet it started just 24 years ago tomorrow.

(Editor's note: Walter Leja died in the hospital on November 24, 1992, at the age of 71.)

Of magpies, chatterboxes and gazettes

[March 16, 1988]

THERE IS SOMETHING ineffably romantic about newspapers.

I'll always remember the day I walked into a newspaper office for the first time. It was in 1965 and at my mother's insistence I went into the old *Gazette* building on St. Antoine Street to apply for a job as copy boy.

The offices looked straight out of the set for the 1940s movie, *The Front Page*. The editors' offices were surrounded by wood panelling, while the journeymen hacks sat with hats atilt in front of wonderful old Underwood typewriters.

And there at the news desk sat a lone copy editor with an old-fashioned green head visor and shirt-sleeves held back by arm garters. I was immediately smitten. Newspapering was for me.

In truth, I always loved newspapers, at least since I started reading *The Montreal Star* as a boy of 7, and started delivering both the *Star* and *The Gazette* in my adolescence.

Most often we take newspapers for granted, one of those things in our daily lives that somehow have always been there. But where did they come from? Who had the brilliant idea of printing news? How did papers evolve?

Well, naturally newspapers weren't possible until the German invention of moveable type in 1456. (Printing and moveable type had already developed in China and Korea but the concept didn't travel.) It took about a century before people started to realize that printing could be used for something other than books.

The first newspaper recognized as such was the *Gazetta di Venezia*, which came out in the mid-1500s. It was a record put out by the city-state government and ever since, the word "gazette" has been used to apply to the official government record.

The word itself is somewhat obscure but it's thought to come either from the Italian *gaza*, which means treasury or store, or *gazza* which means magpie or chatterbox. I like the latter version.

Variations of early newspapers started appearing all over continental

Europe soon thereafter, mostly in the form of court records, and promulgation of laws and edicts. A popular press started appearing soon after. At the beginning they were just single sheets, selling for a penny, which told a single story.

And judging by the sheets on display at the British Museum, pennysheet print journalism then was more along the lines of the *National Enquirer* and yellow rags than the staid likes of *The Times*.

Some of the titles: "News from Scotland describing the damnable life of Dr. Fennan who was burned at Edinborough" (1591); or "Wonderful and strange news of Suffolk where it rained wheat for a space of six miles;" or the more familiar "Baby in Woollich born with two heads."

Much of the early news was either false or very scurrilous, although there were more serious ventures like "News from Holland and Spain." Some sheets appeared more than once, like one in 1645 that had this extremely odd name: *A Preter Pluperfect Spic-and-Span New Nocturnal*; or *Mercurie's Weekly Night News*.

Mercury was a name often used then, and they often were sold by "mercury ladies" who ran through the streets shouting the headlines. The great poet John Milton, who was chief censor and arbitrator of what could be printed in Cromwell's time, edited a *Mercurious Pollticus* in 1659. The first regularly published newspaper in England is thought to be Nathaniel Butler's *Weekly News* (1622-41), while the first in France was the *Gazette*, founded in 1631.

The oldest still-published newspaper in the world is thought to *be Berrow's Worcestershire Journal*, which started off under the name *Worcester Postman* in 1690.

Needless to say, this proliferation of journalism caused governments to take notice. England brought in the Stamp Act in 1712, which required printers to buy paper sheets with a stamp on them costing roughly (in today's terms) $2. Tea houses, taverns and clubs would buy one paper for regulars to share.

The Stamp Act, of course, caused much resentment (and was one of the irritants that sparked the American Revolution). There was one British paper, *The Poor Man's Guardian*, which refused to buy government-stamped paper, instead using its own stamp which said: "Knowledge is Power."

Its printing equipment was smashed about 100 times and the publisher dragged before Parliament.

The first Canadian paper was the *Halifax Gazette*, which started in 1751 and was banned in 1756 for criticizing the Stamp Act and British tariff policy.

Montreal's first paper (and today amongst the oldest continuously published in the world) was *The Gazette*, which started off life as *Gazette du Commerce et Litteraire*. During the American Revolutionary Army's occupation of Montreal in the winter of 1775-76, Benjamin Franklin sent for a French-speaking Philadelphian named Fleury Mesplet and his press, to put out propaganda tracts to persuade the French-Canadian population to join the revolution.

Mesplet arrived just as Franklin and Benedict Arnold decided the cause was hopeless and retreated from Montreal. The British put Mesplet in a stockade for a while, then let him out to start a printing business, and eventually *The Gazette* in 1776. (It was published in French for about a year, then bilingually for a bit, and then in English.)

Within 50 years, literally scores of newspapers were founded in Montreal.

Two Canadian discoveries dramatically changed the nature of newspaper publishing worldwide. First was the discovery by Nova Scotian Charles Fenerty of how to make paper out of wood pulp in the 1830s. Prior to that most paper was made out of rags.

Fenerty noticed how wasps chewed wood fibre to make fine paper for their nests. Out of that grew Canada's gigantic pulp and paper industry, the country's largest source of manufacturing and employment.

And its development led to the burgeoning newspaper industry all over the world with cheap paper.

And in 1869, *The Canadian Illustrated News*, owned by Montrealer Georges Edouard Desbarats, ran a front page picture of H.R.H. Prince Arthur. It was the first photograph ever printed. Prior to that, only line drawings could be reproduced in print.

The *News* had developed the halftone plate and helped make a newspaper revolution.

Big chunk of our history is wrapped up in the Angus Shops

[Wednesday, January 29, 1992]

NEXT WEEK, one of the greatest industrial works in Canadian history closes the gates for the last time.

The fact that the Angus Shops is going out of business with hardly a whimper speaks volumes for the gradual decline of the industrial age, both in Montreal and in the Western world generally. The Canadian Pacific Railway's Angus Shops helped make Montreal the metropolis it is—and led directly to the peopling and settlement of Western Canada and the building of this country.

At its peak, the Angus Shops employed 14,000 workers, making it, along with Northern Telecom later, the biggest private employer in the city. (By comparison, the General Motors plant in Ste. Thérèse going full blast employs 3,000.)

The sad fact is that there is no need now for the Angus Shops, but for three-quarters of a century it was an essential part of Montreal's economic backbone. Its decline in importance in the past two decades accounts for the lack of fanfare accompanying its passing. A pity, because that betrays a lack of a sense of history on our part.

The vast shops and factories were built just after the turn of the century on a 140-acre site located on formerly agricultural land. (Today the area is known as Rosemont, northwest of Olympic stadium.)

The buildings covered 20 acres in 1904, employing 3,000 people.

A 1905 edition of Canadian Engineer describes the shops as one of the most modern industrial works on the continent, incorporating steam heat that maintained a constant 65° F. temperature on the worst winter days, innovative indoor toilets, acres of windows for lighting, as well as huge dining halls, playing fields and a library for the workers.

"A city within a city," *La Presse* marvelled at the time.

The work force was made up of English and French, which explains the strong English presence in Montreal's east end until relatively recently, as evidenced by such street names as Davidson, Hogan and Logan.

The opening of the shops and the ensuing housing boom led the area's annexation to the city of Montreal in 1905.

Angus Shops produced the rail cars and locomotives for the CPR and other rail equipment such as switches, signals and lights.

Around the time that Henry Ford was gaining fame for the assembly line, the same principle was in application at the Angus Shops, using an indoor network of 50 miles of rail line, making it possible (in 1912) to produce an astounding 30 rail cars a day.

At that time, a shortage of rail cars was driving many newly established Western wheat farms into bankruptcy.

To understand the need, consider this:

In 1901, the whole of the Canadian West counted 419,000 inhabitants. In 1916, the population stood at 1,698,000, phenomenal growth in just 15 years.

This was the age of rail, before highways and trucking had made any dent in passenger or freight traffic.

At the turn of the century, the CPR had 584 locomotives, 15,459 freight cars and 709 passenger coaches to handle the traffic. By 1915, it had 2,255 steam locomotives, 88,928 freight cars and 2,781 passenger coaches.

Revenues and profits grew in the same proportion.

Although the Angus Shops were the biggest, the CPR also built complementary works in Winnipeg in 1907 and Calgary in 1914.

During World War I, the factories were retooled to make bomb and artillery casings 24 hours a day, seven days a week.

By the time World War II arrived, the plant buildings covered 80 acres. This time production shifted to tanks and self-propelled artillery.

The first tank built in Canada was called the Valentine because the prototype (a British design) was delivered on Valentine's Day in 1940.

When the workers had produced the 100th Valentine, they decorated it with bunting and a banner that read: "Le Canada sera toujours. This is the 100th Fighting Tank produced by Canadian Pacific Angus Shops employees. Hundreds more will follow quickly. How's that, Hitler? Qu'en pense tu?"

Other tanks produced were the Canadian-designed RAM and the Grizzly, a Canadian version of the Sherman. (The Grizzly earned the unfortunate nickname of "Ronson" because it caught fire easily.)

Most of the 1,420 Valentines produced were shipped to the Soviet Union, where they won praise. (One was discovered recently in a river bed in Russia and returned to Canada with thanks.)

In all, Angus produced about 5,500 war vehicles.

After the war, the shops went into slow decline, employment falling to 7,500 in the late '40s, to 2,500 in the early '80s, to none next week.

"The Canadian Pacific Railway's Angus Shops helped make Montreal the metropolis it is—and led directly to the peopling and settlement of Western Canada and the building of this country."

Do you read this column regularly?
Thank Frank Zappa

[Wednesday, December 15, 1993]

ABOUT 30 YEARS AGO, when I was having a merrily irresponsible time working as a waiter in a downtown restaurant, my mother became worried about what I was going to be when—and if ever—I grew up.

"A writer, Ma," I would tell her, "I'm going to be a writer." In fact, I had no idea what I really wanted to do, except live for the moment and have plenty of fun. But "writer" seemed like a pretty good word of reply for my mother's probing questions.

I actually had scribbled some poetry. I was even employed for a time as resident poet at a beatnik club.

So my mother would look up the want ads for writers and occasionally call me: "There's an ad in the paper for a copywriter, it says here."

"Copywriting, Ma, that's advertising," I'd say. "I'm going to be a poet."

My career plans were not, shall we say, up to Swiss ambition. But she did figure out that the word "copy" had something to do with writing.

One day she saw an ad in *The Gazette* for a "copy boy."

She called me and told me about it, adding a lot of things about me being a shiftless lout, carrying on aimlessly and headed for ruin if I didn't start somewhere.

I promised I'd apply.

Well, I couldn't lie to my mother. But neither was I serious about applying for the job. I went down to the old *Gazette* building at 1000 St. Antoine Street West, intending to fill in the application and then run off to a tavern to meet my pals.

But, lo. I walked into *The Gazette* and it was like walking into a 1940s movie set. There were guys in green visors and guys wearing arm bands to hold up their sleeves. There was wonderful wood panelling, old Underwood typewriters and editors barking "copy!" while young men scurried at their command.

It was love at first sight. This was terribly romantic. I really wanted the job.

Too old, they told me. Twenty-two and I was already too old? Copy boys start at 16.

Well, I found out that back then, *Gazette* newspapermen hung out at Mother Martin's restaurant on Peel Street in the New Carleton Hotel where Place du Canada stands today.

Over I went, lobbied hard and got the job. Thirty-five bucks a week, about my nightly tips in my old job. I was elated. My mother was overjoyed.

As luck would have it, I got arrested one week into my new job. Something to do with early morning carousing on Mountain Street.

There I was sitting in the drunk tank at No. 1 police station, four on a Sunday morning, with bail set at $25. $25? I didn't know anybody who had that much cash.

Well, maybe Gary Eisenkraft had that kind of dough. He ran the New Penelope, a terrific folk-rock club on Sherbrooke near Park Avenue.

He wasn't thrilled at the prospect of coming down to Old Montreal with $25 to bail me out. But I whined and he said OK.

(In court later, I addressed the judge as "your highness," gave some convoluted explanation and then the judge threw both me and the charge out.)

A week later, Eisenkraft called me to tell me I owed him a favour. He had a new, unknown act playing at his club and couldn't get any publicity for it and I had to write a review of the performance for the newspaper.

"But I've never read a rock review, much less written one," I complained. "Besides, I'm just a copy boy. We don't get to write anything."

Bail money from a friend can be a persuasive argument.

So I went up to Walter Christopherson, the entertainment editor, pulled at his sleeves and said: "Mr. Christopherson, Mr. Christopherson, can I? Can I?"

To shut me up, he said: "OK, kid."

So I shuffled off to the New Penelope. I often went to the old Esquire Showbar on Stanley Street where I'd heard Bo Diddley and Little Richard and all the early rock greats. But I wasn't prepared for what I heard at the New Penelope.

This was really a weird group. Bizarre. Like nothing I had ever heard on the radio or in a club. I had a couple of beers with the lead singer next door at the Swiss Hut. Nifty guy. But weird. Funny weird, though.

I knew according to the deal I had to write a positive review. So I made it up, full of what I thought was real intellectualizing and deep meaning.

When it appeared and I saw my byline I was overwhelmed. Must have read it 500 times. It was wonderful. This is what I really wanted to do. Write for newspapers.

Years later, when I was working for the CBC, somebody came up to me and said: "I thought you said you didn't know anything about music?"

Not a thing, I replied. Zilch.

"How do you explain this?" he asked, showing me a glossy promotional brochure-magazine for a group due to play the Montreal Forum.

The front cover had a collage of articles written about the group. From the *New Yorker*, *Time* magazine, the *Village Voice*, etc. The only piece you could read in toto in the collage was my review from years before, my Frank Zappa and the Mothers of Invention review.

What a hoot.

This past Monday, I read a piece in the *New Yorker*, an appreciation of Frank Zappa upon his death last week of prostate cancer written by Matt Groening (accompanied by another tribute by Czech president Vaclav Havel).

In it, there was this great quote from Zappa: "Rock journalism is people who can't write, interviewing people who can't talk for people who can't read."

Twin towers of two churches reflect
resiliency of the Point

[Wednesday, December 29, 1993]

THEY STAND SIDE BY SIDE on Centre Street, the backs of their steeples a familiar landmark for motorists zooming along the Ville Marie expressway on the sharp bluff near Guy Street.

They are the twin spires of St. Charles and the single, truncated steeple of St. Gabriel's, the two churches that serve the 25,000 people of Point St. Charles, one of the more resilient and enduring neighbourhoods in Montreal. In fact, the Point is almost legendary, as neighbourhoods go, a charming collection of homes and businesses and stores and derelict monuments to 19th-century industries, the home of the Irish working class and all the folklore, myth and romance accruing to them.

The odd part, though, is that hardly any Montrealers, except those who live there, ever go to the Point because of its relative isolation. Its boundaries are a bit like fortifications that cut it off from the rest of the city, the Lachine Canal on the north and the autoroutes and highways on the other sides. Its seems only Verdunites, travelling along Wellington Street from downtown, regularly pass through the Point.

I go down there from time to time, mostly to see my regular printer, Vincent Antenucci, whose Impressions Vincent shop stands at the corner of Coleraine and Hibernia streets. From that corner, I look up Hibernia two blocks and see the fronts of those two intriguing churches.

Intriguing for me, because to me they symbolize Montreal, the English and French standing next to each other, close but separate, each distinct but with shared values and history.

At first, in the early 19th century, the Point was French. The parish of St. Gabriel's, an offshoot of St. Henri parish, was French. But with the construction of the Lachine Canal, then the Victoria Bridge, by Irish labourers and the influx of industries along the canal and the railway yards, the population became overwhelmingly Irish.

St. Gabriel's was originally a little church, but by the 1890s the parish was big enough and, more importantly, rich enough to build the present church.

The French parishioners built St. Charles church next door about the same time. St. Charles is a magnificent structure, with an architecturally sumptuous interior that alone makes it well worth a visit.

St. Gabriel's was also a beautiful and ornate church. But after the terrible fire of 1956, all that remained was the stone shell.

The fire started in the roof, which collapsed, bringing down the upper portion of the steeple with it. The entire interior was destroyed.

"I remember the fire well," said the Rev. Murray McCrory, the parish priest, "because it was June 1956, the same time I was ordained a priest at Notre Dame Basilica by Cardinal Léger.

"I only came to this parish in 1980, but I guess the look of the church today had to do with economics."

Presumably the parish didn't have that much money because the rebuilding job consisted of a concrete-slab roof and that truncated steeple without a bell tower.

The interior is, if not austere, definitely sparse. It has stone walls and little in the way of decoration or ornamentation, a stark contrast to the rich interior of its neighbour. (But St. Gabriel's definitely wins in the presbytery department. The adjoining priests' home at St. Gabriel's is a tiny architectural joy, while the one at St. Charles is drab and institutional.)

Today the Point is roughly 70 percent French and the rest English-speaking. But the two churches draw roughly the same attendance, indicating the remaining Irish core is tightly knit and still very much a vibrant community. (Interestingly, St. Charles' parish priest, Gerard Martineau, has an Irish mother.)

Every year for 15 or 20 years, I have been going to Christmas midnight mass with Brian McKenna. This year we chose to go to St. Gabriel's, not only because it puts on a superb celebration but also because it conveys that sense of history and community.

When you walk in, you almost expect to see Bing Crosby walk to the altar, so strongly does the place evoke the feel of an Irish working-class neighbourhood as depicted in those 1940s films.

For in the Point, with its splendid isolation despite being so close to the city core, it does seem that time stands still.

The church was crowded for midnight mass, a mass that felt warm and wonderful.

"It's like a little island we have here," McCrory was saying. "You have to cross bridges to get here. And here we have a real sense of community, as neighbourhoods used to have, because the sense of identity is strong."

In the heyday of taverns, Toe's was biggest and busiest

[Wednesday, May 24, 1995]

THE PASSING of Toe Blake brought back memories not only of his legendary hockey exploits but also of his other great contribution to Montreal life, Toe Blake's Tavern.

For more than 30 years, Toe's was a wonderful downtown institution, the biggest and busiest. The tavern, on Ste. Catherine Street West near Guy, opened in the early 1950s and closed in 1983 to make way for the Faubourg Ste. Catherine.

My father first took me there when I was about 15. That would be 1957, when Blake and the Canadiens were in the middle of their string of five straight Stanley Cups, a record that never has been matched.

Needless to say, the fact the tavern threw an annual Stanley Cup victory party was not bad for business.

A huge crowd used to gather in front of the tavern during the Stanley Cup parades, cheering our heroes lustily but waiting for the last car, a convertible, with coach Blake in it. When the car got near the tavern, Blake would stand up and give the big V sign with his fingers. The noise was deafening. Then Blake would pump that V in the air twice, the way people used to order two draughts of beer in Montreal taverns.

The noise level increased sharply.

And then, like being sucked in by a vacuum, the crowd in front of Toe's would disappear in a whoosh inside the tavern for their free beer.

Later, the players and the rest of the team would have their private party, but I managed to sneak in on more than one occasion.

Montreal tavern culture back in those days was interesting. Everybody, it seemed to me, went to taverns, except women, of course.

Almost all the major downtown taverns—Rymark, McGill College, Coronet, Royal, Tupper, Toe's and the Mansfield—are gone. The Peel Pub used to be the major gay tavern of its day. The Stanley, St. Regis and Dominion Square taverns still look the same, although the ambience is different.

Back in the '50s and '60s, taverns had important social functions, combining elements of a men's club, cheap food, cheap beer and profound, frivolous and cheap talk. Also, there was commercial activity. Goods that fell off trucks were sold in taverns, and in the days before Loto-Québec, taverns were where you placed a bet. Most downtown taverns had runners who sat alone at tables, waiting for somebody to sit down and place a bet. The runner would then take it to the bookies, a few doors away.

After school, I used to walk downtown to meet my father. Depending on his credit standing in the respective taverns, we'd go to either the Royal on Guy or Toe's. This is a habit I have kept up ever since.

Toe's was a great place, peopled by the characters one read about in Damon Runyon stories, ones we saw in those 1940s movies, colourful rogues, seedy down-and-outers. But the downtown tavern was basically democratic, and one could find unemployed guys sitting at the same table as stockbrokers.

In taverns, I got the university education I didn't get in a school.

But Toe's was special, not only because it was my father's local but because it was different from the others. It was big, for one thing, able to seat about 300 people comfortably, while most of the others were limited in size to about 50.

It was also brighter, more open and had great art on the walls, featuring all the greats in Montreal hockey history.

The wooden chairs were big and comfortable, with large, smooth armrests.

It was there that I learned to eat Oka and cheddar cheese with hot English mustard, drop a raw egg into my beer, read four or five newspapers a day—important stuff like that.

Naturally, it was a great place to watch hockey games on TV.

Toe Blake was there most days, especially after the hockey season. Because the Forum was just a short walk away, he'd be in often during the season, although he spent most of his time in his office in the back. People would walk into his office all the time. You could tell whether he liked them or not, because if he did, he'd order a couple of beers on his intercom and you'd see the waiter walk in with them. If the waiter wasn't summoned, you knew the guy would out of there within a minute.

Former MNA Gordon Atkinson says you could set your watch by Toe because every morning sharp at 10:15, he'd walk out of the office, through the tavern and out across the street to the TD Bank to deposit the receipts.

I was impressed by the way Toe always wore a fedora, inside and out. Maybe that's where hats entered my consciousness.

Thanks, Toe Blake, you gave this town a lot to remember.

A Source of Inspiration

Terry Mosher (Aislin)

THROUGHOUT THIS BOOK you will find a selection of favoured cartoons from the dozens that I had drawn of Nick Auf der Maur over the past 30 years.

In the late 1960s, Nick and I met in a Crescent Street bar called the Boiler Room (as people we both knew had been insisting that we get together). Because of this, and being cantankerous times, we were both prepared to hate each other.

We didn't.

Indeed, we got royally drunk, with me having no idea at that time that I was about to become Nick's official cartoonographer. We became fast friends leading to me being his best man at his wedding in 1976. There were many memorable voyages together, some even outside of Montreal. One trip in particular was to Cuba where we both lost our leftist-leaning virginity.

However, in the mid 1980s, dealing with my own demons, I began the long process of sobering up, which meant that I began seeing a lot less of Nick (even if continuing to cartoon him at will). Eventually, it worked to the extent that I didn't miss the drink anymore. But I missed Nick.

I still do actually, and always will.

Hector Berthelot was a celebrated journalist, illustrator and boulevardier here in Montreal in the late 19th century. Quite the rascal, Berthelot was always finding himself in trouble. Whereas the English had their 4 o'clock-tea, Berthelot invented the French tradition of the 5 o'clock-gin (which evolved into the current happy hour). When he died, Berthelot left a generous amount of money at his favourite bar for those to drink who managed the long walk up to his burial in the Mt. Royal cemetery and back again. Notorious in his time, Berthelot is virtually forgotten today.

We can't—won't—let the same thing happen to Nick Auf der Maur.

At the very least, Crescent Street—and God knows, the barkeeps in the area owe it to him—should be renamed la rue Nick; or perhaps, le roué Nick?

Gazette editorial cartoonist Terry Mosher has received many honours, including two National Newspaper Awards. He is a member of the Canadian News Hall of Fame.

NAPS

· NICK <u>DOESN'T</u> RUN IN PROVINCIAL ELECTION!

Sofa so good: No joy equals afternoon nap

[Monday, May 6, 1985]

TODAY, LET'S PAY TRIBUTE to one of the greatest institutions in the civilized world—the afternoon nap.

This past weekend my daughter gave me a belated birthday present, one of those T-shirts bearing a printed message.

"Shhh," it said on the front. "I'm playing rock," the flip-side read. This all refers to an old family joke.

Once, years ago when Melissa was about 3, she wanted to play horsie. You know the game—we've all played horsie—you have to get on all fours and the kid gets on your back and you crawl around and the kid shrieks.

Anyhow, this one time I was feeling tired and didn't feel up to it so I said: "I've got a better game, let's play rock."

The rules to playing rock are very simple. You lie very still on the carpet and pretend you're a rock.

If all goes well, and the kid is gullible enough, after about five minutes you both fall asleep.

It took Melissa about 10 or 12 times before she caught on, but ever since "playing rock" is our code for taking a nap.

In a similar vein, my Christmas gift last December was a "napping blanket" from my friend Johan Sarrazin.

It's a beautiful, quilt-like Indian cotton blanket, perfect for afternoon naps on the chesterfield—one of the simplest and most pleasurable activities known to man.

My appreciation of the afternoon nap explains my affection for countries like Spain, where the siesta is part of the culture.

One of the reasons I like vacations so much is that I get to nap every single afternoon, sort of a two-week-long weekend.

Anyhow, my napping blanket and T-shirt somehow imply that I'm developing a Dagwood Bumstead reputation.

I don't really care. Every time I see a cartoon strip in which Dagwood takes a nap on his sofa (that's the American word for chesterfield) I can identify with him.

For some people, afternoon napping is either for little children or old fogies. But they just don't know what they're missing.

I ask you, what offers greater contentment than lying down for a nap after a big meal?

There's a sense of relaxation and enjoyable indolence that comes with taking a nap.

Power snoozes, cat naps, 40 winks, the afternoon nap is at least as effective as a morning jog and a lot more comfortable.

While there are probably 100 times as many practioners of napping, there are a lot fewer books written about it than jogging.

But if you have trouble falling asleep on weekend afternoons I recommend reading those jogging books.

Napping is the lazy man's road to good health and a sound mind.

It's time to switch the blankets and give thanks for naps

[Wednesday, November 27, 1991]

TOMORROW is the American Thanksgiving, a day of great tradition, for Americans at least.

It used to be, when I was married to an American, that I got to celebrate Thanksgiving twice every year. No more, alas.

But in the past 10 years or so, I've developed my own little way of marking the American Thanksgiving. It's the time of year when I switch napping blankets. During the summer, I keep a light woolen napping blanket, a big shawl really, on my chesterfield. My regular Indian cotton quilt napping blanket, heavier and warmer than my shawl, goes upstairs on to one of the spare beds for the warm weather.

For some reason, perhaps because the American Thanksgiving really seems to mark the advent of winter weather, I've taken to a ritual switch of napping blankets at this time.

Maybe it has something to do with the fact that after the big turkey dinner, I always have a quick nap; or perhaps because this weekend is the busiest travel weekend in the American year, it naturally makes me feel tired. Whatever, I look forward to a nap under that blanket, a Christmas present from my old friend Johan Sarrazin.

She gave it to me in recognition of my long-time great devotion to the afternoon nap, a habit shared by much of the world. Except for a period of adolescent frenzy, I've been a napping aficionado.

This started, I think, when I was about 19 and working in Geneva, Switzerland, where, like most people, I had a very civilized two-hour lunch break.

I lived near my work place, so I'd go home, eat and then lie down for a half-hour. It became part of my body clock.

Now, the afternoon nap—on weekdays at any rate—doesn't fit into the regular North American lifestyle. Fortunately, I work out of my own home, so more often than not, I can indulge myself.

Indeed, I have a hard time walking by my chesterfield, or couch if you will, in the afternoon without trying it out for 20 minutes or so. I have the happy facility, no doubt due to a pure and innocent lifestyle, of being able to nod off in a minute.

Of course, I'm not what you would call a morning person—unless you call 2 a.m. the morning. My body rhythms are more attuned to Latin countries like Spain and Argentina where everybody eats very late at night, goes to sleep late and therefore perhaps needs an afternoon nap to catch up.

There are many theories about napping and I try to keep up on them.

Recently, for example, *The Gazette* carried a feature in which it was claimed the afternoon nap increased one's creativity and productivity.

The story was based on a new book, by some crackpot Californian psychologist named Ernest Rossi, titled *The 20-Minute Break: Using the New Science of Ultradian Rhythms*.

I say crackpot, because it seems to say what three-quarters of the world's population has long known and practiced, that napping is good for you. (To give it credence, the story and book quotes Sir Winston Churchill, a big afternoon napper.)

The book just dresses up common sense with a lot of California-speak about "ultradian breaks" and presto some quack has made a buck.

The story quoted a Larry Dossey, a physician and author of *Space, Time and Medicine*, as saying Rossi's work "will change the lives of many … and could have revolutionary consequences."

Well, maybe those Californians have never checked out the Mexican siesta.

But for every quack on one side of an argument, America will produce another on the other side.

To wit, Ray Wunderlich, a "preventive nutritionist" in St. Petersburg, Florida, who was quoted as saying: "The urge to take an afternoon nap is not a normal habit.

"The real reason for that after-lunch slump at work may have more to do with poor nutrition and late-night television than with natural biological rhythms."

What is astonishing is the number of people who are nap experts, academics who specialize in this business.

There is Professor James Horne at Loughborough University in central

England: "Our natural sleep-wake clock is designed naturally for two sleeps a day, a long one at night and a short nap in the afternoon."

A study at the University of Athens medical school in Greece concluded that men who nap at least 30 minutes a day are 30 percent less likely to suffer heart problems than those who don't nap.

David Dinges, a University of Pennsylvania psychologist who specializes in the study of sleep, notes that "our society looks down on naps" but day sleep is highly beneficial.

The first I suspected that the reform movement in China was coming off the rails was when I read a story that the government was staging an assault on afternoon naps.

In China, office workers are in the the habit of taking naps on the tops of their desks (they are used to sleeping on hard surfaces) after lunch. As part of the modernization program, the government tried to eliminate naps.

See what happened?

Dagwood Bumstead has the right idea.

Nick and Juan Rodriguez at the Rialto Theatre, November 1996.
"Two goons ratcheted our arms behind our backs and ejected us
from the stage."
Photo by Esmond Choueke.

For Love and Honour

Juan Rodriguez

I HAD BEEN AWAY in California for seven years and when I came back to Montreal the first person I saw on Crescent Street was Nick Auf der Maur and, without flinching, he took me under his wing. So to speak.

Things got going and one of them was Nick's outrage at two guys, who will go unmentioned here, who made a movie that intimated that Courtney Love killed her husband, Kurt Cobain. Now, it just so happened that Nick's daughter, Melissa, played bass for Love's band, Hole. Therefore, and by extension, these two guys were impugning the reputation of Nick's daughter. Nick wasn't going stand for that. But—the nerve—these guys decided to show the movie here at the Rialto Theatre. Nick told me he wanted to do something about it. I told him I'd support him in whatever he did.

Well, come Monday of the week of the screening, Nick is in his office at Winnie's and he's fuming. The screening is Thursday, and he's already fuming. I joined him to fume. "How dare they" and "those bastards" are two phrases I remember. We went across the street to Ziggy's to continue fuming. We kept this routine up through the week, until the fateful Thursday, when I walked in to Winnie's, sat across the bar from Nick, and gave him a "I-don't-want-to-go-along-with-this" look.

His eyes bore into me with a "you chicken" look. I wilted, and went to join Nick.

"We've got to get control of the media," Nick said of the impending event. "And the best way to do that is to grab the microphone. We have to have a plan." What plan is that, I asked. "The plan is that we drink, and then it will come to us." OK, we drank. Soon enough, Nick asked our buddy Irwin Steinberg if he could post bail for us, he said yes, and, again without flinching, Nick leapt from his bar stool and announced, "We're off to get arrested!"

I followed.

We sauntered across the street, where Ziggy Eichenbaum was waiting with his 4x4 to drive us to the Rialto. We were feeling no pain, we were on a mission. Ziggy came to a screeching halt, ejecting us from our seats. With the stride of a general, Nick marched into the Rialto and I followed.

Lo and behold, we found out that the movie screening had been cancelled (due to a threatened Love lawsuit), but they were holding a "press conference" instead. So much the better. Nick quickly spotted the stairs to the stage and soon there we were.

He grabbed the microphone and blurted, "I'm Melissa's mother!" and deftly corrected himself. Soon enough, someone from the audience asked me "Who are you?" I found myself mouthing, "I'm Juan Rodriguez, and I used to be the rock critic for the *Montreal Star* and *Gazette*!"

Duh! It was about this time that two goons ratcheted our arms behind our backs and ejected us from the stage. Nick and I were separated. I could not follow.

While Nick was given an escort to the front entrance, I was being kicked and shoved down the stairs leading to the alley. As Dangerfield might say, "No respect!"

I picked myself up, tried to figure out where I was, and staggered around the corner to the Rialto's entrance where I saw Nick … signing autographs! "This is fun, isn't it?" he asked me.

Then he asked, "How do you feel?" And I replied, for some reason, "Takes a lickin' and keeps on tickin." And Nick said, "I feel like I'm 18 again." (I said yeah, yeah, yeah, but the next day I felt 80.)

Exuberant, we went back to the bar and Ziggy said, "You look terrible!" And Nick smiled. A smile I will never forget.

Juan Rodriguez was a rock critic before there were rocks and a Montrealer before Champlain.

"Downtowner's" World was Truly Global

Brian Stewart

I THINK that for Nick life was just too serious to be taken altogether seriously. He was full of such contradictions; a tireless philosopher-clown who held to his own sightlines on relevance. And if you were around him long enough you'd end up surprised how much you learned about life, and eventually about yourself as well.

God knows, he could be a trial. And, let's face it, Nick loved being a trial. Oh, those political rants bellowed across a crowded room; those preposterous jokes; and the fathomless nights on the town that would leave visiting friends begging for emergency medivac out of Montreal.

Still, as a foreign correspondent in the '80s I'd make a point of taking regular R&R in Montreal to gain back a sense of reality. That inevitably meant ditching my suitcase on arrival and heading for whatever bar served as Auf der Maur's current HQ. The scene rarely varied. He'd glance up from his newspaper with the greeting, "Brian, ya bum ya, where have you been?" As if I'd just wandered out for cigarettes.

And then conversation seemed to resume without a beat. It rarely mattered what crisis I may have come from, Nick had his own fascinations to share.

Ethiopia? He'd recall Gibbons' views on its ancient Christianity, and ask all about the stone temples of Axum. The Falklands War? That reminded Nick he wanted to take Melissa on a tour of British Naval Museums. Lebanon? Had I checked out the Roman piping beneath Beirut's streets?, he'd ask. Or the Phoenician wharves they'd just located beneath the town of Tyre? And was it true the last Cedars on Mount Lebanon were really dying of neglect? Who was in charge of post-war planning for Beirut? Nick wanted to write him with some ideas…. Later, he'd tell a bizarre, but true, story of two Quebecers who were dominating Lebanese wrestling, when the ring itself wasn't under shellfire.

We shouldn't forget this: Nick was astonishingly knowledgeable. I could never quite understand how he managed to vacuum up so much information given his lifestyle, but he had a beartrap memory for detail and minutiae, as anyone who debated him quickly found out. And he flourished as columnist and raconteur within a 1940s technological time warp. He had no use for television news at all, and even less for the Internet. Instead he listened to the radio, devoured newspapers and magazines, and worked bar-phones for stories and background.

As for files and magazines—scribbled notes on cocktail napkins. He was one of the few "remarkable characters" I've met who could actually listen, as well as talk.

While we immortalize him as one of the great "Downtowners" of all time, we should also remember his interests were remarkably broad. He was passionately wrapped up in international affairs long before he took to civic politics.

He got himself kicked out of the Kremlin in the late '60s for "ranting" about Czech independence; and in the mid-'80s went to a highly dangerous corner of the Philippines as an election observer. Friends warned him he could be kidnapped or assassinated. Predictably, he went; and stayed an extra week to party.

Apparently comfortable with his own failings, he was happily at ease with the weakness of others. He rallied to defend any who were down, though I suspect he was always surprised if they took being "down" all that seriously. He didn't have to be fiercely loyal to friends; he was effortlessly loyal.

I flew in to visit him just days before his death. He was in great pain, of course, and said he felt the end was very near, but he also wanted to know what I was working on. As it happened, a documentary on 1968, the year I had first met Nick.

"You lived through amazing times, Nick," I said. "A fabulous time to have been alive."

"Right, right, pretty good," he answered in a fading voice.

And then he stirred. "Now about '68. Don't forget Danny the Red in Paris. And the Tet Offensive was in April, I think. Are you covering the Chicago riots, and the Chicago Seven?

"You'd better do the Montreal Left and all those damn manifestos we wrote... ."

We both knew this was the last time he would ever try to guide me; and I profoundly hope he sensed how grateful I was. For everything.

Nick and Brian Stewart were born in the same week in the same hospital in Montreal. There has been speculation they were accidentally switched at birth. Brian first met Nick on *The Gazette* in 1968. Stewart is co-host of the CBC National Magazine and also Senior Correspondent. He has been in television since 1974, much of the time as a foreign correspondent. Now he is settled in Toronto, where he has a wife, a daughter, and a vast storehouse of golden memories of Montreal and Nick.

Les Canadiens sont là... not to mention the Ogilvy Christmas window, Beaver Lake, great early morning radio, Sherbrooke Street in the snow, Edgar Andrew Collard, the Jazz Festival, driving along the lakeshore – even Auf der Maur raving on about something or other...

OUR CITY

When Schnozzola played the Point

[Friday, February 1, 1980]

THE PASSING OF JIMMY DURANTE this week brings to mind an amusing political anecdote from the annals of Montreal's reprobate political past.

It was in June 1960, and "Schnozzola" was playing at the old Bellevue Casino with Sonny King and Eddie Jackson. The trio had a popular act and were big on TV in those days.

Frank Hanley, then in his umpteenth term as both the independent city councillor and an independent member of the provincial legislature for St. Ann's, called up Durante and said: "Mr. Durante, you come from a poor neighbourhood in New York. I represent a poor neighbourhood in Montreal. The boys in the Point St. Charles sports league are handing out trophies Saturday morning and they'd get a real thrill if Jimmy Durante, the famous comedian, would hand them out."

Durante readily agreed. So on that bright June morning Frank Hanley pulled up at the Mount Royal Hotel in a splashy convertible with a big sign on it saying , "Jimmy Durante-Frank Hanley."

Durante, King and Jackson climbed into the back seat, with Hanley sitting on top of the seat, politician-style. They drove down Peel Street and pulled onto Ste. Catherine. And then one of those big. old-fashioned, topless buses pulled in behind Hanley's car. The 15-piece band in the bus started blaring. The bus was festooned with banners saying, "Durante for Hanley, Bank on Frank" and "Durante votes for Hanley." The banners were on the side of the bus, and Durante didn't see them. The little parade rolled merrily down to the Point, with Durante and Hanley smiling and waving to the crowds. It was only when they were deep in the heart of St. Ann's, when they stepped out of the car to pose for a picture that Durante noticed the election banners.

"Jeez, Frank," said Durante, "why didn't you tell me? Let's get to it."

And so, after the sports presentation, Durante hit all the bars and taverns of the district, pumping hands for Frank Hanley. "He only drank milk," Hanley recalls. Afterward, he took the trio to Tony Guinta's shop at

McGill and Notre Dame Sts. (father of the current Tony the Tailor) and outfitted them in new suits. Needless to say, Hanley got re-elected June 22, the election that brought Jean Lesage and his Quiet Revolution Liberals to power.

On Tuesday, Hanley and his pals gathered at the Lantern pub in the Windsor Hotel, to have a few drinks too many in honour of the teetotalling Durante. Hanley passed the hat around and collected $95 to buy memoriam candles at Mary Queen of the World cathedral. "The candles cost $2.50 each, so we'll be able to go about 40 weeks," explained Hanley. True Montrealers that they are, Hanley hits the 9 a.m. Sunday mass in French at the cathedral, while his wife goes to St. Patrick's for the English mass.

"Durante was a good Catholic," said the professional Irishman. "I'm sure he's in heaven with Mrs. Calabash."

Expo 67: The legend lives in the memories we relish 20 years later

[Friday, May 8, 1987]

"Do you remember . . . ?" has been the opening line of half the dinner conversations in town ever since the spate of 20th-anniversary commemoration articles about Expo 67.

How many times in recent weeks have you heard dreamy-eyed people starting off like that? Recalling what, for those of us who lived through it, was the most wonderful summer of our lives? I don't think I know a single Montrealer old enough to remember that year who doesn't think 1967 was the ultimate, the epitome of living.

Those were happy times. They were exciting, thrilling, discovering and just plain exuberant times.

And it's not just harking back to innocence or some picayune exercise in remembering trivia. It was genuine. It was a real "once-in-a-life-if-you-are-lucky" experience.

The fact that we are still talking about it, still relishing the rather incredible and intangible sense of euphoria that gripped our lives for that magic summer, demonstrates the basic truth of the enduring legend of Expo 67.

The year 1967 was one of turmoil, both domestically and internationally. The Vietnam War raged, student and youth revolt was gearing up to the explosions that followed in 1968 in the United States and Europe, separatism was a growing and volatile force here ... and yet from the opening of Expo to the closing, it was as if we had an unwritten truce from the problems that afflicted the world.

We went out and celebrated life, under the official theme of Man and His World. (Only the transit workers who went on strike toward the end of the fair failed to respect the truce.)

I was fortunate in that I had been assigned to report on Expo about 1½ or two years before the opening, as a junior reporter under Bill Bantey who wrote a regular column on Expo for *The Gazette*.

So for two years—while I led a schizoid life as a youthful revolutionary and street activist—I followed the unfolding dream, completely enraptured.

We all have our personal memories of that summer, little and big incidents, the general ambience that is forever imbedded in our consciousness.

My greatest memory of Expo was my Centennial Project.

You remember that in 1967, everybody had centennial projects. Some people roller-skated across Canada. Communities built libraries and parks. Individuals resolved to visit all 10 provinces, and so on.

Since I was assigned to cover Expo and was on the site all the time, and caught up in both the spirit of the 100th anniversary of Confederation and the international aspect of the whole thing, I chose to devote myself to the promotion of country and internationalism.

There were 61 countries participating in Expo 67. Each one was assigned a national day during the run of the fair.

I resolved that on each national day, I would take one of that country's national pavilion hostesses to dinner. Now some may read a euphemism in this, but that would be a rather prurient interpretation.

Suffice to say that I plunged into my self-appointed task of promoting international understanding with the energy and enthusiasm that characterize youth.

In that manner, I visited the whole world. Europe. Africa. Latin America. Asia.

Expo 67. The world was our oyster.

The memories make us wistful and fog up our eyes.

And if only just for that, I'll always have an enormous soft spot for Jean Drapeau for having provided myself and all Montrealers with the most marvellous summer that is humanly possible to imagine.

Anti-anglophone acts should be condemned, just as racist acts are

[Wednesday, December 11, 1991]

ON FRIDAY, many of us wore a white ribbon, part of a national campaign to both commemorate the second anniversary of the massacre of 14 women at Ecole Polytechnique and to get men to speak out against violence against women.

One of the ideas behind the white-ribbon statement was that silence, in effect, condones hatred and violence. It means that we, as human beings, have a duty to speak out against offensive behaviour, against intolerance and hatred.

After a charity function Friday night, I met a friend who informed me about the memorial concert at Église St. Jean Baptiste where marchers had gathered to hear speeches and a concert by the Orchestre Métropolitain de Montréal.

I was appalled to hear that at such an event, a federal cabinet minister was interrupted by a loud outburst of venom and bigotry when he switched to speaking in English.

"Parle français!" an angry man shouted. "C'est Québec. Les familles sont français."

Gerry Weiner, minister of multiculturalism and citizenship, had been specifically asked by Suzanne Laplante-Edward, mother of one of Marc Lepine's victims and master of ceremonies of the concert evening, to include English in his memorial address.

A few other people seated near him in the church also muttered "parle français" and "souveraineté."

The idea that in a setting like that, where people had gathered presumably to speak out by their presence against misogyny and other stupid human shortcomings, someone would feel compelled to utter such bigoted sentiments, shocked me.

Well, I thought, it was such a patently offensive and sick thing to do that it may have a beneficial effect. It would show that some people are really deranged and sick when it comes to Quebec nationalism.

So I picked up the French papers on Saturday to see how they covered that incident.

Le Devoir had a story titled "Poly: un touchant concert de reflêxion."

The story mentioned the presence of federal politicians Benoît Bouchard and Audrey McLaughlin. But not only did it not make any reference to the incident, it didn't even mention Weiner's presence.

I didn't see any mention of it in news stories Saturday in *Le Journal de Montréal* or *La Presse*, and it wasn't mentioned on any of the French radio stations I happened to listen to.

(Columnist Eve McBride wrote an excellent piece on it in Sunday's *Gazette*. As well, the incident was mentioned in a *Gazette* piece on Saturday about various events marking the massacre.)

This lack of reaction saddened me enormously, especially as it came in the midst of 500 or so people pledged, as it were, to speak out against intolerance.

In the same context, if someone had tried to shout down a black, or a Jew, or an Arab, or a lesbian, or just about anybody else, there would have been outrage.

But somebody tried to shout down a male anglophone. And everybody sort of maybe got embarrassed and instinctively decided to cover it up.

Now, I thought perhaps I was maybe exaggerating the incident.

But the other day I spoke to a young McGill student, from a bicultural family, who was at the church and who happens to be making a film about violence against women.

"I think it was the first time I realized that there was such violence and hatred in those feelings of linguistic intolerance," the young man said. "We were there because we're against violence. I don't think I would have made the equation between various forms of violence and linguistic intolerance if I hadn't physically felt the hatred in that man's voice."

He went on to say he felt some people appeared to share the man's sentiments, but that most people at the service were waiting for some response.

The response came from Laplante-Edward, who apparently carried it off with great dignity. People, he said, reacted with enthusiasm to her words.

But like me, he expected the media to react also, especially since it was an event that asked people to speak out about wrongs.

But generally we got almost total silence and no reaction. It was swept under the rug, another family embarrassment we pretend didn't occur. That is a reflection of a cowardly society and cowardly media, afraid to draw attention to something sick in our midst.

Yes, we have racism in our society. And part of the racism is a strain of venomous and virulent anti-English bigotry.

Not long ago a comedian in the West Island insulted some francophones in the audience and the news media made a major controversy out of it. And reporters weren't even present there.

Here a federal minister is shouted at by a racist zealot in front of reporters. And they make hardly any reference to it.

No, it's OK to insult and belittle English-speakers, to behave like a fascist fanatic and utter platitudes about "the best-treated minority in the world."

Just as we have a duty to speak out against violence against women, we have a duty to speak out against verbal violence directed at a language group.

Setting the record straight: the real story behind Expo 67

[Wednesday, April 29, 1992]

IT WAS THE GREATEST summer of our lives. The memories of Expo 67 live on in the minds of those of us who were fortunate enough to have been through it.

It was like a fairy tale, that summer, and as with the mythology that accompanies many fairy tales, this one is full of revisionist history on how it came to be. For one thing, Expo 67 is often seen as the centrepiece of the Quiet Revolution launched by reformist provincial Liberals and the reformist Montreal mayor, Jean Drapeau, both of whom took power in 1960.

The fact of the matter is that Montreal was awarded Expo 67 because of the efforts of former prime minister John Diefenbaker, former Quebec premier Maurice Duplessis and former Montreal mayor (and senator) Sarto Fournier.

In January 1957, Colonel Pierre Sévigny, a Canadian World War II hero, was appointed chief Quebec organizer for the Progressive Conservative Party by Diefenbaker, then the opposition leader, largely because Sévigny had been one of the few Quebecers to support Diefenbaker's leadership bid the previous year.

"Quebec was a Tory desert then," Sévigny recalled. "I couldn't get candidates, funds, or … interest anywhere."

But one day, one of Sévigny's cousins, Louis Tassé, walked into his forlorn office with a man named Barthe, an organizer of country fairs in places like Sherbrooke and Drummondville.

He had an idea of organizing a big fair in Montreal for the 100th anniversary of confederation, 10 years down the line.

"Frankly, I was rather bored with their idea after listening to them drone on," Sévigny said. "Another promoter with a crazy scheme.

"But when I mentioned it to my wife that night, she said we (the Tories) didn't have any ideas—why not pursue it?"

Sévigny went to Ottawa and presented the idea to Diefenbaker. He liked it, but said Premier Duplessis would have to approve it. By this time, there had been much drinking and cajoling. On the fifth vote of the body in charge of overseeing international expositions, the USSR won the right to the fair, 16-14.

Sévigny was heartbroken. He was soothed by an official who predicted the USSR would never stage an expo because it would never accept 20 million foreign visitors and all that would entail.

Sure enough, in 1961, the Soviets pulled out. Canada was invited to pick up the slack.

By that time, Sévigny was a minister in a majority Diefenbaker government. Duplessis was dead and Drapeau back in as mayor of Montreal (elected in 1960), but the new powers proved enthusiastic about the fair idea.

A delegation headed by Sévigny in 1962 won approval for a Montreal fair in 1967.

But Drapeau, who had a more astute sense of public relations, made it out to be his personal victory, even though the federal government was essentially assuming total financial responsibility for it. It was agreed $40 million would be spent on the exposition.

"We had a finance minister who believed in not spending money we didn't have and balanced budgets," Sévigny recalled. "It was different then."

Diefenbaker wanted it to be known as a federal project, appointing his own men to run it. At this time, every big real-estate promoter in town was lobbying to have Expo staged on his site: Nuns' Island, Rivière des Prairies, LaSalle, and so on.

But in the middle of the 1963 federal elections, Drapeau unilaterally announced Expo would be staged on man-made islands in the St. Lawrence River.

Diefenbaker was defeated by the Liberals and Lester Pearson, who, confused with the problems of running a minority government, gave the persistent Jean Drapeau his own way and a carte blanche, ignoring the $40-million spending limit.

Four years and $400 million later, Expo 67 was a triumph.

Without work, without hope, couple choose to exit together

[Wednesday, August 3, 1994]

HE WAS 60, she was 54.

They were victims of our economic times, two people who represent who knows how many others facing similar adversity. They lost their jobs and income, were left with no hope and no expectations, two people lurching along with economic woes for which they could see no out. So they killed themselves. Joann and René Gauthier were together for well over 30 years and were the epitome of hard-working, decent, never-complaining, never-taking always-giving folk.

She was British, orphaned along with her brother during the war, adopted at age 12, coming to Canada at 17, meeting René at 18 and then marrying him and embarking on a life of toil and happiness, difficulty and good cheer.

She was a fixture at the Pique Assiette, the Bombay Palace restaurant at the corner of Fort and Ste. Catherine streets, where she had worked for 17 years as a barmaid.

The Pique, as it is commonly known, has long served as a downtown neighbourhood pub for an eclectic mix of local residents, young and old, employed and struggling or retired, bonded in a family sort of way. A pleasant place to gather and while away of couple of hours, doing the crossword, chatting and sipping.

Joann was the perfect British pub barmaid, the one who was always organizing, collecting money to send flowers to someone sick in hospital, making sure everybody contributed to the annual *Gazette* Christmas Fund, fretting over somebody who seemed to be down in the dumps. She maintained a "swear box," in which patrons who let foul language slip were encouraged to donate to whatever charity Joann was favouring at the time. She was your basic, honest trooper, as solid a citizen as one could wish for.

They were a stable couple, living for 16 years in the same small apartment on de Maisonneuve Boulevard, corner of Fort.

René put in long hours, first as a taxi driver, then as an operator of his own little business, using a minivan to do courier work and pick up ships' crews, delivering them to harbours or airports in the Montreal area.

Every year, for as long as most friends remember, the two of them would drive off to Florida for a winter vacation of golfing and leisure. Joann would often tell friends that that annual vacation, including the long conversational drive down there, was what held their marriage together, was their reward for the rest of the year of work and making ends meet.

Then the recession set in and René's business went into decline. And they went into decline, too. René seemed frail all of a sudden.

A couple of years ago, friends noticed that they didn't take that annual vacation. "Decided not to go this year," Joann said nonchalantly.

Her good cheer sometimes faded and she'd get testy, tossing a dishrag at a busboy or sounding a mite depressed.

And then one February she slipped on the ice on the sidewalk and smashed her kneecap.

After spending time convalescing in a hospital, she couldn't put in the long standing-up time required of barmaids, and her hours and shifts were reduced. Her income and tips were down, René's business was down. About a year ago she stopped working at the Pique altogether.

René's business all but went bankrupt and his health declined. His and Joann's abilities to work were severely impaired. What work is there really for somebody 60, somebody 54 today? Thoughts of retraining just don't enter the world of reality.

And so, a couple of weeks ago, they went on vacation to the Eastern Townships, to play a bit of golf near Sutton, to re-experience that togetherness they so much enjoyed on their annual vacation.

They made sure all their personal bills were paid up, the rent was paid up until the end of August. They planned their vacation well.

And when they finished, instead of driving back to their apartment in Montreal, they drove to a gravel pit and attached a hose to their exhaust pipe and sat in the car with the windows closed and the motor running.

"It was well hidden," explained René's twin brother, Marcel, who lives near Lancaster just across the border in Ontario. "There were trees and it wasn't until three days later that a farmer noticed a glint in the sun off the car."

They left a note in the car.

"They said that nobody was to blame for their problems and nobody is to feel guilty," Marcel said. "They did it by mutual agreement. They just could not see their way out of money problems."

They were hard-working, proud people and I suppose they just couldn't conceive of living on the dole, of not paying their way, of seeing nothing in the future except old age and poverty. They weren't the type to burden anybody, even with a complaint about life.

Theirs is a cautionary tale of life in the recessionary '90s, when young people have it tough but out-of-work older people have it tougher.

Some say they're pests, but squirrels can gnaw at your heart

[Wednesday, October 5, 1994]

"Bubi saw a squirrel with only one paw this morning," my mother's voice said as I picked up the phone the other morning. "But he could hold a nut with just one front paw. Then another squirrel came and tried to chase him away. Isn't it awful? Discriminating against."

Bubi is my brother, Frank, who lives with my 91-year-old mother and my sister, Thaïs, and two big black dogs. My mother phones me just about every day and we converse, usually quite briefly, about a variety of topics. But one that recurs quite frequently, almost every week, is the subject of squirrels.

My mother is, we could say, nuts about squirrels.

Whenever my brother takes the dogs out for a walk, she makes sure he takes a supply of peanuts with him to stick in trees along the route for the squirrel population.

She routinely gives me reports on the little squirrel tribe that lives near her, tells me her observations about which one seems to be important, which one seems timid, about the ones that come into her kitchen looking for handouts, sometimes nudging and scratching her pant leg when she doesn't notice them.

One of the reasons for her passion about squirrels is that her family crest, the Schaelin, has a squirrel on it, squatting on his hind legs holding a small nut.

The family crest goes back several centuries, so she figures it has some sort of mystic message from our Swiss ancestors, telling us something, like work hard and bury lots of nuts.

Thus she has always preached to her children the responsibility we have toward squirrels. So I have always made sure that wherever I lived, I'd leave nuts out for them and get to know the ones who lived nearby.

Once I had a fat squirrel friend whom I called Gus-Gus, after the fat mouse in Disney's *Cinderella*. In the summer, when I left the front and back doors open for a breeze during afternoon naps, Gus-Gus would come in, jump on the couch and gently scratch my head until I woke up. Then I'd have to put some nuts on the porch.

One day, about 10 years ago, my mother found out they often serve peanuts in bars. I guess she saw this on TV because she's never been much of a bar person.

Anyhow, when she found this out, she got on the blower and called me with instructions: "You go to bars. Always take a handful of nuts from the bars and put them in your pocket for the squirrels."

And I have complied with her wishes ever since.

Of course, some people think our family is a bit, shall we say, squirrelly. Once we had a funeral for an old family friend.

My ex-wife, Linda, was there. She hadn't seen or spoken to my brother in a year. At the funeral, when he saw her, he went to her and said, "When you go to a supermarket, you're allowed to take one of these for the squirrels."

And he pressed something in her hand. She looked down. It was a walnut.

* * *

Now I fully realize there are two camps when it comes to squirrels.

When I called Dr. Roger Bider, director of the Ecomuseum in Ste. Anne de Bellevue, yesterday to ask about squirrels, I got the impression he was not as enthusiastic about the little rodents as we are.

"They can be annoying as hell," he said. "They get into attics, make lots of noise … One cut my telephone line … Eat flower bulbs, play havoc in vegetable gardens, haul corn all over the place, get into the bird feeders— the agile little creatures. In the suburbs they are a pain in the butt."

What I wanted to know is why all of a sudden, in the past year or so, I've seen black squirrels in town. I always thought they were black in Ontario and gray in Montreal.

Bider explained that black and gray are the same thing. They can even come "in a beautiful beige, a tan like deerskin. And two varieties of albino, too. The red squirrels are a different species, more woodsy."

When more colours appear, it means the population is rising and a regressive gene is more liable to emerge.

So, the colour of a local population is generally determined by the local gene pool, I suppose.

And yes, squirrels don't remember where they bury nuts. They are just doing their jobs of planting nuts.

That's why it is important to feed them in winter. (I'm saying this, not Bider.)

They often starve to death in the winter.

Bider said they once cut open a dead tree over at the Ecomuseum and found 20 little squirrel skeletons, one on top of another, starved to death inside their winter shelter.

If that doesn't touch you suburban brutes, you have no heart.

Squirrels give life to the city core and make people smile.

Barbecue-chicken debate leaves ex-pats salivating

[Sunday, May 5, 1996]

ONE THING is for sure, the question of barbecue chicken certainly tickles the fancy of Montrealers.

There was quite an astounding response from readers of a column three weeks ago in which I suggested Montrealers were divided into two camps, Chalet and Côte St. Luc Bar-B-Q. About half of the letters and faxes received agreed with that contention, while the rest inundated me with takeout menus from a bunch of other barbecue places in the area. I'm still getting letters from as far afield as California, from former Montrealers expressing hunger pangs for a delicacy that is unique to Montreal.

First, the history of Montreal barbecue.

The three original places were indeed Laurier Barbecue, Chic 'N Coop and Chalet Lucerne, but it is hard to discern which was the first and who copied whom.

Several readers, including Avron Cohen, put forward the case for Laurier. According to Cohen, Laurier opened before the war as Chez Glaby, started by a French couple who sold it to the Laporte family and returned to France just before the outbreak of war.

Apparently, the French couple developed the hot-chicken sandwich there. In the '40s, the Laporte family changed the name to Laurier Barbecue.

The Hill brothers, Cecil, Victor, Elie and Louis, opened their Chic 'N Coop in 1938 and were the first to have built one of those now familiar big, double-rotating rotisseries.

Yvette Lorange started work there at the end of 1938 and recalls that some visiting Americans tried to buy the recipe for the sauce. They escalated their offer to $1,000, but the English-Montreal chef refused to sell, saying "a good cook never gives away his secret recipes."

Lorange's daughter-in-law, Madeleine Defresne of Laval, sent along a staff photograph of the 32 waitresses who worked there in 1940, indicating how big and how popular the Chic 'N Coop was in those days. It was located on Ste. Catherine near Drummond and was linked to the Indian Lounge—where, after the war, war-ace and hero Buzz Beurling worked as a sort of greeter before he went off to be a pilot with the fledgling Israeli air force. He was killed in an air accident.

Chalet Lucerne, on Ste. Catherine Street near Guy was started about the same time by Joseph Bossart, a Swiss immigrant. That closed in 1982, but Bossart's brother had split off from Chalet Lucerne and in 1945 started up the Chalet Bar-B-Q, which carries on the tradition today, although with a different sauce.

My mother chides me for not mentioning the old Swiss Hut on Sherbrooke Street near Park Avenue, which was started up by my godmother, Lena Haefliger, in the same period. But their speciality was chicken-in-the-basket, a variant of Southern-fried chicken that was also a staple at the Chic 'N Coop.

Judging from all the testimony, it appears that Montreal barbecue is the result of a joint French-Jewish-Swiss effort.

Numerous readers recounted visits to those places many years ago.

Alf Harvey, brother of Canadien hockey great Doug, recounts how he returned to Canada in 1953 from England where he played hockey with the Earls Court Rangers. Doug met him and his new English bride, Joyce, at the docks in Quebec City and drove them to Montreal, where Joyce had her first meal in Canada—at the Chalet Bar-B-Q. She's been addicted ever since.

Mary Peate, of Williston, Vermont, tells of being romanced by her fiancé at Chez Glaby and claims it was far superior to the others, but they miss it all terribly—as "all barbecue chicken all over the United States is awful"—and are now reduced to smuggling Chalet chicken and sauce. Her letterhead features the music of "Moonlight in Vermont" written across the top.

Similar sentiments were received from several other former Montrealers now living in the U.S. who were sent copies of my column by friends or families.

Jimmy Berthelet, of Berthelet Food Products Inc., sent a letter longer than my column recounting how his grandfather and his three sons started up their company in the early '60s when St. Hubert barbecue was just starting to expand and had four outlets. They were having problems with the sauce because it took 13 hours to make a batch, but its shelf life was just one hour. After much trial and error, the Berthelets solved the problem by creating a dehydrated version, which they now sell to all 94 St. Hubert restaurants.

Several readers wrote to say the best barbecue chicken to be had in Montreal today is served by Portuguese restaurants, like Jano on St. Laurent Boulevard and Tasca on Duluth Avenue, and others too numerous to mention.

Finally, a couple of readers, including Judge Roland Durand of Quebec Superior Court, wrote that my explanation of the origin of barbecue was wrong when I suggested it came from the Caribbean French and Spanish term for roasting an animal from the "barbe au queue (beard to tail)." It was originally "de la barbe au cul," which, according to the judge, was long ago "a perfectly normal and polite way of referring to the rear-end of man and some large animals (whence culasse, culotte, cul-de-sac, reculer, etc.)."

Sight of ravaged trees is heartbreaking

[Wednesday, January 14, 1998]

I think that I shall never see
A poem lovely as a tree
  –Joyce Kilmer

As POETRY GOES, of course, it's kitsch. But the well-known opening lines of Kilmer's six-stanza poem often spring to our minds when we see an impressive tree. Or when we're impressed by something about trees. One suspects there are few real clods in the world who are so insensitive, so unromantic, that there isn't just a little bit of a tree-hugger in their hearts.

So it's a sad thing that what's been impressive about the trees lately has, unfortunately, been depressing—to witness the awful destruction and damage visited on what are among God's most magnificent creations, or nature's design, if you prefer.

Yes, the massive inconvenience, the human ordeals and suffering brought on by the Great Ice Storm of '98 have preoccupied us.

The awesome power of nature has been impressed on us and we realize we are but puny things.

But still, it is heartbreaking to confront the vista of mangled, split, cracked, shorn, twisted and knocked-down trees everywhere we look. To see work crews pile up little mountains of wooden debris on every street.

The destruction of the trees has been the most visible manifestation of the calamity about us.

It struck me especially on Monday, when I was being driven along Côte des Neiges Road following the funeral of our friend Ron Seltzer, the former publisher of the *Downtowner*, who died of a heart attack on the weekend after several days of strenuous activity helping people out in our neighbourhood.

One image of Seltzer that I carry in my mind comes from one day during the storm. I caught sight of him a couple of times out on the street and in the laneway, directing some effort or another.

"Air-raid warden," I thought. "Seltzer is just like those helpful air-raid wardens with helmets and armbands you see in all those old movies about the blitz in wartime England."

After the sad farewell at Paperman's, Ziggy Eichenbaum drove me by Côte des Neiges cemetery, where we saw the untended trees looking like wrecked match sticks.

And a remembrance came to mind of a time about a dozen years ago, when on a pleasant summer afternoon Seltzer and I went to buy a bunch of Wilensky's Specials and take them to the Mount Royal lookout for lunch.

As we looked out at our wonderful downtown view, we reminisced of what it looked like when we were kids.

Until the late '50s and mid-'60s, I think, the view of downtown from the lookout was one of almost total greenery.

That was when all the streets were lined by that most gracious of the species, the elm tree. They towered over the mostly three-storey buildings that lined all the up-down streets like Stanley and Mountain. They stood upward of 50 feet, providing a vast canopy in summer that gave the whole city an overwhelming green look in summer.

As Seltzer and I chewed the fat and our Wilensky's Specials, we agreed that the greatest tragedy to strike Montreal was the Dutch elm disease that killed off the mighty trees that at one time covered most of the northeastern part of the continent.

The trouble with the disease was that it seemed to spread slowly, although in fact it did much of its massive destruction in a relatively short 15 years or so.

It was just that the elms' disappearance wasn't a dramatic overnight thing. Every year, they just cut down more of the diseased trees so that they went little by little, so it wasn't all that noticeable. But in that period, we must have lost several hundred thousand elms on the island of Montreal, to say nothing about the rest of the continent.

Now all we have left is an Elm Avenue in every town on the northeastern part of the continent, but no elm trees.

But the elm disaster occurred during a period when we equated civic progress with building taller and taller buildings, so the natural disaster occurred in the shadows, as it were, of concrete and steel towers.

I remember Seltzer saying something to the effect that when death and destruction come in one fell swoop, it's a disaster, but when it comes slowly over time, picking things off one at a time, it's just history moving on.

Such have been the ruminations going through my mind in the past few days. I imagine the crisis of the past week has given us all lots of time—maybe too much time—to ruminate on various things.

So we pray that as winter shows off the awful force of nature, the coming spring will show us nature's awesome healing power.

Details, details ...

Leon Harris

THERE'S NO QUESTION Nick was a terrific storyteller and a good writer, but he was also a terrible speller and seemed proud of it in a perverse sort of way.

Several now-bald copy editors working on the city desk at the *Gazette* began their careers with full heads of hair until they were assigned, on a regular basis, to "crack the spelling code" on Nick's columns or fix errors of omission or mistakes.

"Details, details," was Nick's standard reply when tracked down at one of his favourite watering holes and asked to help straighten out his prose for the next day's *Gazette*. Usually jocular, Nick could also be somewhat rude and this once led to a minor falling out. We didn't speak to each other for about 18 months. Last summer, we finally patched things up for good when we bumped into each other at memorial service for *Gazette* reporter Albert Noel. Nick was a buddy. Twenty years ago, Nick was a guest at my wedding in Connecticut as I was a guest at his in Montreal.

As we all know, Nick loved downtown and one of his favorite people was Margo MacGillivray, the daytime barmaid at Winnie's on Crescent Street. Nick wrote a column about Margo and how she was going to sing "O Canada" before the start of an Alouettes game at the Olympic Stadium. (Margo also sang at Nick's funeral.)

Many years earlier, I had worked with Margo's father, Leo, at *The Gazette* and something about the way Nick spelled (or misspelled) Margo's family name didn't ring true. I telephoned Nick to verify the spelling and—sure enough—he had it all messed up.

This might not seem like a big deal, but telephone calls on or near deadline take a copy editor's precious time. We tend to get our backs up when we have to track down a writer to check on something as simple as the spelling of the family name of the main person in a column. On a slow night, an editor might have time to phone the paper's library, but that task is really a columnist's job and there is also a principle involved here.

Nick's columns averaged about 850 words and in one column (we kept it as "evidence") he spelled 54 words incorrectly. Since Nick rarely used complicated prose, this was no mean trick.

He once wrote a column about how he got his start as a reporter. One of the senior editors who Nick kept bugging was the legendary Walter Christopherson. While describing his approach to Christopherson, Nick managed to spell Christopherson's name three different ways in the same paragraph.

Frazzled copy editor on phone to Nick at bar: Nick, nice piece on how you got started in the business. One small question. In your mention of Christopherson in the 13th paragraph, you spelled Christopherson's name three different ways. Which way is correct?

Nick: (loud noises and glasses rattling in background): "I didn't have time to check the library (read: I was too lazy). Think you can do it? I'm in an important conversation right now (with the bartender).

"Why don't you just just pick one of the spellings and make it the same throughout? That'll do it."

Copy editor to Nick: "Yeah, sure, Nick, soon as I poke my eye out with this blunt stick."

One of Nick's favourite topics was Montreal and the uniqueness of the city. He was writing about the track one time—Blue Bonnets horse-race track. Nick was going on about how wonderful it was that a track announcer could call a race in a bilingual fashion, quickly, efficiently and with a certain panache. Did this happen anywhere else in the world?

Copy editor on phone to Nick at bar: "Good column, Nick. By the way, what is the NAME of that wonderful, bilingual race caller (Jean Desautels) at Blue Bonnets?"

Nick (somewhat annoyed): "Details, details. How am I supposed to know that? Who cares what his name is? Not important."

Copy editor: "Think you could make a coupla calls? Try the track. I'm up to my cajones in work tonight."

Nick: "I'll think about it. I gotta council meeting in two hours and I'm in an important conversation here with the bartender."

Copy editor (miming the strangulation of a columnist): "Nick, I said call the track … not go to it. I'll give you back your lousy quarter or maybe the bar will let you use the phone for free? And by the way, Nick, you're not on city council anymore. You LOST in the last municipal election. Remember?"

Nick: "Details, details."

So what are we going to do about Nick's copy? was the late-hour lament as the paper hit the streets—and the beer flowed at the bar.

Somewhat reluctantly, copy editors would approach their bosses with a "raw" unedited version of a Nick column and ask if the more senior editor could get Nick to clean up his act or at least ream him out.

Sometimes these "reprimand sessions" would take place at a bar. The Auf der Maur charm would prevail as the big bosses were regaled with tales of Nick's follies. How can we get angry at this guy?

And then there was the nightly bet.

Veteran newsman Russ Peden worked the City Desk "slot" for a number of years. It was his job—among a host of other chores—to give Nick's column a close, second read. If Russ found three or more errors overlooked by the copy editor, that copy editor owed Russ a post-shift quart of beer. If there were less than three errors, Russ paid off.

Most of the time Russ won the bet. In the end, Nick got me again.

Gazette senior copy editor Leon Harris was a friend of Nick's for 35 years. For the last sixteen years he edited Nick's column on a semi-regular basis.

Nick, Hubie Bauch et al as hamsters.
The Gazette refused to publish this cartoon.

PEEVES

I'm raked over coals over latest
hot potato

[Wednesday, May 1, 1985]

WE GET LOTS of reaction; we even get letters.

In a recent column I stated that Quebec is the last major stronghold of the vinegar-on-french-fries tradition, while other Canadians have switched to catsup (that's the way Americans spell ketchup).

Also, Canadian Yuppies are increasingly putting mayonnaise on their chips. When Yuppies start imitating Belgians you know something strange is happening. Anyhow, my observations on Quebecers' vinegar tradition was greeted with outrage—especially from British Columbians, who maintain that vinegar remains the staple of that loyal remnant of Empire.

Ontarians, Maritimers and, for a while it seemed, half the people I met on the street told of growing up in some part of Canada and putting vinegar on their fries.

"It's not just Quebec," they proclaimed in chorus.

"The Ottawa Valley, you dolt, is the centre of vinegar on french fries."

OK, but my contention based on casual observation on visits outside Quebec is that the vinegar tradition has faded elsewhere in favour of ketchup. But Quebecers remain loyal to vinegar.

Even in some urban centres in Ontario, the vinegar tradition rides with those mobile french fry trucks. And most of them have Quebec licence plates (at least the ones I've seen near Toronto harbour). Some of them come all the way from Aylmer for the weekend.

One more thing, I've been informed that the word poutine (that weird dish of french fries covered with curd cheese and gravy) originated in New Brunswick, where it means an Acadian meat stew.

It's strange, but every time I write about potatoes I get lots of reaction.

It started several years ago when I launched into a tirade against restaurant chefs who bake potatoes in aluminum foil.

The foil defeats the purpose of baking potatoes in the first place, which is to get a nice, crispy skin. The foil makes the skin soggy. If you want soggy potatoes, why not just boil them?

Wrapping potatoes in foil must be a plot by the aluminum companies to sell more aluminum.

At the time, I urged readers not to take it. To send the foil-wrapped potatoes back to the kitchen.

Loud complaints often are the only way to correct a situation.

That column produced a ton of mail, most of it agreeing with me, for once. David Culver, the head of Alcan, sent some aluminum nails with the suggestion that I try baking potatoes with a nail stuck inside. Aluminum, he explained, is a good heat conductor and helps cook the inside.

I've tried it a few times, and it works. But if you like your skins really crisp, as I do, there isn't much point because people usually overcook baked potatoes, anyway. (But full marks to Culver as an aluminum salesman.)

I don't know whether it was a result of that crusade, but I notice fewer restaurants use foil these days.

My next potato crusade was for baked potato skins and it was a qualified success.

On the positive side, many places now offer baked potato skins albeit with an insane variety of toppings, from cheese to guacamole.

The bad part is that baked potato skins have become such a craze that a whole new branch of the industry has emerged: frozen potato skins.

Potato companies now pre-bake the potatoes, machines scoop out the meat, and the skins are frozen. The skins come out sort of soggy, as if aluminum foil had been wrapped around them.

This brings us back to my original potato crusade, the never-ending battle against frozen french fries. There has been some progress on that front, but not enough.

You still have to go to either a greasy spoon or an expensive restaurant to get fresh french fries. (But for some peculiar reason, the greasy spoon variety still tastes better than the ones you get at a fancy place.)

Most in-between places stick to the frozen variety.

Major progress in the war against the diabolical frozen french fry comes from three franchises—Frits, Harvey's, and Dutch Frits, all of which use freshly-cut potatoes.

All three chains were founded by Canajuns, eh?

It just goes to show, we do know how to some things right.

Save us from the foolish rituals of the barbecue

[Friday, August 8, 1986]

HEAVEN KNOWS it's one of the great pestilences to strike us every summer. The outdoor barbecue.

I don't know what it is about barbecues that so captures the imaginations of men, transforming them from innocuous office workers into ludicrous maniacs swaggering around open flames as if they were reaching back to their primitive past as cavemen celebrating the butchering of a hapless brontosaurus. Let's be blunt. I hate barbecues and all the stupid posturing that men adopt around them.

I mean, you get these guys who don't know how to chop parsley. But put them before a gas grill on the back lawn and they pretend they are master chefs.

They wouldn't dream of making a cup of instant coffee by themselves in a kitchen. But let them stick a bunch of raw meat over an open flame and they pirouette around in some bizarre masquerade of primate ritual.

It's like men who don't know how to fry an egg but lay claim to culinary expertise because their spaghetti sauce is superb.

This weekend, all over the continent, there will be hordes of long-suffering guests and neighbours forced to smile wanly as these pseudo cooks plunk mounds of hamburger and steak on their grills.

They wear dumb chef costumes, aprons with silly drawings on them, twirling huge forks as they show off their talents by flipping a weiner over.

"Taste a real steak," the buffoon usually hollers as he dishes out his efforts to some glum victim like me.

The wives have to humour these lunatics by saying things like: "Harold is such a whiz at the barbecue."

That translates as: "The dumb ox doesn't know a spatula from a jar of peanut butter."

Watching these spectacles is enough to turn me into a vegetarian.

The stuff they serve usually tastes awful because it's coated with that garbage barbecue sauce which is probably made from petroleum products.

I like my hamburgers and hot dogs fried in a frying pan instead of smelling like gas and loaded with carcinogens.

Yet, because of social responsibilities and various other exigencies, we're forced to attend these inane functions just about every weekend.

Why people believe eating outdoors with flies and paper plates is better than dining at a kitchen or dining-room table is beyond me. A frozen dinner in front of a TV set is more civilized.

Barbecues are messy and you always have to run in to the kitchen to get the salt, tripping over the dog on the way out.

The reason the guests always get roaring drunk, of course, is because they have to pretend they're having a good time saying things like: "Boy, Harold, this steak is better than Moishe's." Which translates as: "I should have made up some excuse and stayed home and had Kraft Dinner."

Now just so that nobody takes this personally, this diatribe in no way reflects on my two wonderful neighbours, Ron Seltzer and Stephen Phizicky, both of whom are great gentlemen—aside from their predeliction for their gas barbecues.

No, it's the other oafs out there I'm referring to. The ones with real gardens and ludicrous pretentions.

They pay $500 or $600 for those gas grills which, if they worked properly, would blow up when somebody tried to turn them on.

If this column means I never again receive an invitation to an outdoor barbecue, then I've accomplished something. The rest of you are on your own.

I'm just a city boy. Please don't invite me for a weekend in the country

[Friday, August 22, 1986]

SOMEHOW the notion of "the summer cottage" doesn't fill me with the great elation and yearning that seems to afflict other Montrealers.

I'm an urbanite pure and simple. I don't get overcome with the desire to flee the concrete jungle downtown and rush off up north or to the Eastern Townships and the open spaces, to smell the trees and foliage, to escape the din of the city. Why spend good money to rent a summer cottage or buy an old farm so you can sit outside sipping a beer when you can sit outside in your back yard or on the balcony downtown sipping a beer?

But every summer I have to field all these invitations from well-meaning friends who love to rush off on Friday nights to what they always describe as their personal Shangri-La in the country.

"It'll do you good to have some fresh air," they say. "You can go swimming, maybe play a bit of tennis, hike through the woods, shoot some golf, go windsurfing, rent a horse …"

While they go on like that, I usually start to feel a little exhausted and wonder what's wrong with staying in the city and having a long Saturday afternoon nap.

In the country, I find, the visiting city folks are positively manic about organizing activities. You get up there, and they have these schedules of things to do drawn up as if they fear a few minutes of unscheduled repose will get you into trouble, or sin or something.

"Volleyball, everybody!" they shout.

"We're playing Monopoly after dinner," they confide.

"We're going for a swim at dawn," they say cheerfully. "There's nothing like dawn in the lake."

Another part of my problem is that going off to a country cottage always entails a long car or bus ride. And, quite simply, I don't like travelling by car or bus. Being a non-driver, I'm always suspicious about anything that is more than a $3 cab ride from where I live or work. Which is downtown.

It's not that I don't like the country, or feel snobbish about it, it's just that some people have a predilection for city life, while others find bliss in quite rural confines. I figure that if God had meant me to spend time in the country, He (or She) would have had me born into a Swiss peasant family living on the farm.

However, being the good-natured type I am, I usually humour these friends and accept an invitation or two every summer to trek out to some Godforsaken country cottage out in the wilds. This, of course, requires some sacrifice on my part, a sacrifice that is not always appreciated.

My friends usually chortle away and make lame jokes about the fresh air giving me coughing spasms. For some reason or other, they think it's hilarious seeing me without a shirt and tie.

And the next time one of my summer-cottage friends points out of the car window and says: "See that, Nick? That's a cow, spelled C-O-W. That's where milk comes from. Ho. Ho. Ho. Chortle. Chortle"—the next time, I'll murder him or her.

So it was that last week I went to the Laurentians with my daughter and one of her friends to visit at the summer cottage. Two of them, in fact. Since I was going up there, I decided to kill two birds with one stone and visit two sets of friends, one in Ste. Adele and one on Lake Manitou near Ste. Agathe.

In Ste. Adele, we visited some bachelor friends, a couple of lawyers and an advertising man, who rented a cottage for the month. They intended to get all healthy, play a lot of sports and stay on the wagon the whole time.

Well, they said they weren't going to drink for a month except in the case of snakebite.

So they had this plastic snake that they kept picking up all the time and shouting: "Snake attack! Snake attack!" And then they'd pour double scotches and go: "Ho. Ho. Ho. Chortle. Chortle."

Spare me.

And then the kids beat us at Monopoly.

A couple of days of that, and then we moved on to stay with a family at Lake Manitou.

Now there, I must admit, I found it a bit idyllic and relaxing. I didn't even mind getting pushed off the dock into the water about seven times a day by my grinning host.

Best of all, I beat the kids at the board game Risk.

And late at night, when everybody went to bed, I sat outside watching the sky and seeing shooting stars.

While the crickets chirped, or whatever crickets do, I fell to philosophic and pastoral musings. Bizarrely, I found myself contemplating the beauty of nature and the uncomplicated pace of country life.

Well, thank heavens we got out of there before we were completely seduced and lost all sense of purpose. It was a close call, though.

[Tribute]

A Bridge to the Other Solitude

Benoit Aubin

I GOT TO KNOW Nick Auf der Maur long before he became a somebody with rich friends and a cool expense account; even before he started wearing his trademark Borsalinos. Way back when he was just another *intellectuel de gauche* attacking the mayor of Montreal in seedy under-ground magazines. One headline, "Mayor Drapeau Shot By Drug-Crazed Hippy"—in which Drapeau on acid was realizing what was wrong with his karma—got Nick into trouble with the law. It also made his name known to me.

That throws us all the way back to when the Parti Québécois was a nascent force which carried the promise of better things to come, and had a chance of attracting Anglo lefties such as Nick in an enlightened citizens' pledge to derail the Trilateral commission, paint cop cars in psychedelic regalia, and replace then Justice minister Rémi Paul with someone like Robert Charlebois.

During the '70s, as a young reporter, I decided to get acquainted with Quebec's biggest problem: Les Anglais. Once a month, I'd venture to such foreign places as Winnie's or Grumpy's for research, pretending this would be lunch, and knowing I would get very drunk with the extraordinary coterie of hacks and politicos, ad salesmen, film makers, suits and funny businessmen—and the women who hung out wherever Nick was.

Nick was my first guide to the hidden face of the moon, to the other solitude; he was the plank I used to cross the Great Divide between McGill and UQAM, Westmount and Outremont, St. Denis and Crescent; between the universes of *La Presse* and of *The Gazette*. In simple terms knowing Nick Auf der Maur has helped me become a full-fledged Montrealer.

I never viewed him as a friend, really. I could never hang with him long enough to become intimate; he'd drink me under the table long before that. Back then, I sometimes had difficulties understanding what the Anglos were talking about, because I shared so little of their cultural baggage. Nick pinched my bum and I hated it.

But Nick was a big heart on legs, and every time I popped by he would welcome me as his long-lost best friend, fill my glass and introduce me to every one around, making me feel big, important and welcomed. I liked that.

Once, in a column, I branded him *un Montréaliste*, a word I had just coined, which meant, in fact, nothing. But he liked it, and was still quoting that column fifteen years later. I suspect he would have liked this appelation to stick. We all have our vanities.

Nick gave his last interview to the television station where I worked. He admitted very lucidly that his lifestyle was what was killing him. He said that he had been young too long, unable to understand, or believe, that the present time had a built-in ending.

When he passed, we all cried, over and above the Dixieland music of his funeral parade. We all wept on ourselves, as is always the case at funerals, our tears triggered by the sense of the passing of an era.

I don't think history will say Nick Auf der Maur has played a historic role. But it was clear on his departure, that he—and his attitude, and his friends—represented Montreal's best hope of coming together as a complex society, instead of falling apart as a series of disjointed ghettos.

Benoit Aubin is news and information director at Global Television Network in Quebec.

QUEBEC

Nick as the Walrus in an Anglo allegory by Aislin.

Frenglish winners will take a repast

[Friday, December 5, 1980]

OUR INFORMAL little Frenglish contest has ended and top prize, for both sheer volume and delight, goes to Jo-Ann and Caryl UnRuh of Montreal.

The sisters sent in no less that 51 Frenglicisms, plus assorted comments and richly deserve our modest first prize, an autographed copy of the new biography Drapeau, by Brian McKenna and Susan Purcell, plus dinner at some suitable downtown restaurant courtesy of the "big vegetable" (grand fromage?) here at the office (perhaps somebody can explain why "big cheese" translates as grosse legume?).

Herewith a sample from the UnRuh entry:

They "casse" for lunch, and "take" a beer before "commanding" their meal. They always "demand" themselves, instead of asking themselves "pourqwhy?" They often are "stationing" the car, "accusing reception" of letters, and are very often "retarded" instead of late.

They refer to movies that "passed" on TV. As students, they "inscribe" themselves in courses, instead of enrolling. And then, instead of dropping out of a course, they "abandon" it, just as they are "abonning" (subscribing) to a "journal."

And now is often "mainte-now" (which reminds me of an army sergeant we had in cadet camp in Farnham who was always saying "toute bleeping suite").

The UnRuh sisters report that they continue "ameliorating" their French and conclude with Barbara Walters's comment about birds—at least they're biwingual.

Second prize, for originality (almost every Frenglicism was submitted more than once by different people) goes to Ann Silkauskas of Nouveau Bordeaux, for all the "trishing" (tricher) she does to her diet. She'll receive an autographed copy of the McKenna-Purcell oeuvre.

In all, close to 159 entries were received. Many thanks to all.

ANGLOFUN: (That comes from the UnRuhs.) So, perhaps you thought I was going to let the matter drop at that and not go on any more about it all. Well, I received a lot of letters on other questions of language peculiar to Montreal.

R.S. Johnson of TMR notes that the word dépanneur, for handy or corner store, has been in use for only a relatively short time. He started using it without checking the real meaning until recently. He looked it up in the dictionary and discovered dépanneur actually means "break-down mechanic."

"Due to the increasingly shoddy performance of the assembly plants of nearly all the automobile manufacturers," he writes, "I can only assume that it has now become necessary for mechanics to be available on numerous corners in an large city. Since Montreal is a predominantly French city, the resultingly large number of mechanics required are naturally called 'dépanneurs.'"

A fertile imagination, Mr. Johnson has. Actually, the term "break-down mechanic" also has an emergency service connotation in French. And the need of a quart of milk, loaf of bread or case of beer late in the evening is an emergency.

Bob Sancton, news editor of the *Westmount Examiner*, sends along the following English press release from the Montreal Catholic School Commission:

"Le service de l'éducation des adultes de la Commission des écoles Catholiques de Montréal offers courses in Amelioration de mon français écrit and Comment m'exprimer en français oral."

That's four words out of 30 in the opening paragraph. Sancton's note concludes with the usual "I pray you to accept the expression of my sentiments."

This is all perhaps best explained by a letter from Gordon Fisher of Waterville, who writes: "I remarked in my lecture of today's journal that the functionaries are actually planifying the linguistic reglimentations for the national collectivity."

Vince Madigan sends along a flyer put out by Qinincaillerie Goyer Hardware in Chomedey some time ago. It reads in part:

"A reflexion moment..."

"Here is a big news that it might help yourself to shake it or it could help you to break your new snow shovel handle if we try to increase your mind, that the winter season will come very fast...

"And, if suddenly, a snow fall comes very quickly, you should be ready to recieve it and not be in the hurry to get a snowblower because you didn't get it before.

"This program is to help you, for your family budget because when Christmas time is coming, we don't have any spare money. If you use our layaway plan, you will be ready for winter.

"There's a lot of peoples last year, that they missed their shot to buy one. Were you in that gang?"

Certainly not, but where do I put the sic?

Image of tolerance has been scratched

[November 16, 1981]

BACK ON THE FIRST OF AUGUST, I was out in Sutton to celebrate Swiss national day.

It was a big event, attended by upward of 1,000 people, including a delegation of artisans from Vaud canton, visiting an Eastern Townships fête of arts, crafts and working with old tools.

The Vaud craftsmen and women were typical European country stock, bedecked in traditional costumes, long, traditional peasant dresses for the women, flowery embroidered waistcoats for the men.

Their Québécois hosts, who accompanied them to national day celebrations, tended toward the crunchy granola, long-haired North American country look. After all, your average North American farmer doesn't dress up in peasant costume, prefers plastic Massey-Ferguson tractor caps and eschews wooden implements and pottery-making.

No, the Vaud visitors and their Québécois hosts were not only two geographic worlds apart, but for a large part two social worlds apart.

When the band struck up the new Swiss national anthem (replacing the old one which had the same tune as God Save the Queen), everybody stood at attention as is normal.

But when the band, joined by the chorus of Swiss-Canadians, played O Canada, a middle-aged Townshipper in front of me ostentatiously plunked himself down in his chair.

His wife continued standing, and he tugged at her pants from the rear. She put her hand around behind her, trying to slap her husband's hand away.

The Vaud visitors and others standing behind lost the drift of the anthem, as they gazed uncomprehending at this ludicrous performance.

I fumed, feeling embarrassed for the visitors and local community alike. It was just plain bad manners, a lack of elementary respect.

I intended to speak to the boor afterward, telling him he was an childish ignoramus and so on. But like a lot of others, I said to myself: What the heck, why compound it and create an incident? So I let it pass.

The other evening I was in the Monte Carlo, the swank new club in Old Montreal. One gets the impression sophisticates and other civilized people swill there.

I went to the washroom and, as I drying my hands under the electric gizmo, I noticed something peculiar to Montreal.

The sign on the dryer stated: Sechoir CANADIAN Dryer. The directions, English on the right, French on the left, were printed on a metal strip.

But the French words had been stratched out, as were the English words, so the whole strip was one mess of scratchy lines. One couldn't tell who started it.

I thought to myself, what kind of mindless lunatic out for a pleasant evening on the town would feel so much passion, so much motivation, that he would feel compelled to pull out a key and scratch out somebody else's language on a dryer in a can of some bar?

I was thinking of these incidents yesterday as I was reading a speech given by Brian Mulroney in Baie Comeau. Politicians have a habit of extolling Quebecers' tradition of tolerance and generosity.

And by and large it is true. People who don't stand for national anthems and scratch out French words in toilets are fortunately a minority.

Mulroney, as the Tory lore goes, is president of the Iron Ore Company of Canada and is the son of an Irish electrician from Baie Comeau, which is the principal town of Saguenay riding, the staunchest Parti Québécois constituency in the province, represented by Lucien Lessard.

Mulroney had been invited to speak at a handicapped fund-raising dinner by Marcel Poulin, chairman of the Steelworkers Local 8399. One can assume the audience was largely Péquiste.

The speech, before a packed house at the Hotel Manoir, was in many ways the homecoming of the local boy who made good.

As a company president, Mulroney could have limited his talk to platitudes about working together for the good of the handicapped. But Mulroney is nothing if not an astute political and social observer.

His speech was filled with homespun observation and reminiscences, establishing his "authentic" credentials.

He then addressed the current constitutional mess, particularly René

Lévesque's vitriolic bitterness and "theologian civil servants of the PQ."

"(Our) values and liberties … are being taken away from us, quietly, gradually, surreptitiously by our leaders behind a smokescreen called 'democratic collectivism'… like an insidious illness which will, inescapably, diminish our strength and our duties as independent citizens .…

"Individuals in Sept-Iles who would call their neighbors in Port Cartier 'vassals,' 'traitors,' 'public liars' or 'vendus,' and do this every day, would have a problem; not so at the government level.

"The spirit of generosity, the respect for a neighbour's dignity, the acknowledgement of a job well done, the acceptance of honourable compromise as being a step forward, the courage of admitting that you are not always right … all these qualities are being replaced by an institutionalized cynicism and negativism."

Mulroney said, "Mr. Lévesque's bitterness is displayed in full daylight (with) his gratuitous and petty warning this week to the English minority in Quebec."

I called up Mulroney yesterday to ask how this sort of thing went over in Baie Comeau.

"A standing ovation," he said.

Days of Duplessis very like our own

[January 6, 1982]

I WAS BORN in 1942 in downtown Montreal, and grew up for the first few years just east of St. Laurent Boulevard, The Main.

Like of lot of immigrant families, we had our problems—most of which we remember with some nostalgic affection.

As for social relations, I don't recall being too aware of English-French differences. If anything, I was more aware of Catholic-Protestant differences, and being Catholic our feeling of community probably lay more with the French-speaking people.

However, I don't recall much of that ever really being an issue, aside from English-French snowball fights.

Politics I was only dimly aware of. I knew of course that Maurice Duplessis was the premier, but largely because he was pointed out to me on several occasions at mass in St. Patrick's, where he went following his fight with Archbishop Charbonneau.

In short, my childhood days in Montreal, and the time spent in my father's prospecting camp in Charlevoix county, were fairly happy. Not trouble-free, mind you, but with good memories.

It was only later, when Quebec was in the early 1960s and I was in my early 20s, that I learned I had grown up in La Grande Noirceur, The Great Darkness, as the Duplessis era began to be called.

It was called La Grande Noirceur because Duplessis represented a reactionary, insular, church-dominated society.

I quickly took up that theme, once I had learned about it after the fact, and started reading up on all the bad things around me that I had somehow failed to notice while growing up.

I might add that a good chunk of the population was either similarly ignorant of what was going on or else satisfied.

The votes of the majority of people were not affected by the persecution of Jehovah's Witnesses or the crushing of asbestos workers.

These thoughts of the Great Darkness came to mind the other day following a chat I had with a friend who runs a small service business.

In the course of an otherwise jovial holiday conversation, he mentioned in passing that "the inspectors" had come to see his business.

Now it has come to pass in everyday parlance that when an English-speaking person in Quebec says "the inspectors," you know automatically that he is speaking of the language police, or, if you prefer, the tongue troopers.

My friend is a WASP, an easy-going fellow, not particularly prone to being upset or angered over things political.

In fact, if I recall correctly, he even used to vote PQ, not out of any deep conviction, but out of a vague sympathy for French Canadians.

The visit by the tongue troopers did not bother him that much.

His establishment is fully capable of serving clients in French or English, always has been. And so aside from some nitpicking details, the inspectors were satisfied and soon on their way.

"The odd thing about it," remarked my friend, "is that while the inspection was going on, I felt kind of funny."

"Funny in what way?" I asked conversationally.

"I felt Jewish," he said simply.

"What do you mean, Jewish?"

"Well, you know, having to wear a Star of David, being subject to racial purity laws; having special laws for dealing with you that explicitly, written in black and white, discriminate against you; having to produce papers and things for government inspectors, all based on what you are.

"In this case not because of your religion, but because of your language or ethnic origin."

He didn't state that in a strong voice, but rather in a casual, almost uninterested manner.

It being the New Year, and the time for reflecting on such things, I tried to figure out how historians or observers will recall this particular period of time we're going through in Quebec.

Will they see it as a dynamic, positive era like the Quiet Revolution, when French Canada pulled itself out of the Great Darkness?

If Quebec becomes independent, probably. Because if nothing else, historians like to be on the side of a winner.

But in the more likely event that Canada remains united, I think not.

Because Quebec today has more in common with the days of the Great Darkness than it has in common with the social reform days of the Quiet Revolution.

In broad strokes, historians will see this as a time when Quebec society again turned inward, falling back on a nationalism that views les autres with suspicion, a sort of petite noirceur.

Instead of being church-dominated, society is dominated by the political-bureaucrat class.

One major difference, though, is that during the Duplessis era, the intellectuals were in opposition. Today, they are in the unhealthy position of being on the side of power.

More disturbing, there often appears to be an unhealthy conformity of political and social thought in those circles. Quebec intellectuals these days can't be accused of being particularly stimulating of thought.

What passes for a great debate these days is the battle between independantists and sovereignty-associationists in the PQ. It is portrayed as a great debate over vastly different options and principles.

But it is essentially a charade of a debate, and will likely be viewed in retrospect as not much more relevant than the debates indulged in by medieval theologians over how many angels could dance on the head of a pin.

But mostly it will be remembered as confirmation that like the old Union Nationale, the PQ is a coalition party centred on one man, and one major theme, insular nationalism.

And if the dominant new class reproaches English Montreal for voting Liberal all the time en bloc, remember the same reproach was made during the Duplessis era.

A date from our history that can't be forgotten

[Monday, November 17, 1986]

IN OUR POLITICAL PROCESS, there are few dates that stand out in our memories for very long.

Try to remember the date of the last federal or provincial election or the previous municipal election. Most of us can't because even though governments may have changed, our daily lives weren't terribly affected by it all.

But le quinze novembre is different. November 15, 1976, is a date engraved in the consciousness of a whole generation.

For some—I daresay a majority—of Quebecers, it was an evening of euphoria and jubilation. For others, it was a date marked in black, a cause for trepidation.

Sure, one can argue the election of a Parti Québécois government didn't in itself bring about overnight change; rather it was confirmation of evolution from the previous two decades.

However, in terms of symbolism and drama, le quinze novembre was one of those epochal dates in our history.

Who can't remember those flag-waving scenes from the Paul Sauvé Arena that night – René Lévesque puffing nervously on a cigarette, waiting for the tidal wave of applause and singing to die down?

On the other side of town, apprehension was the order of the evening. It would be no exaggeration to say there was even panic.

We all have different memories and emotions from that night as the results poured in.

While some celebrated and danced in the streets, others started feverish plans to pull up stakes. In the days that followed, boards of directors met to plan company moves to Ontario.

Anybody with even the slightest claim of political expertise was sought out to explain what was in store. I recall it as a time when I went though an endless round of lunches, dinners and seminars with foreign diplomats, company officials, academics and out-of-town journalists.

For Sale signs sprouted like mushrooms.

Meanwhile, a whole generation of Péquistes prepared for what they thought was the millenium, the creation of a new member state of the United Nations, the seizure of the levers of power, the staging of vast social engineering projects, the advent of utopia.

The poets were in power.

The "best and the brightest" of a generation of French-Canadians were on the move.

The people who had spent the best part of a decade in opposition, in both the electoral and street activist sense, were going to make a profound impact on the daily lives of all Quebecers. It was going to be dramatic and substantive because the Péquistes were endowed with a sense of mission and a firm belief they were writing history.

This was no ordinary election.

On Saturday, the actual anniversary date, we were recalling the flavour of the times.

"I had just arrived in Montreal from Scotland as a nanny for a Westmount family," recalled Aiso Colston-Fyfe. "I remember arriving on Halloween, October 31, and then on November 15 my Westmount family was terribly upset and started talking of moving to Boston.

"I had just made the biggest move of my young life and didn't want to go anywhere else."

Eventually, that family learned to live with the PQ in power, as did many others who were discomfited.

Yes, many people and companies did leave. But then again, many more adapted to the new circumstances, to the changes that were wrought.

And the PQ also had to adapt to power, to the exigencies of reality and the dictum that politics is the art of the possible.

Is Quebec today a better place, a worse place or the same place?

We all have different answers to that question.

One thing is certain: We all learned something from the roller-coaster experience of the PQ years.

And you had to be here to learn it. I'm glad I was and I'll bet you are, too.

An extraordinary man shaped exciting times

[Wednesday, November 4, 1987]

RENÉ LÉVESQUE was 38 years old and I was 18 when he was first elected to Quebec government.

Needless to say, he played a very important part in my life, just as he has played a very important part in the lives of everybody in Quebec in the past quarter century. And yesterday, watching the faces and emotions of the ordinary people who showed up at the former courthouse and hearing and reading the testimonials of the major figures of our society, it was evident there are an enormous number of people who share not only a sense of loss at his death but a sense that here was a man who led us through history.

He was an extraordinary man who had an extraordinary life. And we lived through extraordinary times.

It's odd, but there are times when one feels prescient.

On Sunday, during brunch at one of those trendy Toronto Yorkville restaurants, journalist Brian Stewart and I had been discussing funerals.

"Who," asked Stewart, a former correspondent with CBC and NBC, "do you think will have the greatest funeral in Quebec? Pierre Trudeau? René Lévesque? Jean Drapeau? Maybe even Rocket Richard, like Howie Morenz did?"

We weren't being ghoulish, but simply indulging our mutual passion for history.

We didn't spend a long time discussing it, but we did remind ourselves of how we marked the deaths of people like Maurice Duplessis, Daniel Johnson, John Diefenbaker, Pierre Laporte and so on.

We both concluded the death that would affect the most number of people in the most emotional possible way in Quebec would be René Lévesque's.

Then on Monday morning, Stewart woke me up in the spare room of his Toronto apartment and told me Lévesque was dead.

I thought he was just trying to get a reaction out of me. But when he assured me that Lévesque had died, I felt a great personal sadness.

Of course, it's hard to measure the impact a public figure has on the life of ordinary people—how a Drapeau or Trudeau or Lévesque affects one's personal life.

But when I think about it, no politician affected my thinking and feelings—and I suppose my times—as much as Lévesque.

I don't remember too much about him when he first got elected, but by the time he had pushed his Liberal government and Jean Lesage into running the 1962 election campaign on the issue of nationalizing the hydro-electric companies, I was a major fan.

Those were exciting times. And the passion of the Quiet Revolution was most eloquently expressed by René Lévesque.

It was inevitable that those of our generation who got their first taste of political passion and ideals from the lips and mind of René Lévesque would be, a few years down the line, the foot soldiers of all the changes that were to come.

Whatever qualities or flaws one may ascribe to him, first and foremost was his ability to inspire and excite the imagination. He made people believe things were possible, that the rules of conventional thinking and conformity could be broken.

By the mid-1960s I was a political reporter, and it seemed if René Lévesque wasn't personally setting the agenda for Quebec and Canada, at least he was extremely well attuned to it and was responding instinctively.

Of course, there were a million factors and many other outstanding individuals who were affecting political and social developments, but Lévesque stood out.

So much so that he was able to start a major new political party and attract, in a few years, the best and the brightest (along with the usual assortment of opportunists later on) to his fold.

He was a very contradictory man, but mostly he was a leader who inspired people. And by and large, we are all the better for it.

Watching the people expressing their sorrow about Lévesque's passing demonstrates there are not many who pass our way who are like him.

[Tribute]

Nick Turned Into a Tiger When Rivals Were at the Tee

Oliver Irwin

WHAT I REMEMBER BEST about the late 1960s was, of course, Expo 67, but also the extraordinarily insane hockey nights at the Novo Rex tavern with Nick and the gang of Rabelaisian roustabouts.

The Rex, now called the O'Blitz Pub, was located beneath the O'Sullivan business college on Mountain Street, just above what used to be Dorchester Boulevard. Back in those days, on Wednesday and Saturday nights, it was the scene of weird antics acted out by a bunch of over-stimulated misfits.

Besides Nick, there was the irrepressible Leon Harris and sports ency-clopedic Terry Haig, both of *The Gazette*, the brilliantly lacerating screen-writer Terry Heffernan, the equally acerbic wit, Craig Cottle, Dave Kerr, cynic son of the great Ranger goalie of the same name, the menacing Charlie Shields and a host of other would-be artists, mad writers and hangers-around waiting for their inheritances.

The group of about 20 rarely missed a game during that era of great Canadien teams of Beliveau, the Pocket Rocket, Dryden, Lemaire, Savard and later Lafleur.

Occasionally more sober-minded individuals, such as Brian Stewart, then of *The Gazette* and later the CBC "National," would join this wild bunch. Nick also seemed to come in a little late after a day of labour for *The Gazette* or later CBC's "Quelque Show." But there was always a place saved in front near the TV for the guy with the Borsalino and the newspapers tucked under his arm.

The crowd was usually fairly attentive during the game, but at about 11 o'clock the Molson kicked in and the merry pranksters began their fun amid the hideous red steer faces that stuck out from the stucco walls.

Once, late after a game, four of the stuplified fans in the front row found themselves with Nick's newspapers draped over their shoulders, poncho-style. They looked like altar boys until suddenly their mantels went up in flames in a flic of Nick's Bic. It took dozens of glasses of gladly-thrown beer to put out the flames. And as usual, no one came out the worse for wear.

Then there was the Saturday Nick and Linda Gaboriau got married in a huge church ceremony on Côte des Neiges Road, attended by the likes of future Prime Minister Brian Mulroney. Later that night, because there was a crucial Canadiens playoff game, Nick persuaded the reluctant bride to take in the hockey match at the Rex.

But enough became enough, and the bride finally persuaded Nick they really ought to leave, but not until the end of the second period. This scene is somewhat more elaborately re-enacted in Mordecai Richler's latest novel, *Barney's Version*—except it takes place at the Ritz instead of the Rex.

It was during these times that I got to know Nick and his affinity toward sports. The same gang got together at the Rex to watch the Alouettes and Sonny Wade in their best Grey Cup years. Nick had played football at D'Arcy McGee High School on St. Urbain Street. He was an end because of his speed. He was also a star sprinter in high school until he broke his leg on the gridiron in his senior year.

(I remember once somewhat after the Novo Rex days that a former colleague at *The Gazette* challenged him to a foot-race down Bishop Street between Ste. Catherine and Dorchester. Nick was a step behind and limping badly when he veered sharply left and ducked into Darwin's bar. His opponent ran full out to the end of the street exhausted and triumphant until he realized he was alone.)

Although he talked about playing a version of stick ball and another game where you threw the ball at steps, Nick never really played baseball. But he was an avid fan and completely knowledgeable about the game.

He was especially keen about the Montreal Royals' contribution to baseball during their time at the old Delormier Stadium in Montreal's east end.

Nick used to come out to watch *The Gazette* softball team play its never-ending series of games against Post Office workers. That is, he would

Nick and Linda Gaboriau at their wedding reception at the
Balthazar Restaurant on Notre-Dame West, May 14, 1977.

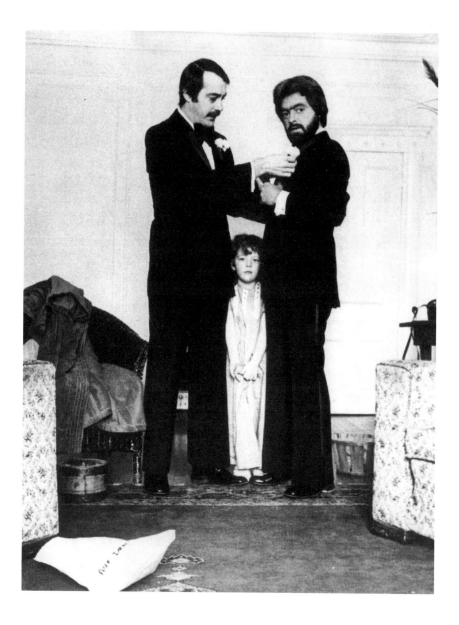

Nick and his best man, Terry Mosher, make last minute
adjustments before the wedding.
Melissa's vantage point ensures that she misses nothing.
May 14, 1977.

show up whenever he could be dragged along out of the old Press Club in the Sheraton-Mont Royal hotel at dawn after Joe Servant had closed the bar and thrown us out.

Nick and I would sometimes take in an Expos game. Although he knew the difference between the hit and run and run and hit, it was the odd and the quirky that he was always exploring, such as whether a thrown ball can actually speed up when it hits the Astroturf.

He once came back from a beer and hot dog run with a baseball. When asked about it, he said a foul ball took a couple of bounces and landed in his plastic tray while he was on the way up a ramp into the Big Owe. Things like that happened to Nick.

Then there was boxing. The bouts I most vividly remember were the two titanic encounters between Muhammad Ali and Joe Frazier which were shown on a big screen at the Forum. For Nick, Harris, Haig, Stewart and myself, it was one of life's metaphors. For four of us, the fight was the oppressed against the oppressor, North Vietnam against the United States, good versus evil. For Stewart, it was the opposite. When Ali lost that first wrenching bout, we had lost the Manichean struggle to the dark side.

Oh how Stewart gloated in the Maidenhead Bar in Alexis Nihon Plaza after the fight.

And oh how glum were we. But we got ours back in the rematch— the Thrilla in Manila.

Then there was golf. Probably Nick hated golf even more than outdoor barbecues or baked potatoes wrapped in aluminum foil. (Once he became chagrined with me when he had to miss a Sunday afternoon at Else's with foreign newspapers and I suggested to the incredulous who had come looking for him that he was out playing golf.)

He actually only golfed one time that I can verify. It was in 1974 at Mayor Jean Drapeau's annual golf tournament for city councillors. That year Nick and a motley crew of maladroit leftists had actually dented Drapeau's Civic Party machine by electing some opposition candidates, including Nick.

So, the new councillors had to be invited to the golf tournament at the Montreal Municipal Golf course, part of which would become the site of the Olympic Village in 1976.

I remember our foursome: Nick, and three of his campaign managers-workers; myself, Paul Ziff, now an oil and gas expert in Alberta and Stuart McLean of CBC "Morningside" fame. We showed Nick a few fundamentals before tee off time. He had the beginner's form—bent left elbow and a clumsy lunge at the ball. The first few holes were miserable for him as he ploughed the ball along the ground in many futile swipes.

Then at about the fourth hole, we crossed paths with the enemy—Civic Party hackers. They were dressed impeccably in bright polyester golf slacks and sweaters and nifty hats and sported top-notch clubs and other expensive paraphernalia. They smugly watched as the rag-tag, ill-dressed political neophytes stepped up to the tee. We three more golf-experienced campaigners sliced, hooked and generally choked under the sniggering gaze of the Civic Party pros.

Then Nick teed up, swung mightily at the ball and watched it sail 220 yards down the middle in perfect flight. It was a small miracle for the good guys as the smirks faded off the adversaries' faces. But it was something other than a miracle because Nick willed beautiful, arcing drives two other times when Civic Party-types were watching. Things like that happened to Nick.

More recently, despite despising cars, Nick took up an interest in auto racing through his friendship with Grand Prix aficionado Jake Richler and with long-time acquaintance and former race driver, Derek Johnson. I remember how pleased he was when I brought back newspapers from Europe with pictures and stories plastered all over the front pages about Jacques Villeneuve winning the World Championship.

Nick's dealings with the Olympics, his book *The Billion Dollar Game*, and his crucial advice to the Los Angles Olympic Committee is, well, another story.

Nick came to view most professional sports and their pampered players spoiled by absurd salaries with increasing disdain. But, for Nick, sports were part of the human condition to be treated with intelligence and perspective.

Oliver Irwin is a journalist in the English newsroom of Radio Canada International in Montreal.

SPORTS

Toe Blake's Tavern sketches during the first game
of the 1972 Canada-Russia hockey series...

USSR
GOAL #1

USSR
GOAL #2

USSR
GOAL #3

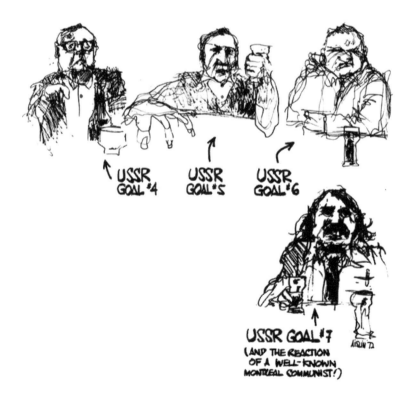

USSR
GOAL #4

USSR
GOAL #5

USSR
GOAL #6

USSR GOAL #7

(AND THE REACTION
OF A WELL-KNOWN
MONTREAL COMMUNIST!)

Rocket Richard riot rocked Montreal
30 years ago

[Friday, March 15, 1985]

THIRTY YEARS AGO today, all the talk in the yard at St. Leo's and every schoolyard in the country, for that matter was the big fight Maurice (Rocket) Richard had had in Boston two nights earlier.

The Canadiens were in a desperate battle against the Detroit Red Wings for first place.

In Boston, March 13, 1955, the Canadiens lost to the Bruins. That left us two points ahead of Detroit. But in the game, Hal Laycoe carved a five-inch gash on the Rocket's temple with his stick.

The Rocket responded in his usual fiery manner.

He floored Laycoe.

Linesman Cliff Thompson tried to restrain Richard, but the Rocket then punched Thompson in the face.

The next day, the NHL office announced that president Clarence Campbell would take disciplinary action March 16.

And so, we stood around the schoolyard wondering and worrying about what might happen.

What would Campbell do to Richard? Fine him? A suspension was unthinkable.

There were only three games left before the start of the Stanley Cup playoffs. (The regular season wasn't interminably long in those days.) Richard had a chance of winning the scoring title for the only time in his career.

The next day, a Wednesday, Campbell's announcement came: Richard was suspended for the remainder of the season and the playoffs.

The news spread like wildfire.

When you're 12 years old, there isn't much news that shocks you. But we were all truly stunned and bewildered. How could they do that to the Rocket and to us?

We went home that day with an awful sense of grief.

That night, with the Canadiens idle, Detroit defeated Boston. The win put them in a first-place tie with Montreal at 91 points.

On St. Patrick's Day, a Thursday, the crowds gathered outside the Forum for the Canadiens' first game since the big Beantown brawl. It was against Detroit.

Here we were, without the Rocket, fighting for first place.

After school, a bunch of us left St. Leo's on Clarke Street in Westmount and walked over to see what was happening at the Forum.

I'd never seen a picket before.

People had signs portraying Campbell as a pig. Others had signs that said: "Vive Richard."

The mood wasn't festive.

We went home for supper and to listen to the game on the radio.

The announcer told us the crowd outside the Forum was getting bigger. There were thousands of demonstrators.

One of the kids on the street phoned me and suggested we check what was happening.

My mother wouldn't let me go. I begged and pleaded. Finally, I snuck out of the house just as the game was starting.

We went over to the old Atwater baseball park, where Alexis Nihon Plaza stands today.

The newspapers said there were 6,000 people there. To me, it looked like a million or more.

People started throwing things. Rocks shattered the windows in the Forum.

We saw a streetcar surrounded by the mob. Its windows were broken, and people were trying unsuccessfully to tip it over. They had better luck with a police car.

Then we saw one of those old wooden newspaper kiosks on Cabot Square go up in flames.

At first, we kids on the sidelines felt a sense of excitement. Then fear. We went home.

Inside the Forum, with the Canadiens down 2-0, Campbell made his entrance. He was pelted with eggs. After a bit, a fan went up to him and extended his arm as if he wanted to shake hands. When he got close, he punched Campbell on the nose.

Then someone threw a tear gas canister on the ice.

People made for the exits. The crowd outside was trying to get in through smashed doors, the people inside were trying to get out.

The police managed to force the crowd east on Ste. Catherine and the crowd broke windows and looted stores all the way down to Morgan's.

The Canadiens forfeited the game and first place. (Detroit was ahead 4-1 by the time fire officials halted things.)

The next day Mayor Jean Drapeau and Richard had to go on radio to appeal for calm.

Montreal made news around the world with the Richard riot.

But Detroit ended up in first place that season. The Rocket lost the scoring title by one point, to teammate Bernard (Boom Boom) Geoffrion. The Boomer had 75 points, Richard 74, and Jean Beliveau 73.

Detroit went on to defeat the Rocketless Canadiens four games to three in the Stanley Cup finals.

Some pundits claim the Rocket riot was the start of the Quiet Revolution—the first howl of rage by oppressed French Canadians.

But I don't at all remember it having an English-French connotation.

There was probably an element of nationalism involved, just as there probably was an element of class conflict. But that certainly wasn't the entire story.

Richard was everybody's idol, our Babe Ruth, a man we all intensely identified with.

In that sense, Richard was Everyman.

And it seemed Campbell was punishing us all.

Spring can't really be sprung until the Canadiens are out of the playoffs

[Friday, April 26, 1985]

SPRING, for some, is a strange time.

Our body clocks tell us it's spring, the time to take in the sun and perhaps play hookey from work to go to an afternoon ball game. The last couple of days have featured glorious, take-a-casual-stroll weather. Those are the spring days when you feel a wonderful sense of exhilaration from walking about town without coats, boots or all that horrible paraphernalia we've stuffed in our closets for the next seven months.

But deep down in our souls we know there is one last vestige of winter we must still confront—the National Hockey League playoffs.

No matter what our body clocks tell us, we know that our Canadian mentality can't adapt fully to spring or summer until we have a Stanley Cup winner (or until the Canadiens are eliminated, whichever comes first).

I know that in a recent column I swore off professional sports, explaining that I felt I was played for a sucker by those extravagant baseball salaries and the silly hockey playoff system.

It's true. I am a sucker.

Here I am hooked again by the Canadiens and their mighty struggle against the godless Nordiques. (In actual fact, I got hooked during the lesson we taught those bad Boston Bruins.)

My colleague Brian Kappler, the baseball writer, used to tell me that the true metaphor for Canadian life was the Canadian Football League:

"The field is too big, everything is confused, it's often very cold, and when it isn't chaotic, its very dull.

"And if you look at the Concordes' goal-line defence, you're speaking about the longest undefended border in the world.

"Hockey on the other hand is almost American. It's lively, spectacular, vivid, colorful, exciting.

"Really, when you think about it, the Canadian national game should be chess—it's played according to the rules, it's methodical, quiet and as unrelenting as our winters. And most often it's inconclusive."

Well, Kappler is originally from Windsor, Ontario. So what does he know about it? He probably grew up cheering for the Maple Leafs. Or even worse, the Red Wings.

Besides, his head is buried in baseball.

No, hockey is as Canadian as maple syrup.

Lately of course, I'm only reminded of that because of the playoffs, when we get a protracted glimpse of the zest and vitality that represent our country. Except too often we're too slow to recognize it as the true Canadian metaphor.

"Absolutely," said another colleague, political columnist L. Ian Mac-Donald.

"And playoff hockey is the essential part of the rites of spring in Montreal. There is a tangible feeling in the air. Everything else is secondary while the Canadiens are still in it.

"There's a kind of anomaly to it, though. It's an exciting time, but the city is quiet during playoff games. Everybody is at home watching the game. The restaurants get murdered, but the staff doesn't mind since all the waiters can watch the game."

(Spring must arrive awfully early in Toronto these years. How do you know it's spring in Toronto? The Leafs are out.)

It's funny, in all my time involved in politics and trying to organize this or that, whenever we've set a date for a meeting for something, we've always taken out our pocket diaries to check two things:

Does the date clash with a Jewish holiday?

Does it clash with a playoff game?

If so, pick another date.

Even provincial budgets get switched to accommodate the only thing people really seem concerned about.

Ralph Allen, the legendary Canadian newspaperman, once wrote that "hockey is Canada's national religion."

At this time of year, most of us become very religious.

Ball-speed argument has them hopping mad

[Wednesday, June 18, 1986]

BOY, do I hate having to write this.

It was a typical baseball argument.

Saturday night the boys were watching the Expos on TV.

At one point, one of the Expos' throws just missed getting the runner at first. "Jeez," said Doug Muncey, "he should have bounced the ball. That would have got it there in time."

I stared at Muncey.

"What do you mean, bounce the ball? How would that have helped?"

"Well, you know," he said. "The ball accelerates after the bounce, picks up speed and gets there faster."

"Are you nuts?" I asked. "Are you a technological illiterate? A ball can't pick up speed after a bounce."

"Yeah," Doug Blomert added, "don't you know anything about elementary physics? You can't create energy out of nothing. A ball starts to slow down right after it's hit or thrown. It can't pick up speed after the fact."

"Oh yeah, Sir Isaac?" Muncey said. "It's like a golf ball. When the club hits the ball, the ball compresses and loses its round. Then when it hits the ground it bounces back into shape and that gives it an extra thrust, like an afterburner on a rocket."

"Muncey," Blomert said, "you're out of your mind. Why do you think a bounce will make it go faster?"

"Because it picks up speed. Chris Speier used to throw that way," Muncey tried to explain.

"It has something to do with Astroturf and gravity or whatever. There's more force added by the inflection of the angle."

Muncey was obviously out of his depth, in trouble with his idiotic argument.

We moved in for the kill.

"According to your theory," I said, "a bouncing ball will pick up speed ad infinitum until it reaches the velocity of light."

Blomert guffawed with delight.

"In fact," I added, "they should build particle accelerators out of Astroturf and save millions of dollars."

More guffaws as Muncey blushed with embarrassment.

At that point, Expos pinch-runner Al Newman was thrown out trying to steal second base.

"He should have started his slide 20 feet sooner," Blomert shrieked. "That way his bounce would have helped beat the throw."

We howled with laughter.

Muncey gamely tried to defend his thesis.

We started drawing diagrams of arc throws and bounce throws. Pretty soon everybody was arguing madly and shouting.

"It's the trampoline effect," Danny Kaufman interjected.

Muncey had an ally all of a sudden.

"Dumkopf," Blomert sneered.

Nick Wrigley tried to come to Muncey's defence.

"If a ball is hit below the centrifugal line," he said with eyes screwed up in concentration, his hands trying to show the motion, "it slows down on the curve and then picks up speed."

"You don't understand a thing about physics, do you?" Blomert retorted.

"You make things up. You probably believe that nonsense about 'hang time' in football, where a ball can hang in the air like Mikhail Baryshnikov."

Naturally Muncey and his allies believed in "hang time" and tried to defend that hoary theory also.

Blomert and I demolished them with wit and logic.

On Monday night while Muncey was listening to the baseball game on the radio, he phoned up Blomert and said: "Did you hear what Duke Snider just said?"

"No," Blomert said. "I was asleep."

"He just said that a ball hit past (fielder Herman) Winningham picked up speed after the bounce. Picked up speed."

"What does Snyder know about physics?" Blomert asked.

"We don't settle this with a PhD in physics, we settle this with Duke Snider. It's baseball, not physics," Muncey insisted.

Well, yesterday I phoned Prof. S.K. Mark, chairman of McGill University's physics department.

"Sorry to bother you," I said, "but some lunatic insists that a baseball can pick up speed on a bounce. There's no way that can happen in accordance with the laws of physics, is there?"

"Oh, yes," the professor said. "It is possible. When you throw a ball, energy is not only put in the linear motion. You can put it into the spin. There can be a lot of energy stored in a spin. And if it hits the ground the right way, that energy can be switched to linear motion, so the ball can be speeded up."

"Oh," I said.

I asked about Muncey's golf ball theory. He was wrong there. A relief. I tried the "hang time" theory.

"Oh, yes," Mark said. "If you throw a ball up, it comes straight down. But if you put the right spin on it, it will come down slower. If you throw a football with the right spiral spin it will appear to hang in the air longer."

I felt sick.

Muncey was right, even though he was wrong.

Millionaire hockey players owe a lot to Doug Harvey

[Wednesday, January 24, 1990]

THE NATIONAL HOCKEY LEAGUE's all-star game and coverage of associated events last weekend made me a bit melancholy.

I saw some of the greats introduced and I read about the politics of the players choosing a new executive director for the NHL Players Association. And then I thought of how sad it was that Doug Harvey, the great Canadiens defenceman who died the day after Christmas, wasn't on hand to share the moment. If some NHL players today can look forward to retirement as millionaires, if the league is to become an even greater success as it expands, it is due in no small measure to the contributions of Harvey, both on and off the ice.

Ironically, one could argue Harvey's decline began after an all-star game in the late 1950s.

Back then, Harvey was a superstar who had a lock on the Norris Trophy (league's best defenceman) and was a key component of the magnificent team that won a record five straight Stanley Cups.

Harvey joined the Canadiens in 1947 after playing amateur hockey, football and baseball and serving a stint in the navy. He was offered, take it or leave it, $6,000 a season plus a $2,000 signing bonus. Nothing for the playoffs.

That was the same year a group of disgruntled NHL players, notably from the Detroit Red Wings, organized the NHL players' pension plan, a move that was discouraged by the owners. The owners contributed nothing to the plan, but league president Clarence Campbell and the owners did go along with the idea of setting up an all-star game, with two-thirds of the ticket revenues going to the pension fund.

The league didn't like the idea, because it meant players might get together to form an association or union. But the NHL still managed to get control of the pension fund—two directors from the six player representatives and two from the owners, plus Campbell.

Fiery Ted Lindsay of the Red Wings was the moving force behind the pension fund. Soon he was joined on the board by Harvey.

"I wasn't used to talking to opposing players. In fact, it seemed totally against the spirit of the game," Harvey once told me. "And it turned out the hardest thing I ever had to do in hockey was associating with Lindsay at a pension-plan meeting. It wasn't easy."

Those meetings were held in conjunction with the all-star game. Soon, Lindsay and Harvey were bringing up various grievances.

"Gentlemen, this is a pension-plan meeting. We'll bring them up (the grievances) at the board of governors meeting next year," Campbell would tell the players.

"That's the last we'd ever hear about it," Harvey said.

The issues had to do with travelling conditions, training camp, payment for exhibition games and even such items as revenue from bubble-gum cards. Sometimes Lindsay and Harvey would want to know why the all-star game receipts were listed at only $15,000 when they figured it must have been $50,000.

At one meeting before an all-star game in the late 1950s, Campbell announced that Conn Smythe, the Toronto general manager, was undertaking an independent audit of the players' pension fund.

Lindsay and Harvey said they'd like to see the audit when it was finished.

Campbell replied: "Well, he's paying for it (the audit) out of his own pocket, and it's his own personal business."

The two players reps stormed out of the meeting. Outside, Lindsay said to Harvey: "To hell with this, let's start an association."

It was difficult and the owners resisted.

But things happened.

"One day," Harvey recalled, "Frank Selke would show up in the dressing room and say: 'We've got a deal on bubble-gum cards. You're each to get $150.'"

The fledging players' association was to have a meeting later with the board of governors to discuss more important business such as the matching of contributions to the pension plan and recognition of the association. The association pressed on with its organization.

Then came the reprisals.

In Detroit, management persuaded Red Kelly and Gordie Howe to get the players to leave the association. Lindsay was traded to the lowly

Chicago Blackhawks.

Montreal militant Bert Olmstead was sent to Toronto. Dollard St. Laurent went to Chicago. Dick Duff was dispatched from Toronto. Harvey's superstar status protected him for a while, until the end of the 1960-61 season when—at age 37—he was traded to the Rangers, where as player-coach he won another Norris Trophy.

The association struggled until a few years later when Alan Eagleson got it off the ground again and gained more recognition from the league.

Harvey played for years, and then there was no room for him in hockey. Back in Montreal, dispirited and broke, he drank heavily, developing the diseases that were to eventually kill him.

In the last few years, he lived in a lavish old railway car parked at Connaught Park raceway in Aylmer, run by Joe Gorman, Tommy's son, with whom he grew up in N.D.G.

A couple of years ago, Ron Corey and the Canadiens—prodded by journalist Tim Burke—made up with Harvey. His sweater was retired at a ceremony at the Forum; he was named a scout in the Ottawa-Aylmer area, and given a car.

"He liked that car," Gorman said. "He spent the best part of his career travelling in trains. It is his monument."

That, the all-star game, and the NHL Players Association.

Speaking of the Stanley Cup, let's tout our hockey history

[Wednesday, February 26, 1992]

SUNDAY, I was all worked up for the Olympic hockey gold medal. It has been, after all, 40 years since Canada's last hockey gold (won by the Edmonton Mercurys in 1952).

But our hopes were dashed.

The game left me feeling a little forlorn. Because politics and the economy are so dreary these days, I find myself taking sports a little more seriously than I normally do. Maybe, I thought, just maybe the Canadiens will win the Stanley Cup this year. That would cheer us up. If they did, it would be the Habs' 24th Stanley Cup, since they first won it in 1915-16, two years before the start of the National Hockey League 75 seasons ago.

That would be the 39th Stanley Cup for Montreal teams.

This is a game I like to play, asking people how many Montreal teams have won the cup. Most people, including many ardent sports fans, say two, naming the Canadiens and the Montreal Maroons, who won it in 1925-26 and again in 1934-35.

But four other Montreal teams have also won the Stanley Cup—the Montreal Amateur Athletic Association Winged Wheelers (3), the Montreal Victorias (4), the Montreal Wanderers (4) and the Montreal Shamrocks (2). As a matter of fact, next season will mark the 100th anniversary of the Stanley Cup, first awarded to the MAAA in 1892-93.

After Sunday's loss, I decided I needed a little hockey cheer, so I went to visit an old friend, jazz pianist Billy Georgette, to talk about the glory days of Montreal hockey.

Billy is a hockey enthusiast, and his enthusiasm is infectious. He's a member of the Society for International Hockey Research, associated with the Canadian Amateur Hockey Association Hall of Fame in Kingston, Ontario.

He's been waging a campaign to have Montreal recognized as the real birthplace of hockey as we know it. In the early '40s, the CAHA designated Kingston as the birthplace, based on a report of game of shinny (or bandy

228

or hurly) played there by military men in 1855 in the harbour with a lighthouse in the middle of the playing surface.

First of all, shinny had no rules, involved any number of players and used a ball. Like lacrosse in those days, the game was played until one side scored three goals.

Georgette's argument is based on historical accounts of the first real game of hockey played on March 3, 1875, at Montreal's Victoria skating rink, our first indoor rink, and the first rink shaped like the modern hockey rink. (Other rinks were generally circular or oval.)

That first game was advertised in newspapers as "introducing the new game of ice hockey." It was the first game played according to written rules. The rules were established by a McGill student from Nova Scotia, J.G.H. Creighton, who captained his nine-man squad against the Victorias. The McGill side was all WASP, except for one Jew, Henry Joseph.

It was the first game played with a wooden disk instead of a lacrosse ball. And the goalies wore cricket pads. All 1,500 seats were sold as Montrealers flocked to watch this novelty. It was supposed to be a two-game matchup. McGill won the first, 2-1, but the second game was cancelled when players and fans got into an enormous brawl which sent the ladies present fleeing. It was a wild success and within a couple of years there were literally hundreds of teams in the Montreal area.

The city went hockey mad.

The word hockey, according to Georgette, was coined here. There are two versions of its origin. One, it was derived from the French word, "houlette," for a shepherd's crook—as opposed to a Bishop's staff, "crosse," from which lacrosse gets its name. The other version is the Iroquois, "hochee," which was chanted when a goal was scored in lacrosse.

Shortly after the game was introduced, the number of players was reduced to seven (the present six-man version was introduced around the turn of the century.)

Then in 1883, Montreal Winter Carnival officials spent $750 to purchase a trophy for what they billed as "the first world championship of ice hockey."

It was played out in the Victoria rink during the week of Feb. 12, by six teams—Quebec, Toronto, Ottawa, McGill, the Victorias and another Montreal team, the Crystals.

They played 30 games in all that week, and McGill staggered out on top.

The Victoria rink, which was the first public building in Canada to have electricity, basically defined hockey.

It stood where the Tilden garage is today, between Stanley and Drummond streets. Because of the distance between Stanley and Drummond, the rink was about 202 feet by 85 feet, the approximate NHL standard today.

In 1892, Governor-General Lord Stanley instructed an aide-de-camp to purchase a trophy, to be awarded to the best hockey team in Canada.

It was first given to the MAAA by some vague consensus. The Winged Wheelers successfully defended it the next year, then lost to the Victorias. (The Detroit Red Wings, incidentally, were founded by an MAAA alumnus who swiped the logo.)

All championships were played at the Victoria rink until the 2,500-seat Westmount arena, which stood where the old RCMP building used to be, was opened in 1898.

The Canadiens were formed as a French team (but also had English-speaking players) in 1909 and originally played out of the Mount Royal arena.

When the Westmount arena burned down it was replaced by the Forum, home of the Maroons.

The new Forum will be built beside Windsor Station, just a block away from the original Victoria rink, birthplace of modern hockey.

Molson, Canadian Pacific and the Canadiens should build an appropriate memorial plaque at the old Drummond Street site. The sidewalk leading down to the new Forum should be turned into a sidewalk of hockey stars, with embedded bilingual plaques commemorating all the greats who made Montreal hockey, including all Stanley Cup winning teams.

We must recapture our hockey history and celebrate it. It is one thing all Montrealers can take pride in.

And next season, for the 100th anniversary of the Stanley Cup, the Forum should display all 38 Stanley Cup banners of the six teams.

Billy Georgette and I urge readers to write to the proper authorities demanding they carry out these very sensible recommendations. It is our history and it deserves to be told.

More data about Montreal's role as birthplace of hockey

[Wednesday, June 3, 1992]

THE SEASON is finally over, the Stanley Cup has been won. And just think, the Canadiens training camp opens in only three months.

Next season marks the 100th anniversary of the Stanley Cup. (This season has been only the 75th anniversary of the NHL.) On February 26, I wrote a column stating that the centenary of the Stanley Cup (first won by the Montreal Amateur Athletic Association for 1892-93) should be used by Montreal to claim its rightful place as the birthplace of ice hockey as we know it.

Remarkably, there is no proper history of hockey, no definitive explanation of its origins and development. In fact, the history of hockey is so poorly documented that it seems no two reference books agree on which teams won the Stanley Cup in the years prior to the formation of the NHL.

For instance, in my column I stated that six different Montreal teams won the cup, for a total of 38 championships. That was based on the book *One Hundred Years of Hockey* by Brian MacFarlane.

My column also detailed a history of the game as researched by Billy Georgette, a jazz pianist and hockey enthusiast who is a member of the Kingston-based Society for International Hockey Research.

The response to that column was quite interesting. I received letters from a number of people who, quite separately, have been enthusiastically researching our hockey history.

Michel Vigneault, a PhD student in sports history who is doing his thesis at Université Laval on the development of hockey in Montreal, writes that, in fact, Montreal teams have won the Stanley Cup 40 times, not 38 as stated in various references.

"The trophy was competed for on a challenge basis before 1914," he writes. "Some seasons saw two winners of the Cup.

"So the Montreal teams that won the Stanley Cup are: MAAA (1893-1894-1902-1903); Victorias (1895-1896-1897-1898-1899); Shamrocks

(1899-1900); Wanderers (1906-1907-1908-1910); Maroons (1926-1935) and Canadiens (23 times)."

Vigneault notes the unreliability of existing references and bases his conclusions on an exhaustive survey of numerous newspapers of the day. (Scores of daily and weekly newspapers came and went in Montreal during the formative years of hockey.)

He agrees that the Montreal Forum should display all 40 Montreal Stanley Cup banners; so did many other readers.

Vigneault says that next season the new Ottawa franchise should display Ottawa's cup banners: Silver Seven (1903-1904-1905) and Senators (1909-1911.)

Quebec City could display the Bulldogs banners (1912-1913), while Winnipeg could display the Winnipeg Victorias (1896-1901). Other teams to win prior to the NHL were the Vancouver Millionaires (1915), Toronto Blueshirts (1914), Kenora Thistles (1907) and Seattle Metropolitans (1917).

The fact that Montreal teams dominated the championship in the early years demonstrates that the game grew out of here.

Both Vigneault and A. Andrew Allan, another reader who has devoted much time to researching our hockey history, remarked on my contention that the first game of hockey was played in Montreal at the Victoria Rink, which stood where the Tilden garage is on Stanley Street just up from René Lévesque Blvd., on March 3, 1875.

"According to the texts of March 3 and 4, 1875, of *The Gazette*," Vigneault writes, "it was not the first hockey match, but the first one publicly seen by outsiders. On the 3rd, we can read the following: 'Some of the players are reputed to be exceedingly expert at the game.' In another article about Henry Joseph (who played in that game) the latter is quoted in the McGill News, 1956, as saying: 'We actually had been playing almost two seasons before we were found out'."

Allan explains how the game developed: "Joseph and some other members of the Victoria Skating Club at first tried lacrosse on skates but gave up the idea after one or two games. It was James George Aylwin Creighton who suggested a game on ice in which sticks and a ball were used after the fashion of shinny. They tried it out and then patterned the game after English rugby, which most of them played. They used similar positions and rules."

Other towns, such as Halifax-Dartmouth and Kingston, lay vague claims to having originated hockey, but today almost everyone, including the Society for International Hockey Research, accepts the fact that Montreal is the true home of hockey. "The Kingston claim was never backed by anything substantial," Allan notes, "just an entry in a diary for the years 1846-47 about shinny being played by soldiers in Kingston harbour. The Kingston shinny never developed or progressed into an organized game … no rules, just hit the ball in any direction and run after it."

What is definite is that the system of scoring, rules and number of players was established in Montreal and other cities gradually followed suit.

"The first public exhibition of hockey in Quebec City took place on February 8, 1879," Allan writes. "They did have some minor rule differences to the Montreal game, but I can't find out any documentation as to what they were, yet different enough to cancel a game with the Montreal Hockey Club in 1880 disputing how they should be interpreted."

As a leader in sports, Montreal has a great track record

[Wednesday, February 3, 1993]

IT WOULD BE FITTING that today, midway between the NFL Super Bowl last Sunday and the NHL All-Star Game this Saturday, we look at Montreal's contributions to sport.

Last fall in this space, we looked at how hockey as we know it was developed in Montreal. The first game, with rules similar to the modern version, was played at the historic Victoria Rink on March 3, 1875. The Montreal Amateur Athletic Association won the first Stanley Cup 100 years ago after emerging as champion of the Amateur Hockey Association of Canada, then the premier league.

But Montrealers made many other significant contributions—so many that this city is a good candidate to be named as the real birthplace of organized sport on the continent.

Consider.

Football was born out of encounters between McGill University and Harvard.

Variations of soccer had been played in U.S. schools for a long time. But in 1871, Harvard started to play a variation known as "the Boston Game," which allowed a player to scoop up the ball and run with it. Other colleges refused to play by those rules.

Harvard then invited McGill for two games at Cambridge, Massachusetts, on May 13 and 14, 1874.

McGill arrived a few days before the matches. The Americans were surprised to see the Canadians kick the ball, run with it and tackle.

McGill members explained that these were part of the rugby rules they played by, rules adopted by the Montreal Football Club in 1870.

Both teams agreed to play half the game according to Harvard rules and half by McGill rules, which—unlike the U.S. rules—had both touchdowns and field goals.

Normally Harvard had 15 players. But McGill could field only 11. So the hosts agreed to 11.

Early in the first half, the Harvard team found they so enjoyed the McGill rules that they agreed to complete the games that way, using McGill's oval ball instead of their round one.

A year later, Harvard, having adopted McGill rules, played Yale University using a combination of soccer and rugby rules, but with Yale's round ball.

McGill and Harvard continued playing in 1876, 1877, 1879 and 1882, refining the game. (Harvard won all the games, except for one tie.)

The two teams' games continued to evolve until we got the separate Canadian and U.S. games.

Montreal was by that time a hotbed of organized sports in North America.

The Royal Montreal Curling Club, the first on the continent, was established by Scotsmen involved in the fur trade in 1807.

The first golf game recorded here was in 1814 on "the priests' farm," while the Royal Montreal Golf Club was the first established on the continent, in 1873, with a course on Fletcher's Field on the eastern slope of the mountain.

The Montreal Racquets Club, now the oldest in the world, was established in 1836. The Montreal Fox Hunt and Jockey Club started in 1830.

From 1840 to 1890, while the city grew rapidly as a metropolis of the continent, there was an amazing creative energy put into both summer and winter sports: an abundance of clubs devoted to every conceivable sport, with the organizers carrying it to other cities with almost missionary zeal.

On August 28 and 29, 1844, Montreal held what it called "Olympic Games," almost a half-century before Baron de Coubertin founded the modern Olympic movement.

Field days had been held in other cities prior to that, but none on such a scale, involving a score of disciplines and team games, including lacrosse and cricket.

The Indians won the lacrosse championship and an Iroquois named Tarisonkwan ran the mile in 4:52 minutes.

In 1886, a McGill engineer, C.H. McLeod, designed the first apparatus to record track times.

In 1874, A.T. Lane imported the first bicycle to North America; he founded the Montreal Bicycle Club in 1878.

In 1881, the MAAA was established as Canada's first substantial sports and social club, a venture created by the affiliation of a gymnasium, the major snowshoe and lacrosse clubs, the Tûques Bleues toboggan club and the bicycle and football clubs—promoting track and field, swimming, billiards, bowling and numerous other activities.

Special note should also be made of Frederick Barnjum, an Englishman who settled here in the 1850s, a disciple of Archibald MacLaren, the Oxford educator who synthesized the British passion for sports with the Scandinavian stress on formal gymnastics.

When James Naismith came from Ontario to McGill on a scholarship, he fell under the influence of Barnjum. (The latter was unique in his day because he was a major proponent of women's athletics.)

While studying theology, Naismith became an outstanding athlete in football, gymnastics, lacrosse and wrestling.

When Barnjum died in 1889, Naismith and another of his pupils, Tait Mackenzie, took over his McGill classes.

Two years later, Naismith, combining his Christian instincts and love for sports, went to work with the new YMCA in Springfield, Massachusetts (the first YMCA in North America was in Montreal), where he invented basketball.

Mackenzie went on to be the first chairman of physical education at the University of Pennsylvania, where he exerted a profound influence on the development of physical education on the continent, including physical and recreation programs for the U.S. and Canadian armies.

There's more, but there's no more room in this column.

Babe Ruth once batted for Ahuntsic against black team

[Wednesday, March 20, 1996]

WELL, we've had a rather remarkable week in Montreal with the closing of the Forum and all the hoopla, culminating in Sunday's monster St. Patrick's Day parade.

The combination of all the events seemed to work as a tonic and morale booster for the city. Sunday's parade especially did that, because there was such an element of spontaneity and enthusiasm that can't be orchestrated unless there is something genuine behind it. This was a show of affection and solidarity by Montrealers.

That element also was evident in the three prolonged standing ovations accorded to Maurice (Rocket) Richard at the various ceremonies attached to the Forum closing.

Richard dominated his game and the fans' imagination and affection like no other in North American professional sport, except for Babe Ruth in baseball.

Which brings me to Babe Ruth's visits to Montreal, events which I and nobody I asked in the past week had ever heard about.

During my research on the old Forum, I asked a friend of mine, Robbie Dillon, who likes to poke around in old archives and newspaper files, to look up some stuff for me. And he came up with an ad that appeared in *The Gazette* on October 11, 1928.

Actually, the ad was for Ruth's second visit here. He first came on October 28, 1926. An article in *The Gazette* explained that "Ruth was signed for his engagement here by the veteran of local baseball promotions, Joe Page, who concluded negotiations while attending the World Series games last week."

That first game, Ruth played for a local all-star team against a team called Beaurivage.

It was played at Guybourg Grounds near what was then the new Forum. Here is an excerpt from *The Gazette* account:

"His exhibition included two home runs, which fairly made the crowd gasp, the first coming in the sixth inning to tie the score for his side 3-3.

"In the (top of the) ninth with the score knotted, Babe faced Paddy Galkin, former stormy petrel of amateur ball here who has been signed for a tryout with the Chicago Sox next spring. Galkin wanted to fan Ruth. He certainly did not want to walk him. The first three balls were wide. Then Galkin grooved two over the plate, both of which Ruth fouled. With the count 3 and 2 and the score tied, Ruth belted the next ball out of the lot and won the game.

"It was what the crowd wanted. They had seen enough and there was no dissenting voice when the announcer came forward to state that the game was called as 36 balls had been driven out of the park by Ruth in practice and in the game and there were none left with which to continue the contest.

"But it was not only at bat that Ruth showed his prowess. Three innings on first base convinced him that the Guybourg shortstop was cracking defensively so Ruth took over the shortstop burden. He immediately grabbed the calcium light with a one-handed stab of a wild throw to chop off an attempted stolen base. Then McCormick, the Guybourg pitcher, blew in the sixth and Babe went to the mound for the last three innings. He chopped Beaurivage off without a hit or a run. In the first half of the seventh he undertook to umpire behind the bat for Ubald Rose, who had his arm injured by a foul ball. Babe handled this assignment perfectly, except that he was unable to extricate himself from the pads at the end of the inning and sent a noisy call for Mr. Houdini to get him out of the harness. (Houdini was playing that week at the old Princess Theatre, now the Parisien.)

"After the game (he) had to smash his way through the crowd in approved rugby style to find his taxi and speed away to the Windsor Hotel where he is quartered. Ruth arrived yesterday morning over the Rutland Railway. He was the guest at a reception at Columbus Hall yesterday noon and leaves this morning for New York."

Two years later, Ruth was back in Montreal with his Yankee teammate Lou Gehrig to play for Ahuntsic of the city's senior semi-pro league against a team composed of local and U.S. blacks.

A crowd of 16,000 turned out to see Ruth hit two for three (but no homers). Gehrig went one for four, but his one hit was a homer in the top of the ninth that broke a 6-6 tie.

Again the opposing team didn't get their last at-bats because the crowd went wild after Gehrig's homer, littering the field with seat cushions and then invading the playing area.

In those days, Ruth would occasionally barnstorm with teams from the old Negro leagues, visiting small towns in New Jersey and the New England states.

The official colour bar in baseball would not be broken until 20 years later when Jackie Robinson came to play for the Montreal Royals in the Triple A International League.

Montreal has perhaps the greatest sports history of any city on the continent.

A card drawn for Nick's 50th birthday celebration.

PETS

Time for a cat-and-squirrel game

[May 15, 1989]

SUNDAY MORNING sitting at the kitchen table, munching on hot, fresh bagels, dully staring out the window contemplating life.

My cat Arthur V, or is it VI? I can't remember clearly. Anyhow, Arthur was anxious to play the squirrel game.

So I go to the cupboard, take out a handful of peanuts and go outside and place them on the window ledge and balcony railing.

Always break the peanuts open because the dumb squirrels will take unbroken shells and bury them somewhere and forget where they are.

This is nature's way of planting, but I have yet to see a peanut plant or tree, or whatever peanuts grow up to be, sprout in my back garden. For that matter, I have yet to see a watermelon plant spring up on any lawn, despite the millions of seeds we spit out every summer.

If you break open the peanuts, then the squirrels sit there and eat them, instead of burying them.

When I first did this last winter the squirrels—there are two, Chip and Dale I call 'em, who live in nearby trees—would sit on a branch that comes near my back porch nervously eyeing both the tempting peanuts and this mad, vicious cat drooling in the window.

After a long tedious standoff, one of squirrels, Chip it was, made a daring run-and-snatch, picking off one of the peanuts and flying back onto his tree in a blizzard of action. Then the other one tried it.

A couple of these run-and-snatch operations later, the two squirrels sort of sat there, quietly munching on their peanuts. And then, I can almost swear I saw this, two light bulbs simultaneously lit up over their little heads.

"That dumb cat can't get through the window glass."

Well, then they casually sauntered over to the balcony and hopped up onto the window ledge.

Arthur went totally frantic, jumping up and down inside the window, screeching away in a "lemme at 'em" manner.

And these squirrels just sat there munching on the peanuts, disdainfully turning their backs on Arthur, their fat, fluffy tails twitching against the window pane.

Boy, did Arthur go crazy, jumping up and down, clawing against the window, racing back and forth on the inside ledge, trying another window.

And I, cruel, sadistic master that I am, chortled away uproariously.

All through the winter, this has been our big Sunday morning squirrel game.

Now ever since I got Arthur last fall, after Arthur IV was killed by an automobile, she—for Arthur is a female—has never gone outside.

Arthur started off life as a barn cat on a farm near Huntingdon. I was visiting there and I saw this mess of about 20 cats playing near an open shed.

When I approached, all the cats scattered off in different directions. Except this one calico, red, black and white kitten who walked up to me and immediately started purring when I tickled her chin.

Well, it wasn't hard to figure out this kitten was going to replace the Arthur, who had died the previous week.

I took her home last November. It was the first time the kitten had ever been inside a home. And did she like the setup.

When I fed her out of a can, it was probably the first time she had meat that she didn't have to run across a field to catch.

And so we played games together.

The first one I taught her was the ginger ale game. This is a great game for kittens.

You pour a big glass of Canada Dry ginger ale and place it on the kitchen table along with the kitten. (Use Canada Dry because the bubbles are bigger.)

The kitten goes up to inspect the glass. And ping. One of those bubbles pings it in the nose.

Baffled, the kitten backs off. Eyes the glass. Sneaks back to inspect, sticks her nose over the open glass. Ping. Hit in the nose again.

Now if you are as simple-minded as I am, this game will amuse you for hours on end.

Because Arthur was a kitten, and I didn't want her getting lost, I kept her inside all winter. And her only connection wiih the rest of nature—aside from visits by my family's dogs—has been those two squirrels who play this wonderful game with her.

And it is a real game. Because last week I forgot to close the kitchen door after I had placed the peanuts on the window ledge.

Instead of sitting at the window, Arthur hid by a corner of the open door.

But when the squirrels came, instead of dashing out the door after them, Arthur went back to the window and went through her futile and frantic "lemme at 'em" bravado.

Arthur, I discovered, is a chicken.

Kitty-litter box hits the fan over church-cat controversy

[Wednesday, March 25, 1992]

"SAW YOUR CAT on TV last night," several people told me yesterday as I went about my business.

Really, I thought, this cat business is taking on a weird nine lives of its own. The people at Newswatch's "City Beat" had told me a few days ago that Catherine the Cat, my new roommate, would be on Monday night, but it had slipped my mind. And now, for almost a month, people have been coming up to me on the street and asking about the cat. Writing me letters about the cat. Phoning me about the cat. Getting worked up about the cat.

Perhaps I'd better explain from the beginning.

One Monday morning, February 24 at 9 a.m., a Mrs. Alison Beaton—an elderly lady, I gathered from her voice—called me to ask for some help in dealing with the problem of Catherine, the cat at the St. James the Apostle Anglican Church.

"It's terrible," she said. "If nothing is done Catherine is going to be sent to the SPCA."

Pause.

"To be executed!"

Now, this is not my idea of one of the great Monday morning wake-up calls.

Hold on, I asked the obviously agitated woman. What's the story? I'll help if I can.

The story was quite simple.

About seven years ago, this cat wandered into the church rectory at the corner of Bishop and Ste. Catherine streets.

The staff and the parishioners, especially the seniors who come for the regular midweek luncheons, quickly took to the cat, which they named Catherine, after the street she had obviously been walking.

The cat had the run of the church spending the warmer days outside with the many people who congregate on its little lawn and garden. Office

246

workers brown-bagging it and glue-sniffers with their heads in bags alike—the downtown community.

Well, Mrs. Beaton explained, a problem had developed. Some parishioners were allergic to cats. Some had been scratched by the cat. After all, when 80 people in a row try to pat you on the head, you, too, might become a little pesky.

It appeared the cat had become a matter of raging controversy in the church. The pro and anti-cat factions were having a go at it, much like pro and anti-smoking factions in an office.

The woman told me she was calling me because she knew I liked cats, that she had often seen my late father looking after strays.

The long and short of it was, if a new home wasn't found for the church cat, she'd have to go and meet her maker.

I said I'd try and do something.

A couple of days earlier, Noel Meyer, the new editor of the *Downtowner*, had called to introduce himself and asked me to keep my ear open for downtown stories.

I called him up and said I had a natural. People like this type of story and probably some do-gooder would take the cat in. Everybody's problem solved.

I went back to sleep.

On Wednesday, the *Downtowner* appeared with Catherine on the front page. Something about "Christians 1; Felines 0."

Mrs. Beaton was quoted as saying the anti-cat people were "hypocrites."

The church secretary, Mrs. Elizabeth Bourgoyne, said some parishioners were almost in tears and that Catherine had "developed a very particular character ... a very independent pussycat. I wouldn't say she is a religious cat, but she does stroll in and out of services."

The new church rector, Rev. Warren Eling, just transferred in from Toronto, said: "For the past three months, Catherine has taken up at least 20 minutes of every church meeting we have had."

Well, the kitty-litter box hit the fan.

The church was inundated with calls, many expressed outrage. We have such a problem with homeless people, how can you kick a cat out? Threats of picketing. That sort of thing.

So I called up and said, "Listen, if nobody else wants Catherine, I'll take her."

"Thank God," said Mrs. Bourgoyne, "the phone's been ringing off the hook. But take your time picking her up, because some of the parishioners would like to say goodbye."

So I waited for a week.

The following week, the *Downtowner* had a front-page story

"City councillor saves Catherine." With a picture of me, the cat and three lady parishioners.

Hell, I can take hero status.

Then the next week, there were letters to the editor in the *Downtowner*.

One read: "Last week, it was a good story, this week it smacks of politics all over the place. Last week, Catherine was on her way to cat heaven, this week she is saved by 'kindhearted councillor.'

"(She) was corrupted by politics. Shame. Shame. Shame."

There was another letter from Rector Eling trying to explain his position.

The phone calls and letters continued. People said I was trying to exploit the cat.

"How," Egan Chambers asked me at lunch, "can you turn a cat into a political controversy?"

"I dunno," I said dumbfounded. "But Catherine doesn't know how to use a kitty-litter box."

Yes, Catherine and I are getting along fine. Except she insists on doing "No. 2" on the carpet in front of the closet in my bedroom. So I put the box in that spot. And then she did it next to the box. The box has been following her around the house.

Oddly, and luckily for me (and her, I suppose), she does the liquid thing in the box. But we're getting there. In the past three days, no mishaps.

Now, we just want a quiet life together. No more publicity.

Pets take centre stage at my family's holiday dinner

[Wednesday, December 27, 1995]

CHRISTMAS is, of course, a family affair. And this Christmas, among other things, it struck me just how much animals are part of the family.

On Christmas Day, my sister Thaïs came to my door to pick me up for the drive out to my sister Terry's in Pointe Claire for the family dinner. As we were walking down the stairs to the car, Thaïs tearfully told me it was "Champy's last family outing. He's going to have his last dinner with us and then tomorrow he's going to die."

Inside the car, my mother and brother sat in the back seat with Champy the dog lying on an old coat across both their laps.

In the front seat, where I was supposed to sit, was Ti-loup, the other, older family dog.

Both dogs are rather large, in the 60-pound range. Not much room to move in the old Peugeot loaded with four adults and two large dogs, one dying.

Earlier this month, Champy, more than 13 years old, was diagnosed with leukemia, not long for this world.

Over the past few weeks, Champy's physical spirit waned, and then for a few days rose.

On Christmas Day, the dog could barely move. The vet was closed and Frank and Thaïs, both of whom are ferociously attached to the two dogs, couldn't bear the thought of leaving him home alone for the day. So they rigged up a sort of stretcher made out of an old coat and some rope to carry him around with them. The dog whimpered.

It was kind of weird arriving at Terry and my brother-in-law Jean-Paul Rolland's place with Mother in tow along with one dying and one rheumatoid older dog. My 92-year-old mother, with failing eyesight and hearing, stumbling along with a cane, was in much better shape than the dogs.

It was a much smaller family dinner than usual. Terry and Jean-Paul's two daughters—my nieces—are in Vancouver now, married with children.

My daughter was having dinner with her mom, Linda, and Grandpa George, in from Boston.

So our dinner consisted of my mother, two sisters, brother-in-law and two nephews, Paul and Mark, in from Ontario.

We sat there, enjoying a fine late-afternoon turkey dinner, watched balefully by the two dogs.

Champy lay on the coat, silent, eyes sad.

Every now and again, Frank would get down on all fours and rub his head, talking softly to the dog.

My brother's grief was total and unaffected. For long periods, he ignored the rest of the family while he commiserated with the dog.

After dinner, my nephew Paul sat there with his cat Toby, with whom he had driven down from Ottawa. Toby is 16, pretty old for a cat. Toby is blind in one eye, with only one visible tooth; most of the others have been removed in $400 worth of dental work.

Toby sits in Paul's lap all the time, sleeps and watches TV with him. The animals in our family are getting old with us. Lots of bonding there.

Afterward, Paul drove me to Point St. Charles for after-dinner drinks with Michele Sarrazin, one of my honorary nieces, and her father, Michael, the actor.

Michelle's sister, Catherine, had gone to Ottawa for dinner with her boyfriend's family.

No sooner had we arrived than Catherine phoned to inquire after Digger, the dog she had left alone at her house around the corner.

Michelle had to go get Digger to join us. Digger is a very healthy, frisky young dog, partly some Hungarian hunting breed.

When he arrived, he ran around manically sniffing everything, becoming the centre of attention and conversation.

Digger is one of those dogs that likes to strut around, tail wagging furiously, with something big in his mouth, a log or a stuffed toy or anything that allows him to say, "Look at me; I have a purpose in life. I accomplish it well."

Michael did a wonderful verbal impersonation of the dog.

I told them about Frank and Thaïs carting a dying dog around with them, how absurd yet touching it was. And we got pleasure out of watching the exuberance of Digger.

Funny how animals affect us, even take centre stage at Christmas.

When I got home that night, I even felt guilty that I hadn't taken home a kitty bag of leftovers for my old cat, Catherine.

I felt even guiltier when I opened a Christmas stocking left at my place, addressed to me. It was signed Lynn & Lucky. Lucky's her dog.

Yesterday, I called Frank to see how things went at the vet's.

"We had an appointment for 4 o'clock," Frank said. "I was outside feeding the squirrels and prayed to God for a reprieve for Champy.

"At quarter to 4, Champy got up and walked out on the deck of the garage roof and had a dump, his first in days. Then he came outside into the alley and looked down to see if his girlfriend was around.

"Then he went inside and got up on the bed with Mother.

"Do you think he knew he had a date with the vet at 4? Do you think this could be a miracle?"

So Champy got his reprieve. At this time of year, anything is possible.

Democratic Alliance candidates Paul Baatz (Ste-Anne)
and Nick (Westmount), listen to Mordecai Richler read telegrams
of support during a candidates' meeting, November 1976.

From the Bar to the Cabinet .... Almost

Brian Mulroney

NICK AUF DER MAUR had many qualities, but his number one quality was his complete absence of malice.

Whether it was in politics or journalism, I never saw any hatred in him. He had many adversaries but no enemies.

And then he was a free man. He was unencumbered. He made his choices in life. He did what he wanted to do, yet he wasn't self-absorbed.

He had a lot of fun. And he was fun to be with.

I didn't see Nick as often as I would have liked, but then we didn't exactly keep the same hours.

But he always impressed me as a completely honest person, very intelligent, and extremely courageous in some of the causes he took on.

I remember in the 1976 provincial election, when Nick founded the Democratic Alliance. I went to see him at his headquarters in a storefront of a building on Sherbrooke Street, across from the McGill music faculty. He was all alone, putting up posters.

"How are you going to pay for all this," I asked him.

"I don't know," he said.

I was then working for the Iron Ore Company, and we sent him a pretty big cheque. He phoned to thank me, and I said we'd send another one, provided he didn't tell anybody.

"Brian," he said, "your secret's safe with me."

I asked Nick to run for the Progressive Conservatives in 1984, and as it became clear in the latter stages of the campaign that we were going to win big, I had high hopes that he would win in N.D.G.-Lachine East. We did a factory tour together in Lachine, and I kept asking where Nick was, because the TV cameras were all up front with me, and we needed to get him on the local news. He was back with the media, briefing them on the campaign. But that was Nick.

One of my regrets is that we didn't get Nick into the House of Commons. He would have been a very colourful addition to the place, and he would have been very good on his feet. I had been intending to put him in the cabinet, possibly as Secretary of State, given his unswerving commitment to minority rights and his genuine embrace of Canada's multicultural communities.

Besides, just watching patrons of Winnie's and Grumpy's having to call him "the Honourable" and "Mr. Minister" would have been worth the price of admission.

But I never had any sense that he regretted losing, and he may have been relieved. He would have been obliged to modify his lifestyle, and he might often have quoted Jean Marchand, that the best thing about Ottawa is the five o'clock train to Montreal.

The only thing he ever asked me to do for him as Prime Minister was the birthday card for Melissa from Ronald Reagan and me on her 13th birthday, which coincided with the Shamrock Summit in Quebec City in 1985.

I explained Nick's request to President Reagan in the car on the way into town, that I had a friend, a bit of a boulevardier, who was particularly close to his daughter, who was both American and Canadian, and part Irish. "I'd be delighted," Reagan said.

He was fascinated by his name. "Auf der Maur," he said. "It doesn't sound Irish."

It wasn't, of course. But he was Irish in the heart. He brought us joy.

Brian Mulroney, Prime Minister of Canada from 1984 to 1993, is Honourary Co-Chairman of the Nick Auf der Maur Memorial Fund.

HOLIDAYS

Gift shopping left me "briefly" embarrassed

[Monday, December 30, 1985]

My candle burns at both ends
It will not last the night.
But ah, my foes,
and oh, my friends
It gives a lovely light.
  —Edna St. Vincent Millay (1892-1950)

WE KNOW what the term "the festive season" is often a euphemism for—overindulgence.

The Millay poem is perhaps a fitting epitaph for the year's end, considering how an awful lot of people carry on at this time of the year.

People whose business it is to pontificate like to go on at Christmas about the cardinal virtues—faith, hope and charity. But we all realize that often more obeisance is paid to greed and gluttony. To be fair, a good many people manage to combine both virtue and vice at Christmas without too much unseemly hypocrisy.

I know that by this point there are bound to be some snickers out there and mutterings about the pot calling the kettle black. However, the fact of the matter is, I'm one of those people who spends quiet weekends at home. I may—rave and carry on on Mondays and Tuesdays—and a few other days of the week – but on Friday and Saturday I'm usually as quiet as a church mouse.

During the holiday season, my tendency is to skip parties and all that and limit my indulgences to second and third helpings of turkey.

As of last year, I'm into a more traditional approach to New Year's Eve. Before that I was one of those terrible bores who liked to blather on about staying home and being sensible on New Year's Eve. (But I digress. We're talking about Christmas here.)

This year, just about the most exciting thing that happened to me at Christmas was during the usual last-minute shopping panic.

Now that my daughter is into adolescence, gift buying is particularly troublesome. One of the suggestions her mother gave me concerned Calvin

Klein ladies' underwear.

Somehow, I've managed to get through life without ever setting foot in a ladies' lingerie department—until last week. I had to go to about six different lingerie departments until I found what I was looking for at The Bay.

Normally, hardly anybody ever recognizes me. But as I was peeking through all this ladies' underwear, a woman came up to me and asked: "Aren't you Nick Auf der Maur?"

Naturally I was mortified and for some reason or other felt compelled to offer a detailed explanation of what I was doing there, with my nose in ladies' underwear. The S, M, L and XL labels were terribly small and I had to get close to the rack to find the right size.

Just as my blush faded and the lady went away, wouldn't you know it, another lady walked up and introduced herself.

Again I was forced into grovelling explanations.

After discreetly leaving the ladies' lingerie department, I rushed out the door on University Street The first thing I saw was a card table set up by some lunatic political fringe group selling pamphlets and books. Against the table was a large poster that claimed the International Monetary Fund was behind the AIDS epidemic.

I had to stop and ask whether they were serious. I enjoy a good screaming argument.

And just as I was about to embark on a harangue about AIDS and political maniacs, I noticed a few people had stopped to listen. Right in front was the first lady who had recognized me in the ladies' lingerie department.

For some reason I was overcome with a vision of this woman going around the Town of Mount Royal or some such place telling people that Nick Auf der Maur hangs around the ladies' underwear department and shouts about AIDS on the sidewalks downtown.

I did the sensible thing: I fled.

A Dutch treat starts the Christmas season

[Monday, December 8, 1986]

Sinterklaas, Sinterklaas.
De zak van Sinterklaas.
O, jongens, jongens 't is zo'n baas!
Daar stopt hij, daar stopt hij.
　　　— A song of St. Nikolaasliedjes.

If you can figure out that, you're a better man than I am, Gunga Din.

Actually, it's kind of easy. Sinterklaas is Santa Claus, and the rest of it is asking young ones whether he'll stop here.

The language is Dutch.

The season is upon us, and Saturday I went to my first Christmas party, a dance put on by the Dutch-Canadian Association to celebrate December 6, St. Nicholas's Day.

Many years ago, a couple of Dutch friends gave me a bottle of Genever gin on a December 6, explaining that in Holland one's namesday is a bigger day than one's birthday.

Ever since, I've celebrated December 6 in my own private little way, but this year I decided to join some Dutch friends in celebrating what, for the Dutch, is perhaps the biggest holiday of the year.

In Holland, and some parts of Germany and Switzerland and, so I'm told, Hungary and a few other places, St. Nicholas's Day is the gift-giving day, the festive time, while Christmas Day is marked in a more solemn, religious manner.

On St. Nicholas's Day eve, St. Nicholas shows up with his assistant, Black Peter. St. Nicholas checks to see who has been a good boy or girl, and the bad kids are threatened with being put into Black Peter's sack and hauled off to Spain. Over the years, it's proved to be a fairly effective threat for keeping under-six-year-olds in line.

Once, when I was about six or seven, I was in my mother's hometown in Switzerland on a St. Nicholas's Day when St. Nicholas arrived in the village square. And I can tell you, Black Peter and his minions who carry switches to smack you with scared the bejesus out of me.

Of course, that was another St. Nicholas than the one I was named after, but Christian history is not our subject today.

However, Santa Claus and our current interpretation of Christmas grew out of the traditions of northern Europe. Legend has it that St. Nicholas came riding out of Spain on a white horse, accompanied by an assistant who was probably a Moor, thus Black Peter, to Christianize Holland and various other parts.

In the checking-out-kids process, Black Peter looks down chimneys into homes, which is perhaps another reason why he got that name.

Little Dutch kids, who learn bribery early, put hay and oats in their wooden shoes as an offering to St. Nicholas's white horse. Here in North America, that tradition has evolved into leaving out a Coca-Cola and a Dunkin' Donut for Santa Claus. And so we adapt time-honoured customs.

At any rate, my Dutch friend Pieter van Westrenen marched me off Saturday night to join about 500 or 600 lowland, highland and Rotterdam Dutch for the big dance at Town of Mount Royal town hall.

"We used to have a big party in the afternoon to give out presents to the kids," said Angie Kruller, the president of the Dutch Canada Association, who has been organizing this event for most of the 19 years she's been in Montreal.

"But now all the kids are teenagers and there are hardly any little kids left. The big influx of Dutch immigrants after the war has slowed to a trickle. The ones who do come usually are single and then they get into a mixed marriage with a non-Dutch and the traditions and language fall away.

"Where the gift-giving for the children was our big annual activity, now we're talking about raising funds for a Dutch old folks' home in Montreal."

Saturday night, they had a brass band, sausage, beer, smoked herring and, of course, Genever gin.

I got there just as they were starting the balloon dance. I'd never seen a balloon dance before.

What they do is tie balloons to the men's ankles. The music starts and the female partner's job is to step on opposing couples' balloons.

It was just like a hockey game out there, with furious forechecking and heavy hitting in the corners as those frantic women went in for the kill, while the men jiggered with fancy footwork trying to protect their balloons.

The last surviving couple with an unexploded balloon won a bottle of wine.

And then St. Nicholas—resplendent in a white beard, bishop's mitre and red-and-white robes—arrived with a couple of Black Peters throwing candies.

They got him up on the stage and MC Fritsi Diepen introduced him along with the new Dutch consul in Montreal, Max Buwalda, who just arrived here three months ago after a stint as ambassador to Uruguay.

Buwalda, a jazz enthusiast, played a bunch of St. Nicholas songs on the piano. Then we all had to get up and do a snake dance with St. Nicholas leading the way.

Then they played a waltz and I had to get up and do the first dance with Buwalda's wife, Elsa, and I only stepped on her foot once, maybe twice.

And so we all had a good time celebrating St. Nicholas's Day.

Kitchen heresy is in bad taste when you're talking turkey

[Wednesday, January 2, 1991]

ONE THING about the holidays, you get to talk turkey.

Sean Noonan, the bartender at Charles Darwin Pub, leaned over the bar as he expressed his genuine concern: "What's this about cooking the turkey stuffing on the outside? Is this some sort of trend that's going to take over? I mean, the whole point of having a turkey dinner is to have that great stuffing with it. I don't like this talk about making the stuffing on the outside.

"I like the stuffing. If they make it on the outside, how can it be— what's the word?—succulent? Yeah, succulent, filled with the turkey juices."

Noonan paused to consider the taste of good turkey stuffing, the way his mother made it. He smacked his lips and resumed, more emphatic: "It's downright stupid, making turkey stuffing on the outside. It wouldn't be turkey stuffing then, would it?"

Noonan's fist hit the bar. "It's outrageous, is what it is. An affront to tradition. In fact, it's worse than what you always go on about, wrapping baked potatoes in aluminum foil."

Noonan had a point there, I had to concede.

I get outraged and upset when I see potatoes wrapped in aluminum foil. The whole point of a baked potato is to have a crisp skin. Wrapping it in foil gives you a soggy skin. You may as well just have boiled potatoes.

But I hadn't heard of the new culinary heresy, turkey stuffing made on the outside.

"Where'd you hear about that method of making turkey stuffing?" I asked Noonan.

"A chef at Carlos & Pepes told my girlfriend that's how to do it," he fumed. "I nixed that crackpot idea."

I could imagine the argument they must have had. In fact, I had a similar one at Christmas.

My friend Johan Sarrazin came over to help with the turkey dinner. She wanted to pour all the drippings out of the cooking pan to make gravy.

"Are you insane?" I shouted at her. "The whole point to having a turkey is the next day when you're making sandwiches, you have the jelly underneath the fat in the pan. That's the best part."

We compromised. She poured out only half the drippings for the gravy.

We wouldn't have had that argument if I hadn't fallen asleep at the switch and agreed to have mashed potatoes with the turkey. Usually, in our family, we have baked potatoes; that way, you don't need as much gravy.

Anyhow, the point of all this is that for most of us, the best meal of the year is the turkey dinner. Somehow, nothing else seems as delicious. Of course, all the preparations and the gathering of family and friends make it special.

And so we develop little idiosyncrasies and passions for what we like about it. For some, it's the stuffing. For others, it's the jelly and bits at the bottom of the pan. Whatever, it's something to which we look forward, and we don't take kindly to tampering with it because of newfangled ideas, not to say heresies.

This business of cooking the stuffing on the outside, my extensive research indicates, comes from the packaged foods industry, which is always trying to make things easier for people, making instant things that require no work. Like Stove Top dressing. That's a stuffing made on the outside. That's why they call it dressing instead of stuffing.

One would think the traditional turkey dinner is so great nobody would want to change things. But no, there are all kinds of bizarre advocates out there, coming up with new ideas on how to cook the turkey.

Some experts get on the radio and tell you that you have to cook the turkey upside down.

The truth is, it does taste better when it's cooked upside down. That's because the dark meat is fatter and it allows the juices to drop through and make the white meat moister and—to use Noonan's apt description— more succulent.

The problem with this is that it just looks weird. Legs and wings sticking out awkwardly, the breast bone crushed like a boxer's nose.

A variation on this comes from the late cookbook writer James Beard, who advocated cooking the turkey first on one side, then on the other, and finally right side up.

The late Jehane Benoît is responsible for the current big turkey-cooking rage, roasting the bird inside a stapled paper bag.

Yes, that's what they are doing these days. It has something to do with keeping in the moisture and eliminating the need for the basting required when cooking it in the traditional manner.

I met a woman named Monica on New Year's Eve who said she followed this recipe, cooking her turkey upside down in a big paper bag, following Madame Benoît's instructions as issued by Royal Orr on his CJAD talk show. She claimed it was absolutely delicious and a big hit.

"Well," I harrumphed, "I like my turkey skin crisp. And I like to look at it when it's cooking. What's the matter with our traditional values?"

Who would have thought Madame Benoît would turn out to be a kitchen subversive?

[Tribute]

The Secret Handshake

Mark Phillips

IT WAS AN ELABORATE RITUAL that, frankly, I'd always found a bit embarrassing. Maybe that's because it was so dumb. For all I know Nick had a private greeting for everybody, but I've come to think of the one he had for me as our secret handshake. Like so much about Nick, there was no point trying to analyze it then. There is now.

The handshake would only be administered after long absences, which in my case was every time I'd see Nick, as life's crooked trail had long ago taken me away from Montreal. But come back into the bar on an infrequent visit to town and Nick would not only still be there, he'd immediately launch into our own little ceremonial rite.

"See where the horse bit me?" he'd ask, pointing to his shoulder. And like a fool I'd lean in for the required closer look. Which is when he'd goose me.

It may not have been quite like kissing the ring, but like all rituals, it served a purpose. It was like being welcomed back home into the world of Nick. No matter how far you'd gone or how long you'd been away, to be a friend of Nick's once was to be a friend of his always.

Which may finally solve the mystery—I've since thought—of why Nick was the only one of my friends who managed to make it to both my weddings. This was an amazing attendance record not only because of Nick's dubious dedication to the matrimonial ideal, but because each wedding required a considerable journey of body and spirit. In other words, each required him to leave downtown. Yet it can all be explained in a peculiar Auf der Maurian kind of way.

Attending wedding one, in the mid-'70s, meant he had to brave the wilds of darkest suburbia. I'm sure he would have come anyway, but I do remember feeling the need to remind him that a clutch of women unfamiliar with downtown Montreal's after-hours charms would also be there. And who was the greatest after-hours charmer of them all?

Attending wedding two a decade later required a journey of greater geographic but perhaps less philosophic distance. He had to go to London, England. This time the added motivation was that the timing dovetailed nicely with his idea of taking Melissa on an educational visit to Europe. The resulting father and daughter tour of pubs near historic British sites is now part of the Auf der Maur legend and is referred to elsewhere in this book. I'm only pleased to finally admit my own and my wife's small part in it. But anyway, for whatever reasons, Nick was again at the wedding and at least one unattached female guest at the affair still remembers it with a special fondness.

I tell these tales not just because I find them amusing, but because they reveal something of Nick's attitude to friendship. His life was all about friendship. He invested in it. He had a sense, before many of the rest of us, of the occasions that consolidated it.

When I look back now it seems that, whether the occasion was mundane or momentous, Nick was somehow part of it—and put his peculiar stamp on it. But let's face it, visits home won't be the same without hanging around with and being goosed by Nick.

Mark Phillips is a correspondent for CBS News in London and worked with Nick at the CBC in the early 1970s.

HATS

THE LAST OF THE BISHOP STREET MOHICANS...

We trend-setters don't talk through our hats

[Monday, July 8, 1985]

"A Borsalino, that's what you need," Charles Dunbar said in his definite sort of way.

"Absolutely," chimed in Terry Carwither. "That will take care of the old noggin and you'll look snappy as well."

I had been complaining about something I've unfortunately become increasingly familiar with in the last few years—sunburn on the bald spot. The bald spot has caused me to rediscover the benefits of hats: remarkable, really, after years of going bareheaded, winter and summer.

I read somewhere that a great percentage of body heat escapes from the head.

It has something to do with keeping the brain warm, so all the blood rushes up to the head, leaving the hands and feet cold.

As a result—as my mother wanted me to when I was a kid—I now wear an assortment of winter caps and hats. Necessity has brought hats back into fashion, at least for me.

"When you get your Borsalino," Dunbar advised, "you'll have to get some proper clothes to go with it.

"You can't go around in those drab things," he said, pointing to my woollen jacket and corduroy trousers. "Go to Henri Henri, get a proper hat—that's the difficult thing—then go to a men's store and get a suit to go with it. Not the other way around."

The idea had some appeal.

Borsalino is the Rolls Royce of hats.

In the late '60s, Alain Delon and Jean-Paul Belmondo played in a movie called *Borsalino*. The two of them played rival Marseilles gangsters and they both wore these great hats.

"If there ever was a movie responsible for bringing art deco back, it was *Borsalino*," Dunbar added.

The other part of the appeal is that for years I've often gone by Henri Henri, a delightfully old-fashioned men's hat store on Ste. Catherine at Hôtel de Ville. I'd looked in the window at the terrific selection from boaters to bowlers, from cowboy hats to fedoras but I had never gone in. So last week, accompanied by my fashion co-ordinators, Iris Dawson and Johan Sarrazin, I went off to buy a hat and suit.

I hate shopping, mainly because I never trust my own judgment. But Dawson does store windows and other designs and Sarrazin knows a bit about everything, so I figured they know about taste.

I didn't want to look too flamboyant.

Henri Henri was founded in 1932 and is apparently the last true men's hat shop in the city.

I tried on various different styles. Unfortunately, there was no Borsalino straw hat left in my size. This, in a way, was fortunate because the Italian hat is quite expensive.

Dawson and Sarrazin then chose a $40 panama by Stetson for me. It was the most expensive hat I've ever bought, but it was fabulous.

The straw was woven by hand in Ecuador, and the hat itself blocked in Guelph, Ontario.

As I was paying, a man walked in and, in a loud western accent, announced: "Name's Murdoch. I'm with Calhoun's in Vancouver."

He handed everybody a card that read: Calhoun's Hat Shop, exclusive hatters for men since 1911, Glenn Murdoch, manager.

The owner of Henri Henri, André Lefebvre, introduced himself.

"I was in town," Murdoch said, "and I just had to drop in. There really are only three decent hatters left in Canada. Henri Henri here, us in Vancouver and Sammy Taft in Toronto."

"Thirty years ago," Henri Henri manager Pierre Manville said, "there must have been 20 or 25 men's hat shops just on Ste. Catherine in the six or seven blocks past St. Laurent."

We hung around a bit, listening to the old hatters talk shop.

Murdoch inspected all the old fixtures and display cases that have been kept intact by Henri Henri since the 1930s.

"Want some western hats?" Murdoch cackled. Since everybody else laughed I supposed it was an inside joke.

They explained that a few years ago there was a western hat craze.

"It was crazy," Murdoch recalled. "People bought them whether they fit or not, even if they were poor quality. They just had to have a western hat."

But the craze died a very quick death, leaving everybody stuck with massive inventories of western hats.

One major company, Biltmore, ended up going into receivership.

How are men's hats doing these days? I asked.

"They've been picking up for the past few years," Manville said.

"Yeah," Murdoch added. "*Indiana Jones* sure helped. Just like *The Sting*. Those pictures helped bring hats back in fashion."

We left the three of them discussing the ups and downs of men's hats, and debating the merits of carrying women's hats. Lefebvre had said he was breaking the ice and bringing in a women's selection in the fall.

Then, just as my friend Dunbar advised, I went into a men's wear shop, pointed to my new hat and said: "I want a suit to match my hat."

Jean-Paul Belmondo, eat your heart out.

Nick in lavish City Hall bathroom, April 1991.
Photo by Richard Arless, Jr.

My hats have turned up but the mystery only deepens

[Wednesday, April 5, 1995]

It sort of reminds me of the Hardy Boys: "The Riddle of the Hats."

Except now I feel I might have been a victim of an April Fools' joke in reverse.

A little refresher: last December, I recounted in my column how I had lost my hats. I had invited some friends and vague acquaintances over to my place for margaritas and to watch my daughter's appearance on "Saturday Night Live."

The next day I couldn't find my hats, which I kept on a table by the front door. We searched high and low for them but could find only one, my favorite Borsalino, which I had casually tossed on top of a high bookshelf the evening before.

Missing were the other five hats in my little collection, including an early 1950s-vintage beige Borsalino, a Colombian fedora, my summer panama and my gray Dick Tracy.

Well, you can imagine my annoyance—hats are a rather personal item to me.

I supposed that one of my guests had taken them as a joke and I expected them to turn up in a few days.

They never did.

Who on Earth would steal my hats? It made no sense.

It could have been anyone, because at that time my front door wasn't functioning properly. I had a new door on order, but in the meantime I couldn't lock the door.

So anybody could have come into my home that Saturday in December and taken my hats. But why? Why not something of more value?

My predicament seemed to strike a chord in many people.

Two readers, complete strangers, called up and offered hats they didn't wear any more. One gave me a formal Borsalino homburg he had worn only a few times since he bought it in the '50s. Another delivered a trilby. Another reader gave a fedora to a mutual friend who turned it over to me.

And until very recently, friends and strangers on the streets and in the shops would inquire constantly: Did you get your hats back?

A TV producer friend took me to Henri Henri, the last of the great men's hat shops, and bought me an absolutely sensational Colombian fedora. (Borsalino, the legendary Italian hatter, has gone down the tubes and the best hats now come from Colombia. Possibly it has something to do with the connection between gangsters and good hats.)

In Florida recently, I bought a sporty but cheap straw hat to replace my prized panama. A good panama—the best come from Germany—costs $250.

Soon I had a proper and varied collection of hats to wear.

Then this Saturday, April Fools' Day, I invited some friends over for margaritas and a game of Diplomacy, the best board game.

Two of my guests, Lynn deGrace and Johan Desrocher, had helped me clean up my office and do some filing in my front room last fall. After the Diplomacy game, I asked them to look for some files I couldn't find.

I heard a yelp: "Look at this!"

They had gone into a storage closet off my office. On the upper shelf, deep in a dark corner (the closet is very wide), they discovered five hats piled on top of one another. My lost hats.

Now at the time of the original loss, another person and myself had scoured my house looking for them. We had both searched that closet. No hats.

So we have the hats back, but we also have a mystery. Who hid them there? And when? And if it was a practical joke, why didn't anybody tell me?

Was it a coincidence that after all this time, the hats show up on April Fools' Day?

Now I have 11 hats. But maybe I should acquire one more—a dunce cap.

In a country built by hats, men wear baseball caps

[Wednesday, March 27, 1996]

Doffed nearly to extinction, the hat is poised to reclaim its place of honour in the wardrobe of every well-dressed man. Because of its position on the highest part of the body, the hat has always been both a useful protective accessory and a mark of identification among men.
—*Il Cappello da Uomo* (Men's Hats) by Adele Campione

It's obvious hats have become my trademark, since I've worn them off and on, as it were, for much of my adult life, or at least for what has passed for an adult life.

About a year ago I wrote a couple of columns about the disappearance from my house of my collection of hats, and its mysterious reappearance last April Fools' Day.

And a year later, people still come up to me on the street or in a restaurant—three or four times in the last month alone—and say they're glad I got my hats back. Or, in the case of some people who hadn't read the second column: "Did you ever get those hats back?"

The thing is, ever since I got into a permanent hat mode, about a dozen years ago, hats have become second nature to me, to the point that I feel naked if I walk outside the house without one. And it's not just because I'm balding.

As Miles Davis once said: "It does something to a man. It completes his whole thing."

Vanity, one could argue. But then again, what are clothes and fashion all about?

Last weekend I was reading this book, *Men's Hats*, given to me at Christmas by my daughter. (It's part of series called *Bella Cosa*, written in Italian and English.)

Mostly, I've been familiar with the English and North American history of hats. But this book is written from an Italian perspective. What is intriguing is the political side of hat history.

The 16th, 17th and 18th centuries of Italian hat history are filled with trade fights between Italy and France, and of the formations of guilds to protect merchants' and craftsmen's monopolies. (In Renaissance Italy, the penalty for making hats without credentials could include hanging.)

It could be argued that our country, Canada, was built by hats. Consider this passage from Il Cappello da Uomo about the 1700s: "The beaver-hat craze had exploded in England and from there had spread throughout Europe and even to South America. In France, La Rochelle was a production and distribution centre for beaver-fur felt. The pelts were brought from Canada, and made into hats that were soft (and) shimmering.

"La Rochelle declined after the revocation of the Treaty of Nantes: 300,000 Protestant subjects, including almost all the hatters in La Rochelle, fled the country. In Brandenburg, the exiles taught their craft to Germans. In England, in 1760 alone, the Hudson Bay Co. brought back enough pelts from America for 576,000 beaver hats, showing just how popular this fur had become."

So Canada assumed its original economic importance because of European hat fashion.

Somewhere along the line, an Englishman discovered that by using a little mercury in the curing process, rabbit fur could be made as elegant as beaver. The resultant rash of mercury poisoning led to the phrase "mad as a hatter."

Hats were worn as status symbols. I found it intriguing that, originally, the top hat was a symbol of revolutionaries and subversives.

In European societies of the late 18th and early 19th centuries, where people of high status wore plain, unfrivolous hats, the black top hat became the symbol of working-class people.

Later, the top hat became the symbol of the dandy and the working class switched to a hardier model—the highly shellacked bowler, or derby.

In the late 19th century, the stiff bowler was regarded as perfect for the industrial revolution, a forerunner of today's construction helmet.

Just as the top hat became the choice of the elite, the bowler also acquired a new status.

In the latter part of the last century, the great Italian hatter Giuseppe Borsalino—who studied his trade in France—popularized a new style, the fedora or trilby, that dominated men's fashion here for the first part of this century.

Then in the 1950s, men started to go hatless. Some people say the trend began when John F. Kennedy appeared at his inauguration without one. But the trend had already set in.

The current trend is toward caps, particularly baseball caps, which some historians compare in popularity to the early top hats and bowlers.

The English word cap, by the way, comes from the Italian for hat, cappello.

Nick greets Michel Benoit (l) and Pierre Gagnier (r)—
new additions to the Civic Party, March 16, 1992.
Photo by Gordon Beck.

The Wedding Reporter

Stephen Phizicky

NICK "covered" my wedding in 1985.

There would have been just another wedding video, but Nick took over and started doing interviews. As he had done on CBC-TV years earlier, Nick brought out the best in people. He prodded them into performance.

One guest, a burly man, looked directly into the camera, pointed at my wife, Shelley Kerman, and said in a menacing Godfather-like voice, "I'm warning the guy who marries this girl that if anything goes wrong he'll answer to me."

Nick let the thought hang for a beat, then turned to the camera and said, "This guy is related to Meyer Lansky!" It was the essence of Nick: Wit. Charm. Timing. And the great beaver-tooth smile too. The one he gave me with his "hello." It always made me think of the lyrics in the theme song of the bar show, "Cheers," "where everybody knows your name and they're always glad you came."

After pleasantries, he would go back to reading his ever-present newspaper if nothing of interest came up. If we had something to say we talked, if we didn't, we read. With Nick there was usually lots to talk about, even when we spent 10 or 12 hours a day together.

Nick was interested in everything and he knew a lot about everything. When we did a show together at CJAD, he once had me so enthralled with a rant about the Horn of Africa, that I let him go on and on explaining what all the factions, sub-factions and splinter groups were doing to each other, and how that related to the U.S., the USSR and the UN. It was so compelling it took us past the end of our program and delayed the news 12 minutes. Our boss, Ted Blackman, pronounced us "insane."

After work, Nick would say, "Come on, we're going to the Cuban consulate for drinks" or the Swiss national day cocktail party or a bar where he would be meeting some politician or Olympic type or a foreign reporter. He disapproved when I didn't wear a tie and jacket because, he argued, with a jacket and any soup-stained tie you could go anywhere. You could get into the bar at the Ritz or, without being overdressed, just go to Rymark's for a pig's knuckle. And who knew what might happen?

That's probably why he didn't like coming to his friends' houses. It was too predictable. Neither the woman of his dreams, nor, say, a guy with the inside story on the Hungarian revolution was liable to be there. It violated Nick's basic Rule of the Bar: that something really interesting could happen at any moment. To get him to family events, one of his friends would pick him up and take him. He didn't have a driver's licence. Often this job fell to me. On the morning of his cremation I woke at seven a.m. with a start—must remember to pick up Nick.

Aieee!

In the wedding video, when he asked my wife's great-aunt Jeanette, "Does Shelley have any faults? She replied, "No, does Stephen?"

"Of course not," said Nick, "he's our friend." And that was it. If you were a friend, you got it all. Fun. Insight. Adventure. Loyalty.

There is no other Nick. I will always consider myself lucky to have had 30 years of him. I'd have settled for 60.

Stephen Phizicky is a documentary producer at the CBC who was a close friend of Nick for many years.

LIFE

Nick gives himself a hot foot.
Montreal Star, 1970.

Sake warms up the spy business

[March 22, 1982]

I'M A GREAT FAN of the spy novel, but my own personal experiences in the world of international intrigue have been more reminiscent of Spy vs. Spy in *Mad* magazine.

Some time ago, for example, I had a pleasant lunch and chat with somebody from the West German consulate. Afterward, she asked whether I cared to be on their mailing list. Sure, I replied.

Soon I began receiving magazines, press digests and other publications from the Federal Republic of Germany, the formal name of West Germany.

One day recently, I opened one of those German mailings and idly started reading it.

Something struck me as odd. The headline read: United in Commitment to Eliminating Dangers with Which Most Aggressive Imperialist Forces are Threatening International Peace.

The publication was from the German Democratic Republic, the East Germans.

Now how did I get on the East German mailing list so soon after I got on the West German list? I had always wondered what all those 300,000 or so spies in West Germany did. One of them, at least, snitches names off mailing lists.

That little story reminded me of a run-in I once had with the Koreans, of both varieties.

Back in the sixties, during those anti-war days, I had made the acquaintance of a North Korean agent here in Montreal.

His name was something like Kim Chung, and his cover was that of being correspondent of the Democratic People's Republic of Korea news agency.

What the North Koreans wanted with a full-time correspondent in Montreal was a mystery.

But I used to see him around and one day he invited me to dinner. I dropped by his office in the Shell Towers on University Street on a Friday.

The walls were covered with about 20 pictures of the glorious, invincible, brilliant, etc., leader Kim Il Sung. Every paragraph in the news copy around contained Kim Il Sung's name at least twice.

We left the Shell Towers at a brisk pace, he telling me to stay right beside him. He led me into the Ste. Catherine Street entrance to Eaton's, down the aisles, out the old Victoria Street exit and into a handy cab.

"What was that all about?" I asked him.

"Security. To fool the fascist agents from the south," he explained.

"Oh," I said, letting the matter drop.

The purpose of the dinner, at a Japanese restaurant, was to invite me to Pyongyang for the 25th anniversary celebrations of North Korea's liberation at the end of World War II.

This got me pretty excited, since no North American newsman had been permitted to visit there since the Korean War.

Toward the end of the meal, after much sake, I asked about that little contretemps in Eaton's.

He said he was having a running battle with the running dogs from the south, who operated out of the Republic of Korea (that's the south) trade office in Place Bonaventure.

It seems they followed each other around and did things like letting the air out of each other's tires, sticking bubble gum in mailbox keyholes (this was in 1970, before Krazy Glue) and indulging in heavy breathing on the phone in the middle of the night.

This had something to do with the battle for the hearts and minds of the 100 or so Koreans living in Montreal at the time. Chung was quite earnest about it and at one point pounded his fist on the table to emphasize "the struggle."

I gulped sake to stifle the giggles.

Within weeks, arrangements had been made for Chung, myself and the late Bernard Mergler, a left-wing lawyer, to travel to North Korea.

I was working for the CBC at the time and they rented me an expensive film camera and gave me a crash course on how to operate it, so I could bring back an exclusive report on life in Pyongyang.

A few days before we were due to leave, I was invited to dinner with a group of South Koreans.

They had heard I was going to the north (how I don't know). They insisted I also visit the south "to get the other side of the story."

They plied me with a great many drinks, asking me questions about my trip and the agent.

While extolling the charms of Seoul, they inquired subtly as to my sexual preferences, intimating I was going to have a much better time in the south's capital than in puritan Pyongyang.

The day of our departure, Mergler and I sat in our respective houses, bags packed, waiting for the North Korean to bring airline tickets and visas.

He never came.

Weeks later, Mergler caught up to him and asked what happened. The agent claimed we were to have met him in Algiers.

Mergler came to the conclusion he had absconded with the airline fare, so he reported him to the North Korean embassy in Havana.

Chung soon disappeared from the scene and I never heard from the Koreans again.

Summer's arrival recalls long-lost days of baseball cards and tree houses

[Friday, June 21, 1985]

No more pencils,
no more books,
no more teachers'
dirty looks.

EVEN NOW that I have reached a period where I show some maturity, the last day before St. Jean Baptiste weekend always brings that ditty to mind.

We all feel a bit of schoolboy excitement over the fact that today marks the end of school and an endless summer of fun awaits.

Memories.

"Sure I remember summer," Ray Pucet, of the Poupart tobacco store said yesterday. "What did I do? I worked. I remember one summer they sent me to a farm. They paid me $7 a week and charged me $7 for room and board."

But Pucet, a war veteran, is 63. Does he feel the same about summer now, as say a 7-year-old boy?

"No. There used to be a joy about not being a prisoner of school," he replied. "I like to see the birds and grass, but really, what's the difference between summer and winter when you're an adult? The difference was so much more fun when we were kids."

"Come on," I said to Ted Blackman as I pulled out my Swiss Army penknife. "Let's play baseball."

I put the penknife on the lunch table, with the blade out at a 45-degree angle.

"What's that?" he asked.

Blackman, a veteran of Rosemont street wars, had never played baseball with a penknife. I guess it depended on where you grew up.

Penknife baseball has always been sort of my definition of summer.

You put the blade at a 45-degree angle and you flip it over. If it landed with the blade sticking into the porch wood, you have a hit. If it landed so that you could fit two fingers under the body of the penknife, you had a double. Three fingers was a triple and so on.

"Did you play that?" I asked Richard Holden.

"No, I'm a Westmount WASP," he explained. "I suppose it was because we all had marble stairs on our porches. But we played that game where you throw the penknife in a square marked out in the dirt. And, depending on the way it landed, you drew a line. I can't remember the rules, but it had to do with taking control of the dirt square and eliminating the other guy. I suppose it was intended to prepare us for life."

Then he sang a ditty Westmount WASPs sang on the last day of school:

Hurray, hurray, hurray
Outdoor fooling begins today.
Chacun à son gout, as the other guys say.

"Summer meant playing baseball cards," said Richard Singer, a 35-year-old Bell Telephone employee from N.D.G. "We spent the summer flipping cards against the wall. And then we'd watch the girls playing that silly game with the tennis ball in a nylon stocking.

"They stood with their backs to a brick wall and bounce the stocking-ball over their heads, under their legs, between their arms. It had something to do with co-ordination, but I don't remember the name of it."

Today's kids don't do that.

Then there was the game called Stand in which you would throw a ball against a wall and call a kid's name. If he didn't catch it on the first bounce he had to get it and yell "Stando." Then he had to try to hit one of the other players with it. If he missed, he got a "baby" and if he hit the other player, the other player got a baby. Once you had 10 babies you had to stand against the wall and let the other players throw the ball against your back.

If your friends were civilized, you played with a tennis ball. But every now and again some macho creep insisted on playing with a lacrosse ball.

Another forgotten game is American Baseball in which you threw a tennis ball against a curb.

"Summer also meant building scooters out of orange crates and old rollerskates," Singer said. "Don't forget that. Summer building projects included tree houses, scooters, forts and hideouts.

"The only thing I can't figure out is where did all those balls go that we hit on to the roof? We were always hitting balls onto roofs and never finding them.

"Sometimes we'd go down to the French school and use the bicycle racks as ladders and go up on the roof and get the French balls. Where the heck did all the English balls go?"

In places like Pointe Claire they'd sound the curfew siren at 9 p.m. and all the kids would have to get off the street and into their homes. That's probably unconstitutional today under the age-discrimination provision.

Summer also meant climbing crab apple trees and eating so many you'd get a stomach ache. And then there was the obligation to steal rhubarb from a neighbour's garden and eat six stalks of the awful stuff.

Summer also means playing Monopoly on rainy afternoons.

That still exists. (Thank heavens some things never change.)

But for the rest, it all seems like I remember summer before they invented batteries, before fast food and before summer became organized.

And one of the best things about the end of summer was looking forward to chestnut season when you'd put a chestnut on the end of a string. You'd hit the other guy's chestnut and try to break it.

"Does anybody play chestnuts anymore?" I asked my daughter.

"Was that in an Eddie Murphy movie?" she asked.

Beware the red (tie) menace, or cravate emptor

[Friday, November 14, 1986]

TIES.

It's funny what columns provoke the greatest reader response, not just by mail, but through comments on the street, in restaurants and other public places.

About two months ago (actually it feels like it was years ago), I wrote a column about two women's views about the phenomenon of red ties. For some reason, these two ladies thought "guys with red ties are jerks."

It seems red ties became a fashion vogue some time ago because they were "power ties"—somehow a whole pile of men seemed to see them as denoting dynamism and power.

But in the views of my two female observers, men with red ties really were insecure people who went in for red ties as status symbols such as BMWs or whatever is fashionable with the Yuppie crowd.

Well, following that column I got an unusually large response, both from men and women.

"Why did you write that?" one fellow said to me. "I went into my office that day and all the women started insulting me, calling me a jerk and worse.

"I had no idea what they were talking about until somebody showed the column to me. Naturally, I was wearing a red tie that day."

Other men said obviously I was anti-Liberal, because die-hard Liberals have for what passes for time immemorial in a young country like Canada, been affecting red ties for tradition's sake.

To tell the truth, I hadn't meant it as any political comment, since I was merely reporting the rather vehement opinion of two women, one of whom worked in a bank, the other at CN. And they had no political bias at all.

No, they were just remarking on a fashion trend that I obviously had not noticed at all.

But a lot of people had.

Secretaries and businesswomen stopped me in the street and said things like: "You are absolutely right. The pushy, trendy guys all wear red ties these days;" or "The guys who wear red ties today are just like the guys who used to wear coloured vests 10 years ago and the young guys who smoked pipes 20 years ago."

Frankly, all of this was sort of news to me. I hadn't thought an iota about it until those two women mentioned it and then when I got all that continuing response.

The funny thing about it, is that a month after that column, I was dressing one day for an important luncheon and I found most of my ties were soiled or dirty a bit.

So with a friend, I went off to buy a new tie at my favorite haberdasher, Fredrick's, on McKay Street.

And what did old Fredrick recommend to go with my suit? A red tie. My friend agreed, and so I acquired a red tie.

Well, the response I received on the street was the same as if I had acquired an ill-fitting toupée.

People pointed at me, giggled and/or muttered "jerk" under their breath.

People gave me a hard time and all I could say was: "Hey, I was just reporting somebody else's opinion."

I still wear my new red tie from time to time and I still get abuse.

Recently, I ran into Charles Cutts, the general manager of Toronto's O'Keefe Centre, and he told me that I had missed the whole phenomenon of yellow ties. I admitted I had.

"Yellow ties picked up in the States, particularly in New York advertising circles, at the time of Ferdinand Marcos's downfall in Manila.

"That's because Cory Aquino's movement in the Philippines used yellow ribbons, and so on, as their symbol. That was borrowed from the song Tie a Yellow Ribbon (by Tony Orlando) which had also become the backup U.S. national anthem during the Iranian hostage crisis years ago.

"But for whatever reason, New York Yuppies and advertising executives took to wearing yellow ties at the time of Marcos's downfall last February. As usual in these cases, the trend reached Toronto in the summer and all the same types started emulating it. But by that time the red tie phenomenon had started elsewhere."

After that explanation, I was ready to admit I really do fail to notice the big trends in men's fashion.

"What's the next tie trend?" I asked Cutts. "Chess pieces. That's what's going on in London. It has to do with a Andrew Lloyd Webber/Tim Rice play called Chess, involving the two male members from the singing group, Abba. It's the big West End hit and people are starting to wear chess-theme clothes. When the play gets big over here, everybody will be wearing ties with chess pieces on them."

There you have it. So get out there and tie one on.

Today, we ask: Was that really me?

IT'S STRANGE, these days, talking about the 1960s.

I mean, our parents get to tell us about the Depression and World War II. We, on the other hand, get to tell our children how insane we were 20 years ago. And sometimes, looking back on our collective hysteria and commitment—which in another era might have passed for fanaticism—it seems so removed from today's experience that we ask: "Was that really me?"

We were wildly taken with the idea that violent confrontation could do good.

In between confrontations, we spent our time organizing political groups, in-fighting, forming breakaway factions and suspecting everybody else of being a police informer.

We also drank huge quantities of beer and liquor and looked down on American radicals as degenerates because they took drugs.

I remember sitting in the Swiss Hut on Sherbrooke Street near Hutchison, one night back in 1968 with a couple of cohorts, wondering what we should be doing. It had been about four months since we had embarked on our last major cause célèbre, a nice little confrontation in the Town of Mount Royal in support of the town's blue-collar workers and the strikers at a 7-Up plant.

Sitting there with my pals, guzzling quarts of Molson, I said: "Why don't we burn down Dorval airport?"

I suppose it was a measure of the '60s that such a suggestion from a young *Gazette* reporter was regarded as a stroke of genius.

The bunch of us had thrown in our lot with something called the Mouvement de libération de taxi, a group dedicated to ridding the airport of its Murray Hill limousine monopoly. In those days, we in Montreal were always looking for suitable working-class issues, as opposed to the "student" issues that seemed to dominate left-wing American politics.

It seems that all it took back then to organize a full-scale riot in Montreal was a suggestion, and lots of beer.

Within two weeks, we had about 200 taxis lined up, every second one of them loaded with a case of Molson Molotovs.

The taxis went off to pick up student stooges at the Université de Montréal and roared off to Dorval to do battle against perfidious Ottawa's awarding of a contract to Murray Hill without public tender.

We didn't manage to burn down the airport, though our taxi guerrillas did attack several Murray Hill limos and buses on the way to and from Dorval.

I tell you this without pride or boasting. The anecdote illustrates the way we lived, however strange it now feels to think we did things like that.

When I say "we," I'm not really sure of how many we were. I just know there was a core of us who hung around politicking, and when need be we could rally thousands to the streets and scare the hell out of everybody. Our endless stream of issues ranged from local strikes to the idea that the annual St. Jean Baptiste Day celebration should be transformed into the annual looting of Ste. Catherine Street.

There was more to the '60s than riots and demonstrations, of course, but those are the images that linger, especially after the FLQ took its own rhetoric seriously and began killing people.

Today, because of their overpowering culture and music and mythology, the official '60s are largely defined by what happened in the U.S.

But Montreal had its own effervescence in the '60s. We had our own causes and our own manic energy.

In the '60s, we were the world.

Days of the strap and Sabre jets

[April 16, 1988]

"The strap," Brian Stewart said flatly.

"The strap?" I asked. "That was your first major impression of education, the strap?"

Stewart, my television journalist friend, and I were mulling over an old first grade class photograph, and trying to remember what first grade was like.

Well certainly the strap made a major impression in first grade, although I can't really list it up there at the top of the big discoveries we all make when we set out on the voyage of life.

"I remember the atomic bomb drills we had in school," I responded, "although I suppose that wasn't first grade. I don't think the Russians got the bomb until I was in second grade."

That was a frightening novelty we encountered when some civil defence expert or other showed up in class to tell us what to do in case of atomic attack. (Nobody used the word nuclear until years later.)

We sat there in our little chairs and stuck our heads under the desks with our arms protecting the back of our heads. It seems to me that was it in its entirety, our atomic bomb drills. I don't remember them telling us anything else to do. For some mysterious reason that drill made us feel a bit more secure.

You have to remember, when I was in second and third grade, the Korean War was raging and every morning before going to school we listened to the radio reports giving us the score from the aerial dog fights. It was almost like a sports score: "Sabre Jets 9, MiG-17s 3."

So the atomic bomb drills didn't seem as outlandish then as they do now. Anyhow, back to the strap.

"The strap loomed large in our life at school." Stewart confessed. "It hovered over us as a constant threat. Certainly it was a more real and tangible threat than the atomic bomb. The strap was our bomb, and we didn't have any retaliatory measures whatsoever.

"We were defenceless against that damn strap."

We sat there and discussed the reality of the strap age, that horrid period that preceded the nuclear age.

For instance, what war criminal company got the order to produce 32,000 leather straps a year? Did they have technicians who measured for the right thickness? Did they a minimum and maximum sting factor?

Did they perhaps take them out and test them on some poor victims locked away in reform schools?

How did they box the straps? Were they polished? If they weren't properly cared for, say like shoes, would they crack? Did school principals —who always had insane names for the strap like "Black Pete" or "The Discipliner"—take them home and lovingly care for their straps, Simonizing them or something?

Or did the strap always remain in that evil little drawer the principal kept it in? And did the manufacturer send a manual along with his shipments of straps?

"When the principal raised his arm with the strap," Stewart recalled, "he always raised one foot off the ground. Then when he hit your outstretched hand with it, the foot would slam on the floor, making a much greater noise. That extra noise made it sound much more painful.

"And of course some kid would really snivel and scream with each thwack of the strap. So the cumulative effect of the noises would terrify any other kid waiting outside the office."

At our school, the strap was administered in the same way, except it wasn't done in the privacy of the principal's office—it was done in front of the whole class. It was like the principle of public executions.

There was real deterrent value there.

And of course there was always a couple of little snits in class who never got into trouble and thoroughly enjoyed the public spectacle of these floggings, smirking away like a bunch of little Madame Dufarges in front of the guillotine.

"All through school, there were always some kids who relished the reputation of being the most strapped kids in class," Stewart said, mystified. "They actually seemed to be terribly proud of if, enjoying the prestige of being sent off to the principal's office, having their heroic stature grow."

And such are the memories of childhood and the beginnings of education.

Sex and the gap-toothed woman

[May 2, 1988]

TODAY we're going to discuss the discovery of sex in Catholic Montreal in the 1950s.

It was a long time ago, but I remember it vividly.

We were sitting in our second high English class at D'Arcy McGee, studying Chaucer's Canterbury Tales—more specifically the pilgrim's tale of the Wife of Bath.

I don't recall being terribly interested in Chaucer at the time, and had some difficulty fully understanding all that medieval English.

And so I put up my hand and asked our English teacher, Mr, O'Neill, for an explanation of a passage that referred to the Wife of Bath as "a gap-toothed woman." What did that mean?

Well, Mr. O'Neill hemmed and hawed a bit, and then proceeded to explain that "in those days, people thought women with a gap between their front teeth were … er, desirable … and, er, sexy."

And then he added what, up to that point in my young life, was the most florid verbal flourish I had ever heard: "Rather like what some people today see in big-breasted women."

I remember being absolutely stupefied on hearing that.

You have to understand, I had your traditional, strong Catholic upbringing, both at home and in school. These were things that nobody, not anybody in authority certainly, ever discussed or even admitted to. Sex was a big, black void that was totally avoided,

And yet, here was someone in authority, a teacher, admitting that it existed. That somehow suggested it was a legitimate area of interest. I mean, they were even writing about it in school texts, or at least this guy Chaucer did.

Now, I was an adolescent, I guess your average adolescent, who was feeling these strange things, those things that brought you to the black void. And here was this teacher, by that reference—mild by today's standards, but absolutely unthinkable to me back then—somehow suggesting that this was normal. That even 600 years ago in Chaucer's day they were thinking about it.

What a revelation.

Up until that moment in English class, that strange feeling business only got people into terrible trouble.

Like the time some guy in first high showed up in school with one of those decks of playing cards that had pictures of naked women on them. Well, he got caught before any of us had a chance to see more than three or four of them. This big Christian brother, Brother Paul, I think it was, grabbed him by the arm, seized the cards and gave him a great big thwack on the head and led him off.

Another time, this was in grade seven in St. Malachy's, a student pulled out a condom—we weren't sure exactly what it was, but we did know it was somehow connected to the black void business. Anyhow, he took out this condom at recess and blew it up and sent it wafting over the fence to the girls' side of the school yard. And before it could touch down in the midst of these shrieking school girls, a teacher came up to the student and grabbed him.

"Where'd you get that?" he roared through clenched teeth at a terrified kid.

Thinking fast, he blurted out "I found it down by the synagogue."

Boy, what a defence. Blame it on the Jews.

THWACK. THWACK. The student got two cuffs on the head, one for the condom, one for lying about the synagogue. And he was led off to some unknown fate.

Another time, well a couple of times actually, one of my friends showed me some magazines his father had hidden. They had pictures of naked women. I remember one in particular was the *National Geographic*, and it had drawings of what life was like in ancient Rome. In ancient Rome a lot of women stood around naked in the bathhouses. There also seemed to be a lot of semi-naked slave girls hanging around the dinner table.

The other magazines were "photography" magazines.

Well, his father found out. THWACK. THWACK. THWACK.

So you can see, up until that time Mr. O'Neill explained about gap-toothed women, all suggestions of sex and those black void feelings ended up with terrible trouble. Awful trouble.

When I was a kid, I was one of those quiet types who more or less just stood around and observed. And what I observed drew me to the firm conclusion that this business was not only risky and to be avoided, it was very bad and dangerous, akin to some dreadful disease.

This was confirmed by the priests, who regularly gave us lectures about such matters, which were always presented in some vague, veiled way. But we caught the drift.

So when Mr. O'Neill told me about gap-toothed women, I felt as if the veil had been lifted from some dark mystery. I can't explain it exactly, but that business seemed much clearer to me. Somehow, I understood that everybody had those strange feelings and that l wasn't alone. It was kind of normal.

And still today when l see a woman with gapped front teeth, I get all kind of woozy and melt. But the problem as I see it, is that around that time Mr. O'Neill laid out this bombshell the orthodontists embarked on some evil plot to narrow all those gaps, putting wire into mouths and trying to eliminate most of the gap-toothed women in the Western world.

The inexpressible joy of ridiculing lawyers

[November 7, 1988]

ONE OF THE RECURRING FANTASIES I have involves getting invited to speak at the Canadian Bar Association's annual convention.

There I am, standing at the banquet podium facing a sea of lawyers, the top legal minds of the country sitting there earnestly waiting for my speech.

And I begin by announcing that Ottawa has decided to ban the use of rats in laboratory testing. Instead of rats, Ottawa has decided to substitute lawyers.

And there are three reasons for that.

One, there are more lawyers than rats in Ottawa. Two, lab technicians tend not to form emotional attachments with lawyers. And three, there are some things that rats just won't do.

Ho ho ho. I'd go, as the lawyers would gape.

Then I'd ask them if they knew how to tell the difference between a dead skunk and a dead lawyer on a highway.

(There are skid marks before the skunk.)

What's black and brown and looks good on a lawyer?

(A doberman.)

Now I know it's not fair to pick on a race, an ethnic group or a profession in telling jokes or casting aspersions. But people do it all the time.

Take for example what people say about politicians as a group. It's often not very pretty the way some people say "all the politicians this," or "union leaders that."

That attitude reflects an unfair tendency to generalize, roughly equivalent to racism.

One of the reasons people tend to single out lawyers for abuse is that we don't usually go to see a lawyer unless we have a problem. So naturally we associate them with problems.

They also deal with something complicated, and we don't understand what it's all about. They seem to speak in bafflegab and turn everything around to mean the opposite of what is intended.

Last week in his speech, Reuben Greenberg, the black, Jewish police chief from South Carolina, typically dismissed lawyers as "people whose profession it is to disguise things."

So it's easy to pick on the poor lawyers. Not fair, but easy nevertheless.

That reminds me of the story about the Pope dying and going to heaven.

He gets to St. Peter's gates and he's waiting to be let in when another fellow shows up and introduces himself. The new fellow is a lawyer.

So the Pope and lawyer chat amiably until St. Peter fInally shows up and opens the gate to let them in.

St. Peter checks their papers and says to the Pope, you check in over here and to the lawyer, you check in over that away.

As they're going their separate ways, the lawyer yells to the Pope: "Give me a call sometime and we'll have lunch."

The Pope is shown to his quarters in heaven. A nicely-designed bachelor pad in a high-rise condo with a big balcony overlooking the lake, the weeping willows and the swans.

The Pope settles in and he's very comfortable and happy.

After about a month, he remembers the lawyer and calls him up.

"Come over to my place for lunch," the lawyer says.

The Pope jumps into a cab and gives the lawyer's address. The Pope is surprised when the cab turns tnto a private tree-lined road leading to a huge estate.

The Pope gets out of the cab in front of a big mansion, goes up the steps and rings the bell. A beautiful angel in a mini-skirt answers the door and leads him through the marble foyer out to the back patio beside the swimming pool.

The lawyer's sitting there, as one sexy angel is lighting his cigar and another is filling his champagne glass.

The Pope is a bit disgruntled but, being polite, doesn't say anything as he sits through a magnificent lunch.

After lunch, he goes directly to St. Peter and says: "I don't mean to whine and complain, but I'm the Pope and all I get is a high rise condo while this lawyer ... ."

St. Peter interrupts him and says: "You have to understand. You're our 112th Pope here. He's our first lawyer."

Ho ho ho.

Do you know the difference between a rooster and a lawyer?
A rooster clucks defiance.

   OK. No more. My apologies all around.

Class of '49. Students at Saint-Leon de Westmount.
Nick, seven, is top right (in crease).

The toothache that turned a grown man into a quivering baby

[Wednesday, May 23, 1990]

ONE THING that always astounds me is how many people treat going to a dentist with great nonchalance.

"You gotta go to the dentist?" I'll ask a friend with a mixture of horror and sympathy.

"No big deal," he'll answer. No big deal, I say to myself. How can he say no big deal? And then I again feel overcome with a sense of guilt and shame.

Guilt because I neglect my teeth, shame because I still feel the terror a child feels at the prospect of visiting a dentist.

Actually, I'll amend that. Children these days display far more equanimity toward dentistry than I could ever imagine.

Today, most kids seem to treat a visit to a dentist as an adventure, better still, a nifty way of getting out of school for a couple of hours.

On the other hand, I feel a visit to the dentist is akin to a summons to Torquemada's Office of the Inquisition.

Perhaps it comes from the very first time I remember visiting a dentist, when I was about 14 or 15. That would be in the mid-1950s.

I had had a toothache and a visiting school nurse had referred me to a dentist on a second-floor Bleury Street walkup.

In great trepidation, I arrived at the dental office, a dank, smelly place, to be greeted by a big, fat, elderly dentist whose breath was heavily whisky-laden, his smock soiled and his hands shaking.

I remember him peering into my mouth, but I don't recall much else except the utter fear.

All I know is that he yanked out the offending tooth and presented me with a bill for something like $5, which I in turn presented to my horrified mother that same day.

We were poor, and my mother had to work hard to make ends meet. As with a lot of poor people in those days, dental care was regarded, if it was regarded at all, as a luxury reserved for those who could afford to lavish money on cosmetics.

A while later, when my teeth bothered me again, my mother marched me up to the free dental clinic at the Montreal General Hospital, where students got to practice their craft on us poor guinea pigs.

I came to view those visits to the dental clinic with unmitigated desperation, thinking the student dentists were all sadists in training, worse, Protestants out to inflict great pain on us poor Catholics.

Needless to say, I didn't get a lot of work done on my teeth there, although they did manage to extract another couple of teeth and install a filling or three before I managed to escape their clutches.

The next time I went to a dentist was when I was 29. My friend Brian Stewart dragged me quivering to his dentist, Dr. Melvin Heft, to see about a toothache.

Dr. Heft peered into my mouth and was aghast.

Then I was aghast at the cost estimate to rectify years of neglect.

Nevertheless, they conspired to persuade me it was something that needed doing.

And so every week I'd go to his office, turn into a mass of jelly, gag incessantly, panic, grip the armrests in white-knuckle hysteria while repeatedly biting Dr. Heft's fingers. Then I'd gag some more.

In addition to the normal apprehensions, I'm also afflicted with an irrational fear that perhaps stems from a dream I once had. Whenever I see the dentist with a needle, I have this vision somebody will bump his elbow from behind and he'll stick the needle in my eyeball. So in addition to closing my eyes when the dentist approaches, I have this insane urge to cover my eyes with my hands and look like an utter fool.

Whenever I'd have a dental appointment, I'd feel the same irrational hope I had when in school on the day of an exam I didn't study for. Maybe a building will fall down or the Russians will attack or something and they'll have to cancel.

Over a couple of years, the good dentist got a lot of work done and transformed my mouth from something resembling an east European industrial wasteland into something approximating an expensive, high-tech silicon valley.

After all that heavy capital investment was done, I even went in for regular maintenance checks every year—well, about three or four times.

By then I found I couldn't take the lectures from the dental assistants, who always said: "Mr. Auf der Maur, you haven't been flossing your teeth."

Then they'd take a gigantic replica of a human set of teeth with a gigantic toothbrush and proceed to deliver a well-intentioned kindergarten lecture that made me feel like a cowardly nitwit.

So for the last 15 years or so, I played hooky from the dentist, thinking everything was all right. I even ignored the minor aches that popped up on the right side of my mouth from time to time.

Those aches popped up again 10 days ago, but I thought they'd go away again, just as they always do.

Last week the pain got worse. Then on Monday night at city council I found my mouth wasn't working all that well and I couldn't speak properly.

The right side was starting to swell up. Soon it looked as if somebody had stuffed a tennis ball in my right cheek.

Pathetically, I went to see Dr. Heft the next day.

Double abscess. Disaster. Two molars had to go.

The oral surgeon managed to get them out while I miraculously managed to refrain from fainting, just barely.

The moral of this is, don't postpone a visit to the dentist. An abscess is much, much worse.

How I got my big break on an
unsinkable story

[Wednesday, August 21, 1996]

THIS is the 30th anniversary of a great breakthrough in journalism. Or at least in my career, which surely amounts to the same thing.

Thirty years ago this month, I got my first "scoop."

I had been working at *The Gazette* for about two years, first as a copy boy, then as a police reporter, then moving up to "general," covering labour, politics, the weather and everything else.

Like all young reporters I was itching for my first "scoop" so I'd be noticed—make my name, as it were.

One Sunday in the middle of August 1966 when very little was happening, Bruce Garvey, city editor at the time, asked me to fill in the night police slot.

Night police was a boring shift, which on Sunday nights consisted mostly of drawing up lists of weekend traffic and other fatalities.

It entailed phoning up the various police departments—before police integration there were about 30 on the island of Montreal—and asking "anything going on?"

Usually there was nothing.

At one point, I asked the guy at the RCMP and he said: "Nah, nothing."

"Nothing at all?" I persisted, desperately hoping for something interesting to write about.

"Well, there was one call," he started to answer, "but nah, that was a nut case."

What kind of nut case, I asked.

"Some woman called to say her husband was lost in a homemade nuclear-powered submarine," he said.

Well, I was off and running, took the woman's number and within days the whole thing was on the front pages of newspapers around the world. And I made a ton of money freelancing it to papers all over Europe.

It started modestly enough with a story in *The Gazette* of Monday, August 15, 1966, about Mrs. Joseph Papp reporting her husband's disappearance.

She said he left Sorel the previous Wednesday aboard a homemade submarine he had been building secretly in a Terrebonne garage for years.

After a 12-hour voyage at 300 mph, he was supposed to call her from somewhere in the British Isles. He never called and she was worried.

Papp was 32, a Hungarian refugee and inventor who claimed to have developed some sort of nuclear power device.

My story quoted a friend, Nicholas Boldog, as saying Papp had completed his submarine after 18 years of research, starting in Hungary.

"The communist government didn't trust him politically," Boldog said. "Joseph didn't trust anybody, not even his wife." He was a bitterly disappointed scientist and would trust only close friends about the project. "That's because some of his inventions, like the motorized water skis, were stolen from him."

It was the summer silly season, and no other paper paid it any attention.

Until the next day, when Papp was found bobbing up and down in a rubber life raft in the Atlantic off Brest, France.

Then the story was on front pages everywhere.

However, I had told Mrs. Papp and her friends that reporters were jackals and I was the only one to be trusted.

Papp was being kept in the psychiatric wing of a French military hospital, because, French authorities said, "he was babbling on about his homemade nuclear submarine hitting a rock."

And we had the only picture, which I got from his wife, of the submarine.

You know how the news media can spin into a frenzy.

This was a mad frenzy and I was in the middle of it, and my editors, Bruce Garvey and Brodie Snyder, were in ecstasy because we had everyone beat.

They had me churning out reams of copy full of detail and nonsense.

Then on Wednesday, French authorities expressed suspicion because they found a Paris-to-Brest train ticket in the pocket of the wet overalls Papp was wearing when found in his raft.

At *The Gazette*, we managed to patch in a phone call to Papp from his wife, while I listened in to his convoluted and contradictory explanations of what had happened.

But the wife and his friends continued to believe in Papp. After all, they had helped finance the $28,000 project.

Then the RCMP discovered Papp had bought an airline ticket to Paris some months earlier. An airline employee had recognized his passport picture as someone he saw boarding the flight the night Papp disappeared.

This, of course, didn't diminish the story. Papp maintained his story and there was a huge crowd at Dorval when he flew back, with TV crews and journalists from all over, the RCMP and hundreds of curious there to greet the man who for a little bit had captured everybody's imagination.

It was a great summer story and everybody had a laugh—except Papp's wife and friends, but even they were rationalizing his acts a week later.

The Daily Express in London editorialized: "Papp leaves Europe a little more exhilarated for his visit. A story so bold and so engaging, backed by such an unblushing lack of evidence, puts Papp in the class of the great hoaxers of the past. And like them, he has caused much hilarity and done no harm."

I, of course, laughed all the way to the bank.

Papp ended up moving to Los Angeles. Years later, when back in Montreal for a visit, he called me up to show me scale models of some inventions he was working on. He was undeterred by what he called "the submarine misunderstanding."

The Best Margarita in Town

Hubert Bauch

HEREWITH, the one true recipe for the official house cocktail of the Hotel Kafka.

It is the product of staggering persistence and copious experiment during the years I was Nick's downstairs tenant in said establishment. In memory he speaks to me still, like those many times he'd phone or come pounding on the door, saying: "Hube, we MUST have margaritas." It was always a signal that things were about to get special. No tale of Nick I might tell could more vividly impart how it felt when the good times would roll on Upper Tupper, than these simple instructions. (Not recommended for children, amateurs or repentants):

Combine in blender: 2 cups ice
1½ cups tequila*
1 cup Rose's Lime Cordial**
1 cup pure lime juice***
1½ cup Triple Sec
½ tsp egg white****

Blend until smooth and foamy. Serve in festive glasses. To salt the rims (optional for health freaks) wet with lime juice and dip in sea salt. A nice crisp lager makes for an excellent chaser.

* Nick liked gold, I liked silver; save the anejo for shots.
** Must be Rose's; substitutes invite disappointment.
*** Bottled is okay in a pinch; fresh squeezed makes the difference between fine and sublime.
**** Any more than this and it'll foam like Vesuvius; don't ask how we know.

We thought we'd hit perfection with this blend, but of all people, we should have known there's no rest for the wicked. Shortly thereafter, Nick went to New York one weekend and came back raving about this bar he'd found on lower Broadway where they served frozen margaritas out of a converted "Slushee" machine. Nick insisted there must be a way to replicate these with a blender—an idea of the sort our Nick was loath to relinquish. Our ultimate success reflects the extent of our dedication and ingenuity.

Per blender (we recommend the Osterizer 10-speed):

—Mix 1 cup pure lime and 1 cup Rose's in a freezer bag. Position the bag in the freezer so that the liquid hardens into a chunk that resembles a large popsicle. Also put bottles of tequila and triple sec into the freezer at the same time. Leave at least 5 hours. (Forget the egg white.)

—Take the hard-frozen chunk of lime/Rose's mix and chop into pieces that fit easily into the blender. Add ½ cup of ice-cold triple sec and 1½ cups ice cold tequila and 2 cups of ice. (Ice cubes shouldn't be too large; bagged is best.)

—Blend until all the ice is crushed. Then, with the blender on high, drop 4-5 more ice cubes, one at a time, through the hole in the blender lid, letting each cube be ground before adding the next. This step is critical to achieving the proper consistency; the mix should form peaks when poured. (Note on blender mechanics: Start at a low speed to let the ice settle on the blades then work up until you get a nice whirlpool effect; hitting high off the bat can have explosive consequences, as we learned.)

—Serve with milkshake-style straws (the narrow kind tend to clog up) and for maximum enjoyment, in styrofoam cups (retards melting).

Cheers to the fearless.

Hubert ("Hubie"-after-a-couple) Bauch is a political writer for *The Gazette* in Montreal.

Everyone Has His Place— and Montreal was Nick's

Jacob Richler

I DON'T ACTUALLY REMEMBER meeting Nick. I only recall that when I was a child, my father occasionally took me along when he went out for an afternoon drink at whatever bar it was that he favoured at the time, and wherever that was, one special man always seemed to have arrived there first. A lean tall fellow with a bushy moustache, a spiffy hat, and a mishievous grin. He'd be telling some people a story, maybe, or chatting on the bar phone, or just quietly reading his newspaper. And I don't remember that anyone introduced him, I just remember knowing his name. Everyone knew his name. It was Nick.

About ten years ago Nick called me at home for the first time and asked me to go out for a drink with him. I found him, as arranged, at happy hour at Winnie's. He was not, as he had promised, at the front bar but rather at the back one, chatting with some attractive young woman, and he didn't seem especially pleased by my timing. All the same he asked what I was drinking.

"What are you drinking?" I asked.

"An Irregular," he said.

"What?"

"Vodka, grapefruit, soda," he said.

That sounded fine. Nick then began a captivating discourse on municipal politics, and, having quickly established that it was the best gig in town, he asked me if I would like to run for his new political party.

"How would I finance a campaign?" I asked him.

"Ask Irwin Steinberg," he said, volunteering a Winnie's regular.

From time to time during our chat, he suggested moving along to another bar, and at each of them, he ordered us a few more Irregulars.

"How many places are there," I asked him, impressed, "where you can order an Irregular and they know what you mean?"

"Oh, one or two," he replied. "Maybe three."

At around the sixth place he told me what a city councillor's salary was, and explained that one could boost that respectably by sitting on a city hall standing committee.

"I'm on two," he added.

"Which ones?" I asked.

Stumped, he took refuge in his briefcase for a time. Then he looked up from his papers suddenly, grinned and said, "Actually, I think one of them is the committee to deal with the problem of there being too many committees at city hall."

I didn't run for him in the end but we became friends that afternoon. A few years later we were spending a lot of time together, and when I then began writing a city column for the *Mirror*, Nick was unbelievably helpful. Whatever the story, he knew exactly which apparatchik or undercover cop or bar owner or politician to call about it, and he had their phone numbers, sometimes even current ones. And whoever it was I called, when I told them who had put me in touch, they were happy to talk.

Almost as happy to talk as Nick was, when I interviewed him for a story about the launch of his 1994 municipal campaign. We met at happy hour and I managed to make it home by four. And after too few hours sleep, my pulse vague, I somehow filed the column.

It was a brief catalogue of things distinctly Nick. A quick account of a death threat from an Iranian heroin dealer, the call placed collect from a local penitentiary. And a story about fixing someone's zoning problem and bringing a new business to the downtown core. He mentioned that his mother, 91 then, still called him at 9:30 each morning to make sure that he wouldn't be late for work. And of course, he talked of his favourite subject, his best friend, his daughter Melissa, who had then just joined Courtney Love's band, Hole. A group with a certain reputation, he knew, but he wasn't worried: he knew that his daughter could handle anything.

Why did his campaign stickers say: "Votez Nick le 7 novembre," when the election was on the 6th?

"Details" he replied, "I hate details."

Why had he switched parties so many times?

"Parties switch on me," he said. "I don't remain loyal to parties, I remain loyal to the decent thing to do."

Late in the runup to the last Quebec referendum, my sister Emma phoned me from London one morning to alert me to a newspaper article which she thought would be of interest to me.

"I was just reading *The Independent*," she explained, "There's a story here on Quebec and in the lead the writer describes a man in a bar wearing a funny shirt and tie, and a hat. And I thought to myself, this must be Jake's friend. And yes, it is."

Sensible foreign journalists on assignment in Montreal always contrived to make a drink with Nick their first stop. And Nick, who had spent twenty years as a city councillor in opposition, and exploited the position for a range of worthy initiatives that comprised exposing the Olympic spending corruption scandal, as well as teaching Jean Drapeau, whom Nick suspected had endured an unfulfilling childhood, how to tell a joke, would explain to these out-of-towners better than anyone else could the history of the city he loved and the politics that made it what it was.

The drinks, inevitably, would turn into a few. But after this time spent with Nick, these visiting reporters wouldn't just come away with quotes to show that Montreal was a cosmopolitan, lively and eccentric place. Something would inevitably happen that proved this was so, too, because that's the way things transpired around Nick.

Take that fellow from the *Independent*, for instance. It's his first time in Montreal, this week in late October 1995, and after an hour with Nick at Winnie's front bar, he has already extracted more than enough quotes about the impending referendum for his story, so the conversation turns to more general things.

"Who's the BBC crew interviewing over there?" he asks.

"Mordecai Richler," Nick explains, "novelist and expert on Quebec political affairs."

"I see," the journalist says, and makes a note of it.

And just then, a crew from Montreal's local CTV affiliate charges into Winnie's and heads for the back bar.

"Who are they here to interview?" the reporter from the *Independent* asks.

"Theresa, the back bartender."

"Is she an expert on Quebec politics, too?"

"No, she's an expert on the real story of the day. The Montreal Canadiens just fired their coach and general manager, and she's a big hockey fan."

The reporter from the *Independent* excuses himself and heads off to the loo. Nick has a look at his notebook, and reads the last entry. "Odd," it reads. "Country apparently fragmenting. Yet, talk of hockey."

When Nick got sick, expatriate Montrealers like me discussed news of the state of his health first off whenever they got together. I ran into a French-Canadian cameraman in Toronto last spring, and he hadn't yet heard that Nick had cancer.

"Non, pas Nick," he said, aghast, even though he had met the man only once, fleetingly. "Nick, c'est le Montréal."

Nick was certainly the Montreal we all liked to project: literate and bilingual, passionate, fun-loving and proud. And much as the city is indebted to him for that, Nick wouldn't have felt so, because he really did have a great time amongst us, a happy life even if it was horribly, tragically short, and he knew that he couldn't have existed as he did anywhere but Montreal.

Jacob Richler is a Montreal writer. His first son, Maximilian Niklaus, was born a few days before Nick's death.

HABITS

Almost quitting smoking was a success
—sort of

[Monday, March 31, 1986]

FINALLY, Lent is over.

A week before Lent started more than 40 days ago, I pledged to give up smoking—no mean feat for somebody used to three packs of unfiltered Gitanes a day for years.

In my usual objective fashion, I think I'll declare the experiment a mitigated success. For the first couple of weeks, I didn't have a hard time at all. In fact, I was surprised at how easy it was, especially since I'd heard all those stories of how difficult giving up smoking is.

Having been a Gitanes smoker proved to be a great advantage. I hate blond Virginia-type cigarettes, which is what just about everybody smokes around here. So if I get a whiff of smoke, it doesn't provoke any particular craving. Unless of course it is Gitanes or Gauloises smoke.

My problems started during a trip to Santo Domingo in the Dominican Republic. I was in a supermarket looking over the local produce when I came across a large tobacco display.

There was a great variety of hand-rolled cigars for which the Dominicans are justly famous.

At the end of the cigar display, I spotted a pile of cigarette packages. The brand was Cremos and the design of the package was old-fashioned and quite beautiful.

I asked the clerk whether those cigarettes were made of black tobacco (as Gitanes are). She said they were.

Well, I just had to try them. But I didn't leap right in. I actually circled around the store several times, but I kept finding myself back at the cigar counter, staring at that beautiful package.

Finally I rationalized it by saying to myself: "Self, you gave up smoking one week before Lent started, so that gives you a bit of leeway here. A few days' grace."

I bought a pack and smoked it over six days. Taking into account the ones I gave away, it meant about two cigarettes a day.

That was a big mistake.

When I came back to Montreal, the ease with which I had made it through my first non-smoking weeks had disappeared.

One day I found myself sitting with Mordecai Richler. I found myself staring at his little cigars, a Dutch brand called Schimmelpenninck, which he buys regularly in New York. They are cigarette-size cigarillos and they smelled wonderful.

Well, again I rationalized. It's not really cigarette smoking. And I won't inhale. And I'll only have one. That sort of thing.

Mordecai let me have one.

After that, I started to seek out Mordecai eagerly. Every time I saw him, I'd filch one of his Schimmelpennincks.

Well, you know what happens when you get into Schimmelpennincks. Pretty soon you're bumming Old Ports off people. Then those little Dunhills.

I was doing one or two, sometimes three a day of those things. But not inhaling.

The terrible thing about giving up smoking, especially when you stupidly blab about it in public, is that everybody wants to talk about it. People feel compelled to tell you all about their experiences. I felt as if I was in a permanent Alcoholics Anonymous-type meeting.

For example, my friend Kenner told me about his ingenious giving-up-smoking scheme.

"I decided to give up smoking by one-hour increments every week," he explained. "The first week, I wouldn't light my first cigarette until 9 a.m., the next week, I'd move it up to 10 a.m. and so on.

"I figured I wouldn't notice the difference. Well, by the time I got to noon, I switched to half-hour increments."

"Did it work?" I asked, noticing he was smoking.

"Nah. I just went nuts," he said, "The whole morning was a zero. I just sat there staring at my watch."

Then there are the people who are always ready with gratuitous advice.

"If you feel like a smoke after dinner," one would say, "take a brisk walk around the block instead."

Well, that's like telling a 19-year-old to take a cold shower.

I think I'll handle it on my own terms.

On the weekend, to mark the end of Lent and celebrate my mitigated success, I treated myself to a whole pack of six weird little Brazilian cigarillos. Smoked four and gave away two. But I didn't inhale.

(Boy. This is starting to sound like True Confessions.)

But now that I've more of less come through Lent, I've decided to keep up the non-smoking routine for another couple of weeks, at least until after my European lecture tour. (OK, so it's only one brief talk in Bern, Switzerland, but "lecture tour" has a better ring to it.)

I figure limited objectives, like Lent or until after this trip, make it easier not to smoke. Saying "forever" has a more daunting sound to it. Makes it seem harder. It's better to stick to the foreseeable future.

In the meantime, I'll try to avoid Santo Domingo and maybe listen to my mother's advice about staying away from people like Mordecai.

Never mind jogging, just munch an onion

[Monday, October 19, 1987]

AND NOW for some advice on eating habits.

It's odd, I hate iceberg lettuce, yet I've always loved the salads my mother makes. And she always uses iceberg lettuce. I was pondering this seeming contradiction the other day as I was preparing a salad for a dinner with my daughter and a couple of her girlfriends. Among my daughter's friends, I have a reputation for being the best salad maker around. This I know, because I've received phone calls from mothers asking how to make salads so that kids will eat them.

Basically, I just follow the extremely simple formula my mother always used. You just use oil and vinegar, with none of that gelatinous guck turned out as commercial salad dressing. I guess you can use any kind of lettuce, but I keep strictly to romaine.

Put in anything else you want, from tomatoes to cucumber to carrot sticks, but you must always put in onions. Nice chunky pieces of onion, not thin slivered stuff. They impart a flavour that is vital to the salad. After a while, you'll find even the most fastidious kids wolfing down the onions. If you feel like it, sprinkle on freshly chopped garlic.

Another thing—always use olive oil.

Then the other major trick is to serve it to the kids about an hour before the meal. Obviously, they're hungry and they'll eat anything you put in front of them. However, a simple salad like that grows on them, and it has become a trademark of my house.

My tenants' two kids, who live downstairs, positively swear by my salad. And the youngest, Niki, insists on making all their salads according to my specifications.

A word about the onions.

It has long been my contention that raw onions are a major key to good health. This is, of course, an old wives' tale from way back, one which I have subscribed to wholeheartedly since my childhood.

We used to have a roomer, Alexander Roy, an old man who was a business associate of my father's and who looked very much like Col. Sanders. He used to sit in his room and read Zane Gray and other western novels, and every now and again he'd burst into operatic arias.

Mr. Roy used to play the horses and if he won at the track he'd give me a dollar. And when I was 10 years old, a dollar was really big time.

Obviously, I liked the old guy.

But Mr. Roy taught me two things that remain with me to this day.

One: On Saturday afternoons always listen to Milton Cross and the Texaco opera broadcast from the Met. Well, Milton Cross has long gone, but I still faithfully play the Texaco opera in the background every Saturday.

Two: Eat lots of onions.

When I came home from school, Mr. Roy always fixed me an onion sandwich. He explained that onions were the key to good health. Maybe the fact that we were often too poor to have peanut butter and other stuff around had something to do with it, but the fact is Mr. Roy lived well into his 90s and I believed him.

So I now have this evangelical thing about getting kids to eat onions.

I haven't bothered to really check the theories in any systematic way, but I am convinced there is something in onions and garlic that maintains health.

I humbly offer myself as evidence. I lead what most would consider a pretty hectic life, yet despite the fact I do no exercise and generally don't look after myself, my annual checkups show me to be in good health.

This I attribute to onions, olive oil and, to a lesser extent, garlic. I say a lesser extent because I really don't eat enough garlic.

There's a town in Spain that is called the "garlic capital of the world." It is their single resource and naturally they also eat massive amounts of it. And the 2,000 inhabitants of the region have virtually no heart disease. "You may die of boredom here," the locals say, "but never of heart disease."

Several years ago, I read of a nine-year medical study comparing the health of policemen in New York and Italy. The study found that the Italians had significantly fewer heart problems than the New Yorkers.

And while nothing was proved, the study noted that one of the major differences in diet was the fact that Italians consumed lots of olive oil.

It didn't mention it, but garlic and onions were probably involved there, too.

My physician, Dr. Sydney Smith, says that my onion/garlic/olive oil theory is not so crackpot as some may think. Fact is, he advises people to eat sardines mixed with fresh chopped onions. He recommends the sardines because of both the value of fish and the oil used in the canning.

So there, for what it's worth, you have my basic nutritional advice.

Follow it, and you can probably dispense with jogging, Nautilus and all that time-consuming other stuff.

Stand up for what you believe in, even if it's Donald Duck

[Wednesday, July 15, 1992]

PERHAPS I am becoming an old grump.

I often sport a Donald Duck lapel pin and if people ask me why, I launch into a tirade against Mickey Mouse, who I think gets an undue amount of publicity. Look at TV reports from EuroDisneyland and all you see is the little rodent. The boring, uninteresting rodent who gets on all the watch faces while our hero duck gets ignored. And here it is, the middle of the strawberry season and people ooh and ah about strawberries. And I find myself going into a funk and denoucing strawberries because basically I'm a raspberry guy.

Strawberries get this terribly pretentious image that was most likely manufactured by some big PR machine. Ladies' auxiliaries at big museums organizing "strawberry and champagne balls," the swells at the Wimbledon tennis championships scarfing down individual strawberries at one quid a pop – big mutant strawberries probably grown at some radioactive dump site.

So that's it.

I'm irrevocably, completely in the Donald Duck and raspberry camp and I feel it's time to make a statement.

Ever since I was a kid, I loved Donald Duck and all the characters in Duckburg. They were interesting types. Scrooge McDuck, Gyro Gearloose, the Beagle Boys, Huey, Dewey and Louie.

Donald always screwed things up and lost his temper. You could indentify with him. In other words, he was Everyduck.

But who did Mickey Mouse hang out with? Goofy, Pluto, Minnie Mouse. Goody-goody two shoes. Wimps all.

Why people identify with his persona is beyond me. Why the Disney people make him the big star is beyond me. Why Nikita Khrushchev wanted to go to Disneyland and be photographed with Mickey Mouse is beyond me.

Bo-orring.

When I was a kid, I learned about things like the Philosepher's Stone, the Fountain of Youth, lost cities, ancient Egypt and such from reading the comic book adventures of Donald, Scrooge Donald Scrooge and those three ingenious Junior Woodchucks, Hewey, Dewey and Louie.

Still today, I buy Scrooge McDuck comic books. But almost always in French, because they are thicker and better in French.

What did anybody ever learn from Mickey Mouse?

Diddley-squat, that's what.

And yet who gets all the recognition when he turns 50?

The big American networks, the magazines, Knowlton Nash—they all go on about the little rodent and show Steamboat Willie and natter on about how much the whole world loves him. Saccharine drivel abounds around the characterless mouse. Donald Duck turns 50 and barely a mention.

Who won an Oscar?

Donald Duck in 1942 for Der Führer's Face.

Donald was right up there on the front lines in the fight against fascism.

They didn't even bother to draft Mickey Mouse.

One of the reasons I identify with Donald might have to do with the move we made when I was 11, when my father managed some mining deal and we ended up like the Beverly Hillbillies, moving from being janitors on Coloniale Street to a house in lower Westmount.

The address was 313 Elm Avenue which, of course, was Donald Duck's exact same address in Duckburg.

Wow! I exploded in my dim pre-adolescent mind.

Anyhow, I retain a deep sense of loyalty.

In the same vein, I have this feeling for raspberries, when you consider that nonsensical luxury, good-life mystique that surrounds their rivals, the strawberries.

All the oohing and aahing about strawberries just makes me a more determined and convinced proponent of the underdog raspberry, a good, honest field berry. Not for us, the upper-class twit strawberry.

Each of those little raspberry buds are like flavour bombs when you bite into them and chew them.

Blackberries and blueberries are fine, too. So long as you don't get those big, fat mutant blueberries imported from cultivated farms in

Michigan or Maine. But we're getting off on a tangent here.

My point is, stick up for what you believe in.

If you feel strongly about ducks and raspberries or anything else, speak up and let people know. Don't just sit there following the conventional wisdom and trends foisting second-rate rodents and berries or whatever on you.

Pound your fists and defend the values Donald Duck defended in the fight against fascism. Feel free.

Free men and women and ducks and wild berries everywhere depend on it.

*   *   *

(from a followup column, July 22)

Apropos of why Donald Duck was terrific and more relevant than Mickey Mouse:

I stated, among other things, that Donald Duck was on the forefront of the fight against fascism because he won an Oscar for Der Führer's Face in 1942 and was used prominently to sell U.S. war bonds.

I also said Mickey Mouse was such a wimp he wasn't even drafted for use in war propaganda.

The day after that column was written, I received my regular mailing of the Week in Germany, a press review.

It contained a piece about an International Comic Salon held in June in Erlangen.

This is what it said in part: "Discussion of the role of Mickey Mouse in the Third Reich drew great interest at the meeting.... Mickey had fans in high places in the Nazi regime.

"Propaganda Minister Joseph Goebbels, for example, noted in his diary that Adolf Hitler had been 'very happy' about Goebbels's 1937 Christmas present to him: 18 Mickey Mouse films. 'I hope that this treasure will bring him much joy and relaxation,' Goebbels wrote." Hitler also ordered five Mickey Mouse films from Disney for private screenings.

I rest my case.

My recipe for healthy living: a little touch, a hearty laugh

[Wednesday, December, 1, 1993]

As I was walking over to the washroom, I noticed the back of the head of an old friend of mine who was sitting at the bar.

As I passed by, I gave him an affectionate little pat on the rear and continued on my way to the washroom. What I didn't realize was that it wasn't my old friend. It was a total stranger, an old friend of Grumpy's barman Doug Muncey, a fellow he hadn't seen in years. He'd heard Muncey was working there and dropped by to say hello.

After I had patted him, the astonished man called Muncey and said: "That guy just pinched my ass!"

Muncey looked at my receding back and said: "Oh, that's OK, that's just Nick."

The man furrowed his brow, looked up and down the bar, and said to Muncey: "What kind of bar is this, anyway?"

Every now and then, you do something that you know is going to get you into trouble, or at least misinterpreted. Writing this column is one of those times, in this time of political correctness and raised consciousness.

The fact is, I'm a bit of a bum-fondler. But don't get me wrong; let me explain.

Oh sure, somebody is thinking. He's going to rationalize, justify some sort of sexist, crude, juvenile behaviour.

It's not that I've worked this out in any great detail, as a matter of philosophy or weighty thought. It's really just that I need a column subject today and it occurs to me that every now and then I get into a bit of trouble over this habit I have.

And habit it is. I've been doing this as long as I can remember. And not, I like to think, in some sort of crude, sexist, juvenile manner. It's not sexual at all. Rather, it's a tactile reflex, an ecumenical reflex applied to both men and women. But not to everybody and not to all friends.

Some instinct tells me who would be receptive and who wouldn't appreciate it. Of course, mistakes do occur.

I can't say it's a cultural thing with me, although obviously some cultures are more tactile than others. Russian and other Slavic men will readily embrace each other in greeting. Italians and others are prone to touching each other when talking, a hand on the arm or some such. (Napoleon was in the habit of affectionately tugging at people's ear lobes when he talked to them.)

Now, I don't really pinch derrières. It's more partway pat, partway fondle, or a pat with a bit of finger movement. Brief enough so that it won't be regarded as a grope. I use it as a greeting.

Now, I realize we live in a society where this is considered gauche or forward or unacceptable.

But this is a society where people get on elevators and scrunch up their shoulders, arms tucked tightly in so as not to alarm any other passenger by accidently touching. Many people are so untactile and afraid of physical contact you'd think they think everyone else had bubonic plague.

It's the same thing with emotions. People are reluctant to express them publicly, even privately.

But the fact is, we need human contact, physical contact, just the way children need hugs and kisses for reassurance and love.

This is healthy, both mentally and physically.

Years ago, I remember reading a newspaper story about a surprising finding of a University of Ohio study on cholesterol intake.

They fed various groups of rabbits only high-cholesterol diets. All groups, save one, showed 40-to-50-percent increases of the bad stuff in their bodies.

The one exception showed a 20-percent decrease. They did much painstaking study to find the mysterious variable in that exceptional group.

The researcher found that the person responsible for that group stroked, touched and talked to the rabbits during feeding.

That, they concluded, was the reason for their better health.

The fact is, alienation tends to promote illness.

That's why studies (one was done by the Centers for Disease Control in Atlanta) also show that some illness is connected to a lack of a sense of humour.

Laughing boisterously for a few minutes a day is a good physical exercise —as good as jogging, I'd suggest.

Living and laughing and patting go hand in hand, just as illness and constipated personalities do.

Yes, I can see where some people will see this as a bit of rationalization.

But with my recipe for life and a bottle or two of red wine, at least you get to smile and chuckle while others frown.

Why I steal peanuts from bars to feed the squirrels

[Wednesday, August 14, 1996]

WE HAD LUNCH at the Alpenhaus Restaurant, as we always do on these occasions, to celebrate my sister Thaïs's birthday several days ago.

While the other family members were nattering away, my mother slipped me an envelope. She's 92, and her hearing and sight are going, but she's mentally as sharp as ever.

"Open it," she told me. I opened it and inside there was a photocopy of a 1639 Swiss woodcut of one Peter Shally, Shally being a variant of Schaelin, my mother's maiden name.

The woodcut shows a medieval warrior wearing full body armor seemingly in conversation with a squirrel. On the photocopy my mother had written "military man with great-great-grandfather's emblem."

And in case her son was dull-witted, my mother had thoughtfully penned the word "squirrel" next to the squirrel, as if I didn't know that the squirrel was on the family crest.

I also noticed there was a $200 cheque in the envelope. I tried to say, "But ma, it's Thaïs's birthday, not mine," but she's hard of hearing and she didn't want to know anything about that.

"You write about the squirrels," she instructed.

And she has phoned me several times since, demanding to know where the squirrel column is.

My mother has instilled in me our family obligation to squirrels and the need to feed them, especially in winter. This I do faithfully.

I steal peanuts from bars, wash the salt off and leave them for the squirrels—on the front porch for the two that live in the street trees and on the back porch for the family of three in the lane. It is these squirrels that I suspect scurry around inside my roof, driving my cat crazy with the noise.

As you might have guessed, I'm stretching this column to keep my mother happy. She didn't specify what I was to write about squirrels— just general promotional goodwill stuff, I suppose.

But after that birthday lunch, there was a front-page story in *The Gazette* about a proposal to kill gray squirrels in Britain. It seems the gray squirrel was imported from North America and has prospered in Britain, much to the detriment of its smaller relation, the British red squirrel. Something called the Joint Nature Conservation Committee wants to cull the gray squirrels.

As it happens, I bought the *London Sunday Telegraph* the other day and found a piece by one of my favorite columnists, the crotchety Auberon Waugh, titled: "Resist the red squirrel menace."

He wrote: "Last week the committee launched a campaign to kill huge numbers of one group of squirrels—whether by poisoning or by shooting or by preventing births within the group—so that another group of squirrels can expand and prosper.

"If we transfer that program to a human context—poisoning, shooting or sterilizing blacks, to make way for whites—you have a clear case of genocide crying out for immediate action by the United Nations.

"Yet many animal-lovers will support the move to cull gray squirrels if it helps the native red squirrel to survive. Once again, there are fascist, or at any rate jingoistic, undertones to all this. We have all been brought up on the myth of the pure, sweet red squirrel, English bred and born, being thrown off its ancestral woodlands by hordes of invading American tree rats, as these red supremacists call the only squirrel that most of us have ever seen.

"I have lived in the English countryside for 56 years and never seen a wild red squirrel, although I once saw one in Wales. So far as the west country is concerned, the red squirrel has been more or less extinct for the past 40 years. Most of us have been able to live happy and fulfilled lives without it. Why do so many urban folk worry about wild animals?"

Waugh, son of writer Evelyn Waugh, dismissed the committee as "a front for Nazi-style racial supremacists."

My mother and I agree.

He Could Draw a Crowd

Margo MacGillivray

NICK AUF DER MAUR first walked into my bar in the late 1970s or early eighties. I'm not sure of the exact date, but whenever it was, it changed the bar forever.

Nick was always surrounded by his cronies: a diverse group of journalists, radio people, lawyers, salesmen and writers. Great discussions went on all the time.

He could even draw a crowd watching him read his newspapers. Nick read anything from *The Globe and Mail* to *This Week in Germany*. He was a sponge for knowledge; anything you needed to know about almost any subject, Nick was sure to respond to—especially if having to do about his beloved Montreal.

On Wednesdays, Nick's column was required reading at the bar. When he would arrive pinching bums and smiling, we would make our comments. (Often one or more of us was mentioned in print, which pleased us all.)

"Good column, Nick," we'd say and he would grin. When confronted with the "absurdities of life," his opinions would be expressed in the paper by his alter ego, Claude Baloune. The bar was Nick's drop-off point for mail and phone messages. I will miss taking his messages and phoning him at home at noon to remind him that his lunch date had arrived and was waiting for him at the bar.

Media crews were always hanging around waiting to get Nick's opinion on one subject or another. This was especially true during his years as a city councillor. When Nick did his television series on the old Forum, we would turn down the music, turn up the TV and focus. It was some of Nick's best work and we all told him so.

Nick's drinking habits changed through the years; he invented various concoctions to suit his moods. After a few cocktails mid-afternoon, Nick would put down his papers and join in whatever discussion was going on at the bar.

The heated ones were his favourite and the most fun; he called it his "aerobic workout."

"Lunatics!" he'd cry and his face would turn red and his heartbeat would increase. His best discussions were with his dearest friends and at the end they would agree to disagree and carry on to the next subject. Nick's friends were part of his family and he felt at home at the bar; we are now missing our "favourite son."

His body may have tired but his spirit lives on around us. Thank you Nick for letting us be a small part of your wonderful life.

Margo MacGillivray is a daytime bartender at Winnie's. Over a period of 18 years she has also worked at Grumpy's and Woody's. Nick was a regular at them all.

[Tribute]

Nick had Rules

Lisa Van Dusen

I FIRST MET NICK at the Press Gallery Dinner in Ottawa in 1985. He was wearing a tux, a white silk foulard and a bow tie adorned with flashing red lights.

My date that evening was my then-future, now-ex-husband, L. Ian MacDonald, one of Nick's closest friends. After dinner, about ten minutes into Prime Minister Brian Mulroney's speech, Nick leaned forward and muttered "Hey, Lisa, baby...whaddaya say you meet me outside in 15 minutes?"

"Are you out of your #$%&ing mind?" I replied.

He leaned back, probably just long enough to suck a drag off a Gitane, leaned forward again and cracked, "Alright, then...make it 10."

Despite his berating me, as the evening wore on, for a whole list of offences, including fear of spontaneity, lack of discernment and, at the top of his lungs, frigidity, it marked the beginning of a cherished friendship.

There are two kinds of womanizers: the kind who love women and the kind who hate them. Nick loved women. Which is why, as a feminist, I never had trouble reconciling our friendship with my otherwise inviolable notions of offensive and inoffensive male behaviour. He was so unerringly democratic in his bum-pinching, leering, eyebrow-wagging approach to just about every female who crossed his path that it would have seemed downright peevish to take it personally.

After we'd been friends a few years and lived through enough of his entanglements, and I'd actually sulked out the odd domestic dispute of my own, astonishingly unmolested in Melissa's room, it reached the point of my complaining that his bum-pinching had become insultingly perfunctory.

But I was gratified that my status had evolved into something between one of the boys and a favourite, wayward niece. And it was heartening to know that, arcane and flexible though they may have been, Nick had rules.

For all his ranting at politicians and whipped up righteous indignation on any number of issues, from baked potatoes in aluminium foil, to the future of Confederation, Nick was possibly the least judgmental person I've ever known. And it was an unspoken condition of his friendship that you not judge Nick, no matter how concerned you might be for his health or safety.

When my marriage finally ended, Nick was one of the few friends we shared custody of, and it was a testimony to his open-mindedness that he was unfailingly loyal to both of us in the last few years of his life.

Nick was always proud of the fact that, among the things he could offer his daughter was the sense of life's endless possibilities. And the fact that Melissa grew up to be the bass player for an all-girl rant band may just prove that, in the end, Nick Auf der Maur was, along with all his other contradictory qualities, a closet feminist.

Lisa Van Dusen is an editor with UPI in Washington and a columnist for the *Ottawa Citizen*.

CLAUDE BALOUNE

Disenchantment with foreign affairs of the non-romantic kind

[Friday, November 21, 1986]

"Sometimes I feel Lenin had it right," a dejected Claude Baloune said.

"When the Bolsheviks formed their first cabinet and government and handed out the important posts, like police chief and army commander, somebody said: 'What about foreign affairs?'

"And Lenin said: 'Do we have to have them?'

"I think that demonstrates the important principle—that when it comes to foreign affairs, Lenin innately understood they should be limited to the romantic or sexual kind."

I must admit that anecdotal outburst left me a little perplexed.

"What," I asked Baloune, "does that have to do with the current state of affairs ... er, state of the world? Why do you seem so depressed?"

Baloune seemed uncharacteristically glum. As an aging roué, with a spreading bald spot he likes to call his breakdancing scar, he's weathered the vicissitudes of political life fairly well, travelling the road from the left to the right.

"Foreign affairs are mucking everything up," Baloune responded, his baggy eyes staring somewhat vacantly.

"You know I started my life as a jaded observer with the likes of Larry Zolf, mouthing left-wing platitudes until I found out the road to Damascus leads, after all, to Damascus and to all those other sordid and squalid ideological capitals.

"So, after being tricked by everything from Stalin to Pol Pot and all the wretchedness that passes for Utopian salvation, I hitched my horse to neo-conservatism and all the promise that seemed to be incarnated in the Reagan revolution.

"As you recall, their buzzwords and phrases were 'fiscal responsibility' and 'balanced budgets'. They bludgeoned us with tales of how, if government deficits continued to rise, nobody alive today would get an old-age pension; that we were mortgaging our children's future.

"Despite the fact I don't know a thing about accounting and actuarial practices, I instinctively agreed with them. After all, I didn't want myself to feel I was a fiscally irresponsible idiot.

"So then what happens? After six years of the Reagan revolution in the U.S., the deficit has doubled, from an incomprehensible $100 billion annually to a stark raving lunatic $200 billion. "That's conservative politics? The liberals might have held it to $150 billion simply by not giving the California defence industry a blank cheque.

"But anyhow, when you're committed and convinced, you tend to fudge on details like that. You want to remain convinced, so you refuse to consider the facts and make excuses.

"But now it's getting harder. No, not harder—impossible. Because of foreign affairs.

"Look at the record. Not only do I get sucked in, Brian Mulroney gets sucked in and believes what the Great Communicator says: Canada and the U.S. are the best of friends; free trade is the answer.

"As soon as free trade talks get under way, the first thing Canadians find out is what (cedar) shakes are. Nobody ever had a clue that we even had a shakes and shingles industry until they torpedoed us.

"While we discussed the Utopian idea of eliminating tariffs and promoting efficient free trade, the American administration piled on protectionist measures.

"So again, you try to fudge it off.

"So Reagan is a bit obsessed with Nicaragua. We'll overlook it because he is, after all, a master communicator and must know something we don't. We believers balanced off the Reagan administration's inconsistencies with notions that, after all, he had a strong resolve against international terrorism.

"Reagan stood up to pipsqueaks like the Libyans.

"And now what do we find out? They're arranging arms shipments to Iran, the very country that did so much to humiliate America in the hostage affair.

"Reagan's secret diplomacy has made idiots of all those who supported him. It makes you wish he stuck to screen affairs instead of foreign affairs. It makes you puke having to use that phrase 'after all' all the time."

I tried to commiserate with Baloune, another victim of failed political promise.

"Let me buy you a beer," I said.

"To hell with beer," Baloune said. "We'll have Mumm's. If Reagan can't balance the American budget, I'll just follow his example and go into total folly with my MasterCard."

Nick and Linda's wedding reception,
May 14, 1977.
(Back row) Nick's mother, sister Thaïs, Elsie Murphy,
Bob Chodos, Drummond Burgess, John Richmond.
(Front) Nick, --?, Rae Murphy.

Apocalyptic argument produces a revelation

[Monday, January 26, 1987]

IT'S A QUANTUM LEAP from discussion of the Super Bowl to biblical scholarship, but my friend Claude Baloune managed it over the weekend.

And it proved to be another example of everybody thinking he knew something, and everybody being wrong.

We were sitting in my kitchen, having a late Sunday brunch, when discussion turned to the Super Bowl. "A mismatch," Baloune harrumphed with his usual authority. "Just like last year. The Giants will steamroller 'em and then you can use Grantland Rice's lead if you want."

"What was Grantland Rice's lead?" I asked.

"You tell him, Brian," Baloune said, pointing to Brian McKenna. "You're the authority on Notre Dame."

"The thing about the Four Horsemen of the Apocalypse," McKenna said. "You know, when Rice covered the (U.S. college football) game between Army and Notre Dame for the New York Tribune back in Knute Rockne's days."

"How did it go?" I asked.

"Well, he named the Four Horsemen of the Apocalypse and … " McKenna tried to recall, "then I don't know, something about war, famine, death and pestilence."

"No, no," Baloune interrupted. "The Four Horsemen of the Apocalypse are famine, death, plague and conquest."

"I thought Christ or conquest was one of the four horsemen," I countered.

So we sat there arguing about famine, death, war, conquest, pestilence, plague and other nasty things until we concluded that there must have been six or seven horsemen of the Apocalypse. Later we were to find out we were right, sort of.

Then we got into a big argument about just what the word apocalypse meant in the first place.

"Sort of the end of the world," Baloune said.

"Yeah," I agreed. "Like a Götterdämmerung."

"No, no," McKenna said. "I think its one of those words everybody gets wrong, but it means something totally different, like eternal peace."

Well, since I had to go down to *The Gazette* yesterday afternoon, it was agreed we'd end the argument in the library and see just what the facts were.

First off, I decided to go right to the major source, *Bartlett's Familiar Quotations*, and looked up Grantland Rice.

The first quotation listed for Rice, was his most famous: "When One Great Scorer comes to write against your name . . .

"He marks—not that you won or lost—but how you played the game."

For a hardbitten sportswriter, he certainly had a kind of religious bent.

Then I found his great lead sentence used to describe a 1924 Notre Dame football game: "Outlined against a blue-grey October sky, the Four Horsemen rode again. In dramatic lore they were known as famine, pestilence, destruction and death. These were only aliases. Their real names are Stuhldreher, Miller, Crowly and Layden."

So I asked Donna MacHutchin, *The Gazette* librarian who seems to know the answer to most literary and scholarly questions, who the four horsemen were.

She came out with another variation.

So we decided to look it up in the *World Book Encyclopedia*.

It listed them as conquest, war, famine and death.

We tried the *Maryknoll Catholic Dictionary*. It said: "The first horseman is usually interpreted as being war; the others are civil strife, famine and plague."

So we tried the more authoritative looking *New Catholic Encyclopedia* (It has 1,200 pages versus only 600 for the other.)

It had a long chapter on it, explaining that it comes from the sixth chapter of the Book of Revelation by St. John the Divine in the New Testament.

In this particular revelation, God is seated with a scroll that has seven seals.

"As the first four seals are successively broken, four horsemen appear— white (representing either the victory of the Gospels or imperialism), red (war), black (famine) and pale green (pestilence and death)."

You'll be interested to know that the next two broken seals don't produce horse visions but things like earthquakes and martyrs praying. While the seventh seal (now I finally understand that Bergman film) produces seven trumpet blasts, each representing another litany of woes.

By this time I was thoroughly confused, still without a clear idea of who the four horsemen really were.

So I asked Donna to get the actual source: the Bible.

Well, without quoting directly, that left us even more confused.

So if anyone ever asks you who the Four Horsemen of the Apocalypse were, just remember that any of the 10 or so mentioned above, including Christ, can be interpreted as correct.

Finally, the word apocalypse has nothing to do with destruction or the end of the world. It is ancient Greek for revelation or disclosure.

It is only used in the current sense because some of the revelations in that book of the Bible are sort of, er, apocalyptic.

We're fair-weather fans—but who knows why?

[Monday, August 31, 1987]

Winning isn't everything, but wanting to win is.
—Vince Lombardi

"YOU'RE JUST LIKE THE REST," Claude Baloune said to me contemptuously one day last week. "This city only likes winners."

We were sitting at lunch reading the newspapers. And Baloune noticed one of my traits. I had come to the sports section and I rapidly skipped through it, ignoring most of the stories—because the Expos had lost the night before.

When the Expos win, I sit there reading through all the stories, poring over the boxscore, spending long minutes looking at the standings. When they lose, I don't want to know the details.

"The old saying that everybody loves a winner really applies to here in spades," Baloune said. "Here nobody has time for a loser. Here it's all bandwagon, whether in sports or politics.

"That's why we have such wild swings in politics. Federally, provincially or municipally, if a party wins a lopsided majority one election, the next time they get all but wiped out.

"Look at the Expos last year. Miserable attendance. This year it's up by almost a half million, almost 1.5 million paid attendance this year compared to just a million last year at this time. And look what happened to the Alouettes."

It's true, you know. We do have a funny attitude toward these things. What is it in our psychological makeup that gives Quebecers and Montrealers such a propensity for backing only winners?

Sure, there are exceptions, but the majority seems to be like that. And it's not just a French-Canadian thing. English Montrealers are like that also.

We all sit and wonder how Torontonians go on supporting the Maple Leafs and Argonauts, losing season after losing season. If they played here, we'd stay away in droves.

Other cities may back athletic teams out of civic pride or for tribal reasons.

For example, take British soccer. In Glasgow, you'll have supporters of the Rangers (the Protestant team) and those who back Celtic (the Catholics), win or lose. That's tribal.

Compare that to, say, Chicago, where they have the Cubs and White Sox in baseball. What makes the difference?

I don't know, but back in the '60s there was a comedian who used to suggest people from Chicago made great soldiers because every year White Sox fans learn how to die. Aside from the Bears football team of recent seasons, Chicago teams hardly win anything.

Our friend Neil Cameron, the John Abbott College history teacher, was sitting with us and suggested maybe our attitudes have something to do with our historical viewpoint.

"You have people, like the Arabs and the Irish, who have a sense of being on the losing side all the time," he explained.

"Most of their history in the past few centuries has been losing.

"They get the attitude that ever since some battle in 732 or 1688 or something, it's all been downhill.

"French-Canadians may see their history in a similar manner, just as maybe English-Quebecers as a group see their lives as downhill for the past many years.

"So maybe we don't like being associated with losers on the athletic fields and get very demanding of our teams. We end up with this feast-or-famine support for teams and political parties, kind of making up for historic reverses."

That reminded me of one of Pierre Bourgault's great speeches (most great orators have two or three set pieces) where he talks about how all the great heroes in French-Canadian history were losers: Montcalm, the Patriotes, Dollard des Ormeaux, Jean de Brébeuf.

That's characteristic of the minority mentality, a fear of losing coupled with pride in the valiant heroes of the past who tried and lost.

But, Baloune pointed out, there's a contradiction there. Somebody once said the British like to celebrate their defeats—say Dunkirk—as much as their victories. Ditto with the Americans when they go on about the

Alamo, or Canadians as they commemorate Dieppe. Everybody likes to savour victory, I suppose, but remembering defeat, so long as it was noble and served some purpose, also can be stimulating.

However, does any of this explain our insistence on winners?

When it comes to sports and, often, politics, we seem to forgo that through-thick-and-thin loyalty in favour of the fair-weather-friend attitude.

Are we, with our unquenchable belief that champions are the only ones who deserve our support, somehow unconscious victims of our view of historic forces?

Or is there a simpler answer?

Like, we're poor losers?

Or—and this has a ring of truth—maybe the Montreal Canadiens have spoiled us.

Of course history repeats itself, but is anybody listening?

[Wednesday, August 22, 1990]

"Do you remember a year ago?" Claude Baloune was saying. "Last August the world was full of optimism as we watched on television when the Hungarians allowed East Germans to escape to Austria.

"The Berlin Wall fell. The Cold War thawed to the point where we believed the impossible had come through. The threat, the great confrontation, was over. At home interest rates were low, business was booming and Quebec was enthralled by media hype about how our entrepreneurs—our new secular saints—were going to bring us to the promised land of clean streets, a well-scrubbed, healthy, robust, yogurt-eating populace of, if not world-beaters, then free-trading capitalist continent conquerors.

"So today how do we feel? In one year we've gone from total unmitigated optimism to apprehension. War looms in the Mideast. Meech Lake has become another Gulf. It makes you think of Vienna in the prewar years. Both wars. Cocky and confident, yet in retrospect oh so stupid."

We were walking on Sherbrooke Street. "Time and context is the vital component of confidence," Baloune exclaimed. "Look at that building," he said, pointing to the old mansion on the south side of Sherbrooke near St. Urbain that today is the headquarters of the St. Jean Baptiste Society.

"In the 1940s and '50s, the time of darkness or La Grande Noirceur, as the Duplessis years were called by the conventional thinkers of the Quiet Revolution, that building used to be the Reform Club, the club Liberals used to call home.

"The federal movers and shakers hung out there, along with their forlorn counterparts from the provincial opposition. The bleus, the Union Nationale, hung out down the road at the Renaissance Club (corner of Berri). At the time everybody must have thought it would be there forever.

"At the time, all those things seemed impermeable and immutable, like the Catholic Church. But what seemed so solid collapsed.

"But institutions don't collapse before your eyes, as in an earthquake. They are big and powerful, then they go into decline, and when they decline they are not so important, and then when they disappear as a factor people even forget they ever were even a factor.

"Today the people going into that building, the St. Jean Baptiste nationalists, are cocky and confident. So cocky that they think it's a good idea to cut off cheap Western Canadian oil and gas.

"The media tell us business leaders think sovereignty is great thing. They have yachts, Mercedes, money and influence, so they must have intelligence.

"Well, the last thing you want in life," Baloune said as his voice rose, "is to let business run social and political policy. They are nitwits when it comes to that because they are so convinced they know the bottom-line truth.

"Look at the record of the Chambre de Commerce. Two years ago they gave a standing ovation and hero's welcome to Robert Campeau after he took over all those American stores. Now he's a bust and a bankrupt. A year ago they gave Michel Gaucher a hero's welcome and standing ovation when he took over Steinberg's—with our pension money. Now Steinberg's is as healthy as Campeau.

"And in their emotionalism, they gave Lucien Bouchard a standing ovation when he declared for sovereignty. I say, watch out for standing ovations from the Montreal Chambre de Commerce. They are about as sure a thing as the Chicago futures market. You can lose your shirt."

We continued walking, and by this time we were at McGill University.

"Remember when we all congratulated ourselves that this was one of the top universities in the world?" Baloune said. "It was once. Now the only reason people from around the world come to study here is because the fees are cheap.

"The old days—and this is only 25 years ago—is when Caughnawaga was Caughnawaga and we used to go across the Mercier Bridge to see Chief Poking Fire. Now it's called Kahnawake and when we're standing in the shower trying to listen to the radio news in the morning and they mention troop movements we're not sure whether it's in Châteauguay or the Kuwait border.

"A year ago we were talking about the 'peace dividend,' how we'd put all our military savings into tax reductions or saving the environment. Now we're thinking of sending the Sûreté du Québec to Saudi Arabia because of their gas-attack expertise."

Now we were standing at the corner of McGill College looking down to Place Ville Marie.

"Buenos Aires must have looked like this," Baloune said wistfully, "before Peron and all that nonsense sunk Argentina. The analogies are all around us but most people won't see them until 20 years from now. By that time they'll have forgotten everything."

A Complete Absence of Malice

Anthony Wilson-Smith

THE PRINCIPLES that carried Nick Auf der Maur through life were, according to him, simple. "Deny everything," he would cackle, flashing his enormous beaver-toothed grin, "and make wild accusations."

But being Nick, he challenged conventional wisdom—even his own—so that his wildest stories invariably featured himself. Did he really, as he claimed, once try to take Conrad Black to a gay leather bar just to take the stuffing out of him? Maybe, maybe not: Black just smiles at the mention of Nick's name.

For a reporter seeking stories in Montreal for most of the last three decades, there was only one piece of advice—and one adviser—that really mattered. "Stick with me," Nick would say, "and you'll learn everything you need."

Seeking a leader in, say, the city's Greek or Italian communities? Nick always knew at least five—who were usually feuding with each other. Perhaps there was a requirement to cultivate a source within the Parti Québécois—no easy thing for an anglo reporter. Nick—who once paired with the late, great Péquiste Gérald Godin to represent Canada at the World Table-Hockey Championships—would, and could, supply one. Part of Nick's charm was that he brought together people who had plenty of reason to dislike each other—and whose only trait in common was their fondness for him. From his command posts at Woody's, Grumpy's, Winnie's, and Ziggy's, Nick held court with cabinet ministers, judges, journalists, undercover cops and underworld hard cases.

Once, a friend of Nick's received an anxious call in the small hours from another friend reporting that Nick had just been spotted in the back of a speeding police car, its lights flashing. A check the next morning revealed the reason: the cops had decided that their pal, a bit the worse for wear, could use a safe and speedy ride home.

For Nick, nothing succeeded like excess. His Borsalino hat and huge walrus mustache seemed to sweep into a room ahead of the rest of him. He was, as someone said of Bruce Springsteen, a "notorious heterosexual" who dated hundreds of women—and remained friends with them all. He ranted at everyone, and anyone who disagreed was pronounced a Lunatic! and Clearly Insane!

No one took offence, because he was so clearly without malice. Despite his remarkable memory and unmistakable writing style, Nick was never a great journalist in the classic definition—because he would much rather be in the thick of an event than watch it from the sidelines. He was a natural politician: Claude Ryan once wrote that Nick was the one anglophone capable of filling a church hall with admirers in the east end of the city. But even his talents in that area were sometimes obscured by his huge appreciation of the absurd—which can mean most facets of a politician's life.

In the end, Nick was one of those rare people who are so gifted in so many ways that they can be and do almost anything they want. What a great gift to so many people, then, that he devoted those talents to two things in particular: living—and giving.

Anthony Wilson-Smith is national affairs editor of *Maclean's* magazine.

TRAVELLING

Aislin's first cartoon of Nick, drawn for the
McGill Daily, 1968.

Breaking the sound barrier on a fast flight to nowhere

[Monday, June 8, 1987]

IT WAS ONE of those ideas that seemed terrific at two in the morning.

"We must go to do the Concordes," Alvira (Woody) Widman said earnestly.

"Alouettes, Woody," I replied. "They've changed the name back to the Alouettes. But I didn't know you liked football." Woody thought for a moment. Then he paused for another moment. Then it hit him.

"No, no," he shouted. "Not the football. The Concorde. The airplane that goes supersonic."

Woody, my hotel- and bar-owner friend, has a Uruguayan accent that gets ever more pronounced when we have drinks together. At 2 a.m. sometimes it's difficult to follow.

"We go up, we eat, we go supersonic, we go down," he explained rather vaguely.

"Sure, Woody, we go supersonic," I humoured him, ordering another round.

A few days later, I ran into Woody and he was beaming.

"I got the tickets," he said.

"What tickets?" I asked.

"For the Concorde," he replied.

I vaguely recalled our vague conversation.

"Where are we going?" I asked.

"Nowhere. We go up, break the sound barrier and come back," he said, smiling.

Sensing something amiss, I asked: "How much is this going to cost?"

"No much," he replied. "No much."

"How much no much?" I asked.

"Eight hundred," he said.

"Too much no much," I said.

But Woody was adamant. He went on about having to have a sense of adventure, of how many more chances would I get to go supersonic and the need to have a feeling of romance, describing how beautiful the Concorde was.

I think that was the point that got me.

Many times I've seen the Concorde on the ground at airports. And each time the sheer beauty of the aircraft impressed me. Sleek, elegant, the lines of a jet fighter.

What the heck, I thought, you only live once.

So Friday night the two of us set off for Mirabel airport. The traffic was bad and the going was slow. And we were late.

"Why they put the airport so far?" Woody asked. "It no makes any sense."

"It's a personal thing," I explained. "When the Queen Mum comes in, she lands and departs at Dorval. The same with the prime minister of Greece. When the Pope left for Rome, he flew out of Dorval. When the president of Gabon came in with his wife last year on a plane leased from Elvis Presley's estate, he came to Dorval.

"When Prime Minister Chirac of France arrives, he gets to land at Dorval. When President Mitterrand came in on his Concorde from Quebec City they let him land at Dorval.

"Big shots get to go to Dorval. Taxpayers like you and me, we have to go to Mirabel. It's one of those personal things."

"I see," Woody said.

What we didn't get to see was the Concorde. We did catch a glimpse of it on the runway about a mile away when we drove in, but otherwise it's difficult to get a view of any plane at Mirabel because you have to travel to the plane on one of those lunar transit vehicles.

But as we neared the plane, everybody was up peering through the transporter's windows, trying to get a look at the most magnificent passenger plane in the world.

The 120 seats were sold out, as they were for the seven or eight other flights scheduled on the weekend. One travel agent in Val d'Or sold 100 tickets.

Woody and I were seated in separate rows, me next to a 70-year-old foot doctor, Marcel Rivard from Trois Rivières, and Woody next to a 74-year-old retired man from Quebec City.

The average age was fairly high. Most of the passengers were male.

People I talked to said they just felt they had to fly the Concorde through the sound barrier once in their lives but they couldn't afford the $2,200-plus one-way fare from New York to London or Paris.

Inside, the Concorde has the feel and look of a 30-year-old narrow-bodied jet—not surprising, since it's basically a 20-year-old plane, using 23-year-old French and British technology.

But on takeoff, one can feel the power. It lifts off after only about 30 seconds on the runway. And it climbs at a terrific rate.

Our flight path took us toward the Massachusetts coast at a speed just under the sound barrier. (It only flies above the speed of sound over the ocean because of regulations.)

About half an hour into the flight, as we were starting to eat our passable airline dinner—Iranian caviar and filet mignon—it was announced that we were going to cross the sound barrier. We all watched the Machmeter in front as the afterburners were turned on and we went into another steep climb.

We all cheered at we hit Mach 1. We climbed. Mach 1.2 and then on until we hit Mach 2.02 (or 2,200 km/h or 1,350 miles per hour at 60,000 feet. By comparison, a regular jet flies at about 30,000 feet.)

At 60,000 feet, the sky below us was a deep purple, while above us it was the dark blue foreshadowing space.

Passengers were scampering around snapping photos and shooting video. But the windows on the Concorde are only about six by three inches.

We flew out over the Atlantic at twice the speed of sound, then turned around and came back.

Flight time: two hours.

Everybody was given a certificate saying he or she had broken the sound barrier.

Woody was exceptionally pleased, like a kid who had taken a roller-coaster ride.

"It was beautiful," he said. "But next time maybe we should go somewhere."

We're not unique

[Wednesday, March 8, 1989]

BUENOS ARIES–I was sitting in the Gran Café Tortoni, a wonderful turn-of-the-century café with 20-foot ceilings supported by Corinthian columns, in a leather chair at marble tables in a 150-foot-long wood-panelled room with billiard tables in the rear, on the Avenue de Mayo a few blocks from the Casa Rosado (the Pink House), seat of the Argentine government.

With me was Simja Sneh, a Polish Jew, a Yiddisher who fought in the Jewish Brigade of the British Army in North Africa and in Italy, all the way up to the Tyrol when the war came to an end.

He had come to Argentina ("to get as far away from Europe as possible … I tried to go to New Zealand but they wouldn't take Jews …") in 1947, having lost all his family.

He didn't speak a word of Spanish, but he became a writer, winning the Argentinian writers' association award for best author in 1977 for El Pan y la Sangre, a collection of short stories that helped earn him a reputation as the South American Isaac Bashevis Singer.

"So tell me," I asked him, "I was surprised to learn there are 350,000 Jews here in Buenos Aires. What do they do?"

"Well," he said, "a lot of them are in, what we call here, the schmatta business—clothing, leather…."

Sound familiar?

In Monday's column, I mentioned that Buenos Aires reminds one of many European cities, and that Argentina resembles Canada in many ways.

Well, in the late 19th century, when there was massive immigration from Europe and the Mediterranean, the Spanish-speaking population evidently felt threatened, so the government adopted a Spanicization law, a sort of Bill Cento Uno.

Among the provisions was a requirement that newborn children be given Spanish first names.

So I met a Japanese guy named Tadeo Suzuki, an Irishman called Miguel Collcutt, an anglo-Argentine named Jorge Simpson and noticed a major newspaper editor's name was Emilio Weinschelbaum.

354

So you see, French Quebec's worries are not so unique.

At the time, the British were the major traders and investors in Argentina, building the railways and setting up banks, while the Germans, French, Dutch, Belgians and Americans came in later.

(In 1850, there were some 10,000 English in the capital city when it had a population of perhaps 90,000. Today, there are perhaps 100,000— 15,000 registered with the Anglican church out of a population of ten million-plus.)

Today, the descendants of the original Spanish conquerors are a minority in Argentina, with only 35 percent of the 33 million people of Spanish descent, while more than 40 percent are of Italian origin.

There is a Welsh town in the south, in Chubut province, called Trelew, where they have been speaking Gaelic for six generations, and, while I was there, in the Buenos Aires *Herald*, an English daily, there were notices about the upcoming celebrations for St. Patricio Day.

The Germans have their own paper, the *Argentinsches Tagesblatt*, while the ubiquitous street kiosks offer papers and magazines from Italy, Germany, England and the United States.

But remarkably, there's a great degree of homogeneity about the Argentinian people, who display a greater degree of national identity and cohesion—except in the political sphere—than, say, Canada.

It is more akin to the U.S. melting pot—with the exception of race— than the Canadian multicultural experiment.

I'm not familiar with the rest of the country, but in terms of race, Buenos Aires is a very white city, unlike far away Rio de Janeiro.

One of the reasons for that is there wasn't much of a slave trade in Argentina, and what there was came mostly from the Portuguese in Brazil who brought them in from their African colony of Angola.

It is said that most of the blacks were killed off in the many wars fought in the last century. (Slaves were freed if they enlisted in the army.)

One such was the war of the Triple Alliance, when relatively tiny Paraguay, under a military dictator, decided to wage war simultaneously with Brazil, Uruguay and Argentina in 1865-70.

One of the results of that war was the build-up of the professional Argentine army, which later came to be heavily dominated by Italians.

Until then, a small portion of the country, which is the size of continental Europe, had been settled by whites. The vast areas of the pampas and Patagonia in the south were largely in the hands of ferocious unconquered Indians, who harassed encroaching settlers.

And so the Argentinian army embarked on the big Indian wars, clearing those territories. (As late as 1876, Indians raiding 200 miles from Buenos Aires made off with 300,000 head of cattle and 500 white captives.)

The resulting clearances killed off most of the remainder of the native Indians who hadn't been killed off during the epidemics, or by forced labour under the Spanish regime.

At the time of the Spanish conquest in the 1500s, it was estimated the Indian population was 750,000, far smaller than the 25 million in Mexico, central America and Peru.

And so today, there are only small pockets of Mapuche in the Andes in the south, along with the Guarnis and Quechas in the north near the Paraguayan and Brazilian borders.

One of the results is that unlike most other Latin American countries, there is little visible racial trace of Indians or blacks in Argentina. Visibly, the population is very European.

There are large numbers of Syrians, Lebanese and Moroccans. All people of Arab descent are called Turcos, as they came from the Ottoman Empire, while all Jews, no matter where they come from, are called Russos, because the big immigration started in the late 1800s by refugees from the pogroms in Russia.

(Sneh's wife told me they play the tango with balalaikas, and have asados—the traditional big barbecue—with gefilte fish. Also, the Jewish gaucho is no myth.)

One day I went to have a look the Jewish neighbourhood of Once, a kind of St. Urbain Street area near the Plaza Miserea. And most of the many shops are now run by Koreans, of whom over 100,000 have arrived in recent years.

One community that has become more discreet lately is the once very powerful anglo-Argentine, although their contribution is still very visible in terms of street names, companies, shops, cafés—London City, Richmond Salon de tea, cocteles y salon de billares—and domestic whiskey brands—Blackjack, Breeders' Choice, Hunting Lodge.

The Falklands (Malvinas) war had that impact.

One of the major landmarks in Buenos Aires is a tall clock tower next to the Retiro railway station (which looks like a copy of one in Liverpool or London.) The area is known as English Town.

The clock tower was called Torre des los Ingles—Tower of the English.

Now it's called Tower of the Argentine Air Force.

Sort of like what happened to Dorchester Boulevard.

Sipping from Imelda's teacups

[May 3, 1989]

HONG KONG–Peel Street seemed like an immensely daunting climb, especially in the hot and muggy heat of a tropical afternoon.

Peel Street in Hong Kong is a heck of a lot steeper than Montreal's Peel Street. It's so steep that the sidewalks are actually stairs. Hong Kong is very hilly, with narrow, winding and twisting roads snaking up ravines and Victoria Peak, which dominates the city's central core.

I was staying at Davie Kerr's place on Staunton Street, which runs perpendicular between Peel Street and Old Baily Road, not far from Rednaxela Street, so named because many years ago the Chinese signmaker inadvertently spelled Alexander backwards.

Kerr is an old friend from Montreal who moved here a few years ago. He's a hockey nut and we used to watch the Montreal Canadiens and the Junior Canadiens together years ago. (His father was Davie Kerr Sr., one of the first Canadians to appear on the cover of *Time* magazine, back in 1938 when he was the star goalie for the New York Rangers. He won the Vezina trophy in 1940, when the Rangers won the Stanley Cup.)

Anyhow, one day last week, we had just finished watching a two-week-old replay of the Los Angeles-Edmonton seventh game on Hong Kong TV and Kerr had given me directions to the laundry on Caine Street, at the top of Peel Street.

I looked up Peel, daunted by the effort it would take to walk up that incline in the steamy heat, and decided there must be some other, less arduous route up to that laundry.

And so I was huffing up Old Baily Road when I walked by a fancy antique store, Theodore & Alexander Goff Ltd. It looked air-conditioned so I walked in to take a break and look around.

Now, I had just that morning been reading in the *Hong Kong Standard* about the arrest in Switzerland of billionaire Saudi arms dealer Adnan Kashoggi, accused of helping Ferdinand and Imelda Marcos plunder the Phillipines. (There was also another story that morning about Pamella Bordes, described as "a tiresome tart," the centre of the latest political sex scandal in England, who was used as sex bait by Kashoggi in business deals.)

Among other things, Kashoggi was accused of ferrying millions of dollars of antiques out of Manila for a period of 18 months prior to the Marcos overthrow. He is said to have used a private Lear jet and his luxury yacht (now owned by Donald Trump) to bring much of it into Hong Kong.

What a bunch of venal jerks these people are, I had thought to myself as I read the stories.

Those stories came freshly to mind in the antique store as I found myself standing in front of a glass cabinet staring at pieces of a beautiful Limoges dinner set, gracefully designed in cobalt blue and gold.

And right in the middle of the plates, in 24 carat gold leaf, was a highly-flourished monogram with the initials "IRM," for Imelda Romaez Marcos.

"They come from Limoges's 'Grande Prestige' series at the turn of the century," the manager told me. "It was probably owned by a royal family, and some time later Imelda's monogram was added. It could have been a gift from someone like the Shah of Persia."

I peered at the price list: $2,700 for a dinner plate. (The Hong Kong dollar was at about 6.5 to the Canadian dollar.)

I sat down on a silver-framed velvet armchair. It turned out to be an 1860 Anglo-Indian chair, one of four given to Imelda Marcos by a maharaja.

They were going for $73,000 each.

I peered across the room into an elaborately gilded arched mirror, on a carved century-old French console. Hers too. Price, $74,000.

The manager said they had a terracotta bust of the exiled First Lady, but styled after Elizabeth Taylor. That had been snapped up.

All the pieces came from a Manila antiques dealer, she said.

But she was vague on the details because, she said, they were acquired before she came to this antique shop.

I asked to see some of the other items from the 60-service dinner set and she brought out teacups, side plates, salad plates, demi-tasses, soup bowls and some other oddly-shaped porcelain we couldn't figure out the use for.

She showed me a letter from Haviland, the Paris firm that produces Limoges, authenticating the set. (But the exact provenance was not given, because the Paris office couldn't locate the records.)

It's kind of funny reading about such things in the morning papers, and then stumbling on them on the way to the Chinese laundry.

The next morning, l woke up early and asked Kerr if he'd like a coffee.

"Sure," he mumbled from his bed.

I brought the coffee and the morning paper into his bedroom.

"What's this?" he said looking at the cup.

"Cheers," I said lifting up my cup. "These are $2,000 teacups. Does the coffee taste any better?"

Later that day, quite by accident, I bumped into Channel 12's Don McGowan, who was in town doing his "Travel Travel" show.

We shared a beer, and he showed off some of the things—pearls and the latest Walkman he had bought in Hong Kong, which is one great shopping city.

"What did you get?" he asked.

"Oh," l said casually, "some of Imelda Marcos's teacups."

It's amazing how there is a bit of the snob in all of us.

Far-flung travellers' tales sometimes end up covering same ground

[Wednesday, November 25, 1992]

THERE'S BEEN a lot of to-ing and fro-ing among people I've chatted with recently, so today we have some notes about travellers.

Last week a bunch of us gathered together for drinks, sort of a send-off for Brian McKenna, the evening before he went to join his brother Terence for a well-deserved vacation in Florida after all that controversy over his TV series "The Valour and the Horror." We were joined by our former CBC colleague Mark Phillips, the red-haired ex-Montrealer who works for CBS News out of Washington, D.C., in town for a family visit.

Mordecai Richler was there, just back from a trip to Germany, Israel and Egypt.

"Tell them the typewriter story," I badgered Richler.

Reluctantly, Richler repeated his story.

He can't use a computer and prefers to work on old manual type-writers, which are hard to come by these days, and even harder to find a repairman for.

Anyhow, for this trip he purchased a new electric typewriter. On his arrival at Tel Aviv airport, the typewriter was inadvertently left behind on a luggage cart.

When he arrived in Jerusalem, he had his hotel call the airport to see if they had found the typewriter.

"Yes, we did," an airport official said. "We blew it up."

Being security-conscious, they get very serious with lost luggage.

So, we got to telling travel anecdotes.

McKenna recounted a story about an eight-part TV series he made some years ago, for sports networks, about bigtime stars.

The idea was that they'd do profiles on individual athletes, but combine them with some other angle to produce a travel piece, too. So they'd do quarterback Joe Montana, and take him back to the University of Notre Dame and add in some sports history. They'd do baseball catcher Gary Carter, and take him to Japan, etc.

They decided to take boxing star Sugar Ray Leonard to England and do some historical stuff about the birth of boxing.

As an extra fillip, McKenna decided they should travel aboard the Queen Elizabeth II and have Leonard spar with the ship's boxing champ while they all had a pleasant trip.

Leonard's wife couldn't make the trip by ship, and arranged to fly over and meet them in London. Leonard travelled with his young son.

When Leonard's wife arrived in London, she asked their son how he liked the boat trip.

Terrific, he answered, except that sometimes he didn't get much sleep in their suite because of all the noise from daddy's parties.

But the ladies were real nice, he added.

Well, Mrs. Leonard got real frosty. In fact, it was difficult to get her to co-operate with the filming over there. Mr. Leonard acted sheepish.

McKenna went on regaling the folks with travel anecdotes, but I had to leave Grumpy's and go over to Le Soubise, a Ste. Catherine Street restaurant where I had arranged to meet Otis Nixon, the Atlanta Braves' star outfielder who had those two dramatic last at-bats—two outs, bottom of the ninth, ditto bottom of the 11th—in the last game of the World Series last month.

Nixon was visiting Tony Macklovitch, a real-estate man and friend of mine. The two became friends when Nixon was with the Expos and was the only player to live in Montreal year-round.

Despite what one may think because of his well-publicized incident over cocaine use, Nixon is a quiet, diffident man, mild-mannered, intelligent and very likable. Also he's a teetotaler, but I can overlook things like that.

I've met a lot of athletes in my time. Nixon doesn't fit the usual athlete's image, since there isn't an ounce of braggadocio, affectation or swagger in him. If comparisons need to be made, he's a Bob Gainey type.

Anyhow, he was here with his girlfriend Juanita to relax in a town that he feels close to, just to chat quietly with friends.

After a couple hours, he left to return to Macklovitch's house for an early night, leaving me and Macklovitch to finish our drinks.

"A really swell guy," I said to Macklovitch, "but I didn't get that part about building two houses in different suburbs of Atlanta."

Nixon's girlfriend had said they were both building large, new homes and the two of them hadn't decided which house to live in together.

Also, I noticed she was very elegantly dressed, with a fair amount of discreet but expensive-looking jewelry.

"Who was she?" I asked.

"Oh," Macklovitch replied, "she used to be Sugar Ray Leonard's wife."

Small world, eh?

Don't make enemas while abroad

[July 6, 1994]

TODAY'S TOPIC is vacation travel tips. The first tip concerns language. Make sure you know what you're saying in a foreign tongue. The other day, I was sitting in an outdoor café with a Chilean businessman, Patrick Davila, and his niece, Stella.

We were discussing travels and travails.

Davila informed me that former Chilean dictator Augusto Pinochet was kicked out of Holland after it was discovered he checked into a hotel under an assumed name. Asked if I had ever visited Chile, I answered no, but volunteered that I had spent quite a bit of time in Argentina.

Oh, Davila asked, you speak Spanish?

Well, in my travels in various countries I have mastered certain key Spanish phrases and words.

To impress him, I asked in my flawless Spanish: "Donde esta el lavado, por favor?" The two of them broke out in laughter.

What, I asked, did I forget to put an upside down '?' at the beginning of the question?

No, they informed me, you asked "Where is the enema?"

Lavado is enema while lavabo is washroom.

This would explain all the funny smirks those Buenos Aries maître d's and waiters were always giving me.

I always thought it had to do with the way I used to order beer in Buenos Aires: "Por favor, dos cervezas und mach schnell schweinhund."

Ho, ho, I got a lot of laughs with my clever use of language.

Next travel tip: stay away from massage parlours.

A few years ago, I was visiting Hong Kong.

It was the end of the day and I felt exhausted from walking around (it's a very hot and hilly place).

I spotted a sign announcing a massage parlour. Now this being British Hong Kong, a massage parlour is exactly that, not a sex emporium.

So I went in and asked for a soothing massage.

It was one of those affairs where the lady walks up and down your back.

It was most relaxing and pleasant. I fell asleep during it.

When I woke up, I noticed a sign advertising various other extras. One of them was a pedicure for something like three bucks.

Well, I had never had a pedicure in my life. My feet were still sore from all that walking so I decided, why not?

I was escorted into an informal lounge with a TV set, showing a Chinese movie, and three guys sitting there smoking cigarettes and drinking cognac (a very popular beverage in Hong Kong).

One guy was getting a pedicure from a man who looked to be about 60. The other two were waiting their turns. I sat down and ordered green tea from a waiter and flipped through Chinese magazines looking at the pictures.

After about 20 minutes, the pedicurist got to me.

One peculiar thing I noticed is he didn't have scissors or a nail clipper. Rather, he had a scalpel-like instrument. This was all new to me, you understand.

Well, the man busily set to work doing whatever it is pedicurists do, pulling my toes this way and that.

After about three toes, I lost my fascination and stopped watching, going back to the magazines.

Several minutes later, I glanced down and saw blood on one of my toes. His scalpel must have slipped.

Then this incredible thought materialized instantaneously in my brain: Wait a minute, he pedicured who knows how many people with that same scalpel that I didn't notice being sterilized and maybe I'm going to get AIDS and nobody in Montreal is going to believe me when I say I got AIDS from a pedicure.

COGNAC! I bellowed. DOUBLE COGNAC, I indicated by alternately waving my hands up and down, and showing two fingers and shouting just in case they understood English.

The waiter came running over with the snifter full of Remy Martin.

I grabbed it and immediately poured it on the cut. The pedicurist moved back in alarm. The waiter looked befuddled.

There was still some cognac in the snifter. Maybe if I soak my toe in it, it will work better as a disinfectant, my brain suggested.

Neither the pedicurist nor the waiter spoke English so I couldn't explain to them why my toe was stuck in the cognac snifter.

For fun, I tried walking with the snifter on my toe. An odd sensation.

Anyhow, fortunately I didn't have to go around explaining how I got AIDS from a pedicure, a story, of course, nobody would have believed.

So to summarize: when travelling, keep your mouth shut and your socks on.

I could have been in Havana with the Pope

[Sunday, January 25, 1998]

THE POPE IN CUBA. Sort of helpful in taking our minds off our weather. And reminding me of my youth.

About 25 years ago, aside from whatever day jobs I may have had, I was involved in publishing a left-wing, muckraking magazine called *Last Post*. It was sort of semi-underground and low-budget, but we had a lot of young talent involved, people like Terry Mosher (Aislin) and Mark Starowicz, later to be the CBC wunderkind.

Back in those days, I was always trying to promote the magazine. It used to be my habit to go to the Metropolitan News shop on Peel Street at Ste. Catherine and pull out all the business-reply cards from *Time* magazine, take them to the tavern and write insults on them, then send them to *Time*. The trick was they were business-reply cards, so *Time* had to pay the postage for the insults.

Hey, we were revolutionaries.

One day, I was in Metropolitan News, surreptitiously taking out all the *Time* business-reply cards, when I noticed a man in the back pick up a copy of our magazine, *Last Post*.

"Hey!" I yelled so everybody in the store could hear me. "I see you're buying *Last Post*. Terrific magazine. Great reading. Everybody should buy it."

This was my idea of promotion.

Well, the odd thing was, the man got very nervous. He threw down the magazine and bolted for the front door.

I followed him out, but he started running. Strange. I raced after him. It took me about two blocks to catch up with him. But when I did, he thought I was going to arrest him.

Well, it turns out he was the international director of *Prensa Latina*, the Cuban press agency, and he had been sent to Montreal to try to set up an operation here.

He thought I was with the police, but I was able to convince him I was one of the editors of the *Last Post*. In fact, he was looking at it with the vague idea of contacting us for help.

"No problem," I assured him. "Me and my associates will take charge of everything."

There were problems, like AT&T having the only cable to Cuba from Florida and they wanted to charge *Prensa Latina* an outrageous $29,000 a month for its use.

In those days (this will require an explanation some other time), I used to have a valet, David Crandell. I put him in charge of the *Prensa Latina* project, and decided to make Drummond Burgess, our full-time editor, the official *Prensa Latina* representative in Canada.

At the last minute, Burgess declined, saying he didn't want to be a Cuban agent (he's now the editor of the Ontario legislature *Hansard*, the official record of proceedings and debates). So we scrounged around, and came up with an out-of-work Argentine journalist, Alberto Rabiolta.

Before the operation was up and running, Terry Mosher and I decided to go to Cuba to check things out.

Back then, the only cheap, practical way of getting to Cuba was to take a tourist-package tour to Varadero Beach. So we ended up on the beach, trying frantically to contact Havana for them to send someone to fetch us.

Finally, two cars arrived at the same time, one a Volkswagen driven by a guy who had fought in the hills with Raul Castro, and the other an Alfa Romeo driven by two government hotshots.

The hotshots won out and took us to Havana for what I remember was a lot of rum, a baseball game and touring some cultural institutes.

The government placed at our disposal a 1955 Cadillac and driver. Needless to say, we had fun. But I categorically refused to go visit any model farms or factories or anything.

Some time later, back in Montreal, we got the *Prensa Latina* operation up and running, short-circuiting AT&T by going through the United Nations.

As the *Prensa Latina* representative, Alberto Rabiolta had a habit of quoting me in practically every story he wrote out of here. Back in Havana, the officials—little of this stuff ever got into print—must have thought the two most important politicians in Canada were Pierre Trudeau and Nick Auf der Maur, because that's who got quoted all the time.

Then I'd get invitations to go to Havana. A funny thing happened when

I did go. The *Prensa Latina* people and people from Minrex, the minister of external affairs, would both be at the airport to meet me, both claiming I was their guest. They used to fight over me.

The thing was, back in those days, all sorts of left-wing blowhards were making pilgrimages to Cuba to do things like voluntary cane-cutting work and other stuff to help the revolution.

I refused any of that. All I wanted to do was bars, babes, restaurants and baseball games.

So as you can imagine, my Cuban handlers much preferred my company than the dour revolutionary types.

After a couple of trips, they made an arrangement that *Prensa Latina* would get me for three days; after lunch on the third day, they'd turn me over to Minrex.

This was all fine when I was naive and waxing about the wonders of the revolution. But after a few visits, the scales started falling from my eyes, and things weren't as free and delightful as I had thought—it was basically a totalitarian regime.

So, basically, my relations with the Cubans cooled and I lost contact with them.

But a couple of years later, there was one of those public inquiries into the RCMP and subversive stuff.

One day, I read that an RCMP agent at the enquiry identified Alberto Rabiolta as the head of DG6, Cuban intelligence in Canada.

Well, I thought, if Alberto was head of Cuban espionage in Canada and I recruited him for the job, what did that make me? I've always wanted to see the RCMP files on me.

There was one other thing that could have been an interesting turning point in my life, but wasn't.

When I was a teenager, my mother thought I was heading for trouble and misfitdom, so she made enquiries to see whether she could enroll me in the Pope's Swiss Guard in Rome. Nothing came of it, thank heaven.

But can you imagine, if she had succeeded? I might be in Havana today. Head of the Pope's security detail.

Ah, Spring! Time to plot!

Brian McKenna

IT WAS SPRING in Montreal, and conspiracy was in the air. On Mountain Street, downstairs at the Bistro, Nick was at the zinc bar, angled in newspaper Zen, absorbing the latest on Vietnam from *Le Monde*. He was alone, sipping pastis and water, a cloud of yellow haze in a glass tumbler. A fellow conspirator moved through the regulars, greeting him with a touch on the shoulder, sotto voce:

"How you doing?"

"Oh, you know, stumbling along."

Nick looked just fine. He was wearing a blue cotton Mao jacket, plain and unadorned, just like the crazies of the Cultural Revolution. But Nick set himself apart, with among other things, a tie, the same yellow as the Pernod. This was before the Duck, and the Borsalino, when there was still a sheaf of black hair. The look, half revolutionary, half vagabond, was completed with a khaki shirt, wool pants, and espadrilles.

"Hear about the wooden horse…" he started. Eyes rolled at the old ritual joke.

On the bar this evening was a pressing question—where to find the ingredients for a bomb, wholesale.

"There's a place on the Main where we can get gallons of ketchup. But we're still looking for cottage cheese in bulk."

Nick received the report solemnly. Ghosts curled up from a Gitane, just stubbed out in the bar ashtray. He pulled out another, last in the blue box. He took the empty pack in his fingers, gently jangling the copper bracelets on his wrist.

"Georges!," he said, hailing the bartender. Everyone looked up to watch the nightly performance. Georges was Parisian, vintage in a white shirt and black vest, busy washing glasses. Nick gestured at him to back away. From a distance of some 30 feet, Nick let fly at a stainless steel pail. There was a smattering of mock applause, as he dunked the cigarette box on the first try. "Voila!", he uttered in triumph, the same grin, roguish, toothy below the bushy mustache, that erupted for victorious revolutions, and all matter of conquests, large and small.

The latest revolutionary act was proving difficult to organize, and time was running out. Richard Nixon was soon to make a state visit to Ottawa. The United States was bombing the shit out of North Vietnam. So the plan was to stage a kamikaze protest, bombing the U.S. embassy in Ottawa from the air, then landing on Parliament Hill in front of the Peace Tower to surrender. Two more conspirators made an entrance. There were greetings all around. Said Nick: "Any news on a pilot?"

"There's a lot of American deserters around, but so far no helicopter guys. It would be great to find a gunship pilot."

Nick addressed the problem by unwrapping a new pack of Gitanes. This was a ritual enjoyed as much as midnight mass, but more often. The cellophane crinkled like fire. He pulled off silver foil, sniffing the incense of fresh tobacco, and selected the middle cigarette in the perfect white row. From a pocket he produced a lighter, a brass type favoured by doomed World War I officers. There was a sudden flare of flame. He lit the cigarette as carefully as an altar boy, taking a deep drag, and blew out smoke in a steady stream: "What if we can't find a deserter?"

"Maybe we can get Jesse Winchester to do it," offered one of the conspirators.

"You lunatic," Nick said with a sudden shout. "You're insane. He's a draft dodger. He's never flown a plane. You think he's going to bomb someone with his guitar!" At the sound of the word bomb, the crowd at the bar stopped talking, and looked over. Nick was undeterred.

"Idiot!" he shouted, but it was the coup de grâce. Now he realized that he might be going too far. The RCMP had been poking around too much recently. The bartender delivered a fresh round of drinks. The regulars went back to more important things, the Canadiens having won seven in a row. The plotting went into high gear. "Maybe Barbara Emo will do it! She's got her pilot's license."

"Good idea! All she has to do is fly over so one of us can drop a garbage bag on the embassy."

"We'll need back-ups in case the first one misses."

"Claire Culhane demands a spot on the plane. She says she's earned the right to be arrested."

"What if there's a no fly zone, and they shoot us down?"

"Details!"

"What if the bag plummets down and nails some poor security guard?"

"We're not going to kill anyone with a garbage bag full of cottage cheese and ketchup."

"I dunno, its not like flinging a Gitanes pack."

Nick grew thoughtful. He stroked his mustache... "From that height, you never know."

This gave everyone pause. The idea of headlines around the world had been too delicious for words. Anti-war Protesters Bomb U.S. Embassy with Nixon's Favorite Lunch. Now we grew gloomy at the prospect of sanity prevailing. The meeting adjourned to the back of the Bistro. On a sheet of white paper laid as a tablecloth, Georges scribbled orders for bifteck, frites, and red wine In the silence, Nick lit another Gitane. "Wait a minute. The other night I met this guy... ."

Journalist and filmmaker Brian McKenna first conspired with Nick in 1966.

[Tribute]

A Warning from the Goddaughter

Robin Siobhan McKenna

"THIS IS MY GODDAUGHTER," Nick announces.

"He's my moral compass," I add.

My parents' choice: their spiritual heir, the guy to teach me my lessons in life. "I ruined her baptism!" he chortles, gleeful about some marital disaster. That was the beginning. Nick taught me to be a troublemaker.

Valentine's Day, I'm 20 years old. Forget the boys I know. I want a date with Nick.

I sit on the barstool beside him, drag him out of his newspaper, torment him with questions about life. Shouldn't we rescue society by building communities, like the town in New York State that's replaced money with a barter system?

"RIGHT, Robin, we'll all go live in COMMUNES!"

"Oh, now you're a practical realist?" My irony is lost. Nick puts down his drink, yells my argument down. I'm reduced to tears, he takes me out to dinner.

He's excited about the pasta bar: baked garlic on the menu, I have to try the baked garlic. He's yelling at the bartender about his Italian mother. Me, I have more questions for Nick the radical. If he were my age now— what he would be fighting for? He thinks and pours red wine from a jug and tells me: "That's for you to figure out."

No big answers just now. He leaves to "check the plumbing," he comes back excited, there's Italian lessons playing in the bathroom, do I know the story of the Roman emperors and the lions and the ship that sank?

I love my godfather because he's excited about life.

Campaign rooms, pinball machines, stolen fedoras, margaritas "LUNA-TICS" (from him that's a compliment). When Nick bought me sandals for travelling I jumped through a skylight in Paris, kept the bloody shoe to show him. He squirmed. I think he was proud.

My godfather kept forgetting how to spell my name. He gave me huge books, Sherlock Holmes, Mark Twain. He never, ever took me to church.

Growing up with Nick. How to work without really trying. How to make onion sandwiches, crash parties, break hearts. Why stories have to be told—and the world turned upside-down. How to live like a free spirit: the real thing.

Danger since the beginning: my parents threatened me with military school. They should have known, it was all their fault.

Watch out, Montreal. I learned from Nick Auf der Maur.

FAMILY

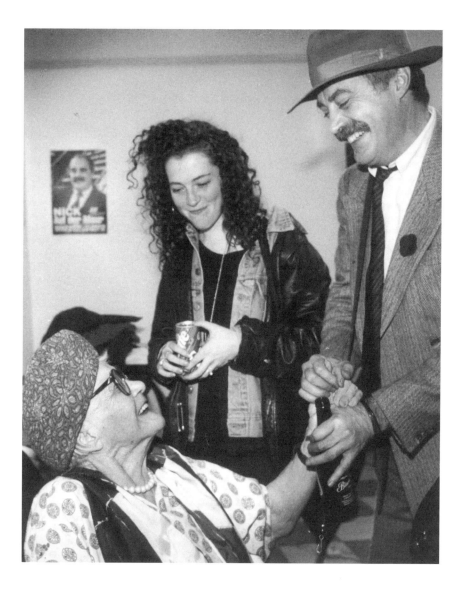

Nick, with Melissa, is congratulated by his mother,
November 4, 1990.
Photo by John Kenney.

That first job is a major step toward adulthood and independence

[Friday, January 25, 1985]

QUICK NOW, what have been the most exciting, enthralling moments of your life?

There probably have been many, but one of them probably was your first job.

This week, my 12-year-old daughter, Melissa, landed her first job.

She has joined the company. Melissa is now a *Gazette* delivery girl, or person, or whatever they call them these days.

This had absolutely nothing to do with either myself or her mother. She, on her own initiative, with encouragement from friend Anna, applied for and got a paper route.

I only learned about it after the fact.

When she told me about— it the prospects, the money, the plans and all—memories of that first innocent, starry-eyed enthusiasm I felt when I got my first job came rushing back.

As it happens, my first job was as a *Montreal Star* delivery boy. I then moved into the corner grocery beer boy line, then I got four *Gazette* routes on Côte des Neiges that paid me more money than my first regular job with this paper ($35 a week as a copy boy).

What does a first job mean to a kid? Well, I suppose independence is the biggest part of it. The first step toward being able to support yourself, of not being totally dependent on others.

It's only a paper route, you may say. Talk to a kid who has just started one. It's as big a thing in their lives as the day some of us get promoted to vice-president.

It's a big deal.

Listening to my daughter talk, telling of her first days delivering papers in the cold, dark morning, the enthusiasm was infectious.

The third day on the job, she and Anna found their pile of 35 papers outside the house along with one of those "fault notices."

The notice said that 2168 such-and-such a street complained of "erratic delivery."

Here they were at 6:15 in the morning, new in the business. It was cold, snowing and very dark. The two girls checked their subscriber list and 2168 wasn't on it. They looked back at the notice.

"What does erratic mean?" Melissa asked Anna.

Anna, who is a year older, pondered the question. With rather sensible logic, considering that 2168 wasn't on the subscriber list but 2170 was, she concluded that "erratic" meant noisy.

So the two of them tiptoed up 2170's steps, whispering "shhh" to each other, and 2168 continued to go without delivery.

It was terrific just hearing these anecdotes.

Melissa told me of the grumpy lady (every newspaper route has one grumpy customer) who gave a 15-cent tip after haranguing the two girls for 10 minutes for the faults of the previous delivery boy.

Then Melissa told me about the dark, scary inside stairway at one particular address. "The first day we went in, we heard a dog barking, so we just threw the paper in at the bottom of the stairs. The second day, we heard burping."

"Burping? You heard burping in the apartment?" I asked.

"Well, it sounded like burping," she said, "so we threw the paper at the bottom of the stairs again."

All of this was told with the gusto of an Amazon explorer recounting details of some perilous adventure.

Stairways, normally unremarkable, are harrowing; quiet street corners become major landmarks; the district manager's chance remarks are gospel.

Of course, when we were kids there weren't any newspaper girls. That's just the way it was.

"Now, about 20 per cent of our carriers are girls," *Gazette* circulation manager Michael Kirby said yesterday. "And most of our district managers say that girls are probably better at the job. They're a little more reliable, more conscientious—a little more mature, I suppose.

"They don't last as long as boys, though. The average stay is a year or so. But in general our carriers are now lasting longer then they used to.

"Also, the average age has moved up to about 14 or 15 from 13 or so. That's because of the lack of other part-time jobs and the fact that we pay more now. The kids used to make 22 cents a week per paper just a couple of years ago. Now it's 57.5 cents. On average, they're now taking home about $30 a week plus tips."

To conclude, here's a tip from Ted Blackman to all newspaper delivery kids who worry about one of the most perplexing problems in the business.

What do you do about all those people who pay for the paper at the office, thereby depriving the kid of a tip?

"You're allowed," Blackman told Melissa, "to drop by every month or so and ask the person: 'Has the delivery service been satisfactory? Is everything OK?'"

Funny, as a delivery boy, I never twigged to that.

Baby Nick and family.
August 26, 1942.

Turkeys Switzerland-bound: Baggage handlers must hate to see me

[Friday, July 19, 1985]

MY 82-YEAR-OLD MOTHER'S sense of frugality comes, I suppose, from having survived the Depression.

Whenever somebody in the family is going on a plane trip, mom worries that he or she won't take the full baggage allowance.

Until a few years ago, transatlantic passengers could take 20 kilograms of baggage. Now travellers' luggage is limited by volume.

Back in 1968, our whole family decided to go back to visit Switzerland together.

My mother arrived at the airport with her own bags, plus a clanging collection of other baggage.

When my own bag only registered 11 kg on the check-in scale, she rummaged around and gave me a cardboard box, a bunch of aluminum pots tied together and a lawn chair. These items brought my luggage up to the weight limit.

Why we had to take aluminum pots and lawn chairs to Switzerland, I wasn't exactly sure. But my mother was adamant that we weren't going to waste any cargo space.

So my two sisters, my father and mother and I flew off to Switzerland loaded down like war refugees fleeing with our meagre possessions.

A few years later, I was flying to Italy on my honeymoon. Before we left for the airport, my mother showed up with a big suitcase filled with old clothes.

The suitcase was labelled: "For the poor of Rome, care of the Pope."

"Ma, I don't want to drag around a huge old suitcase," I told my mother. "We're travelling light because we don't want to be weighed down. Besides, we're not going to Rome."

"Well," she instructed, "just take the suitcase to the Milan train station. Leave it sitting somewhere in public. And when somebody steals it, it will probably be because they're poor. So it'll be delivered."

Once I embarked on something called the "Nick Auf der Maur-Stephen

Phizicky-CJAD Personality Tour of the Soviet Union."

My mother loaded me down with individually packed plastic shopping bags, stuffed into my luggage. Each contained items like old jeans, shirts, socks and underwear that she had acquired at rummage sales. She gave me about 20 of these bags and told me to give them to deserving people.

"Leave some of them in church pews, or even a synagogue" she said. "I want some believers to get a little present."

So in Kiev and Leningrad and Moscow, I went on these little side trips, dropping off plastic bags on buses, in churches and just giving them to old ladies selling flowers on the street.

It was as though we were operating our own foreign-aid program.

My mother is a very practical person who believes in practising her Roman Catholic virtue of charity.

Last week, my mother, my daughter Melissa and I were preparing for another visit to Switzerland, to show Melissa her roots.

Now that baggage is limited by volume rather than by weight, I was wondering what approach my mother would take.

She called me up and said:

"Turkeys, they're heavy and don't take up too much room. We're going to take frozen Butterball turkeys to Switzerland."

"Frozen Butterball turkeys!" I exclaimed. "Ma, they're richer than we are in Switzerland. It's Ethiopia where they're starving."

"They don't have turkeys in Europe," she answered. "It's a North American bird and we're not going to leave all that weight unused."

My mother went out and bought the turkeys and Melissa and I loaded up on real Montreal smoked meat—plus a ham and a tin of cranberry sauce.

While you are reading these lines, we are in Switzerland—we left on Monday—preparing a Thanksgiving meal for our Swiss relatives.

City kid goes back in time—and gets a renewed appreciation of his roots

[Monday, August 12, 1985]

EVERY SUMMER, Europe and Africa and just about everywhere, I suppose, are awash with North Americans out to discover their roots.

In little town halls in Normandy, there is a steady stream of French Canadians looking up old birth and parish records, trying to trace ancestors who were among the first immigrants to hit Canada. For some it's a compelling search, for others merely curiosity. But for whatever reason, most of us at one time or another go back to discover our roots.

This summer, I decided it was time to show my daughter from whence we came—Switzerland. So we, along with my mother and joined by my two sisters, went to visit relatives and the towns my parents left in the 1920s.

My father comes from Schwyz, a little town off the big lake that Lucerne sits on. That town, which is the capital of a canton called Schuyz, gave Switzerland its name—Schweiz in Swiss German. The Swiss flag comes from the canton's white cross emblem.

The canton of Schuyz formed the Swiss confederation in 1292 along with the cantons of Uri and Unterwalden, which is where my mother comes from.

As do many Europeans, both my mother's and father's family keep family trees; my mother's goes back several hundred years, while the Auf der Maurs' goes back to the year 958 or thereabouts.

Schwyz was a walled town, and the first Auf der Maur (which means "on the wall") ran a tavern in the town wall. (Whenever I go into a bar and have a drink, I can validly claim to be maintaining 1,000 years of family tradition.)

Today, Schwyz is a quiet little place that express trains zip through and, among other industries, boasts the Victorinox factory that makes Swiss Army knives.

My mother's home town is Sachseln, whose chief claim to fame is that it is the burial place of St. Nicklaus von Flue, who is Switzerland's patron saint as well as mine.

Sachseln also boasts the home of Birkemuesli, the original Swiss crunchy granola factory.

Most early Swiss history occurred in that area of central Switzerland. That is the locale of William Tell and Heidi and the various battles where the Swiss were beating off the Austrians or Burgundians or Napoleon. When they were at peace they sent off mercenary troops to fight for just about every crowned head of Europe.

So, on arriving at Zurich airport loaded down with my 83-year-old mother's army duffle bags we headed off to Sachseln, a town that easily fits the cliché image of as-neat-as-a-pin, story-book Swiss village, nestled in a lake valley surrounded by beautiful mountains. This is Heidi land.

My mother's family were farmers—peasants in the vernacular. And they made cheese.

So we're talking basic Swiss here.

In the summer, they take the cows up to the high mountain valleys. The lower pastures are used to produce hay for winter feeding.

They've been doing this for over 1,000 years, but lately some farmers have increased the use of commercial grain feed. As a result of the cows' changing diet, the holes in some Swiss cheeses are coming out smaller and the Swiss cheese industry is alarmed. Research teams are looking into how to keep the holes big.

However, one of my cousins operates a small herd in the old manner.

The cows all have these big bells and the men all yodel and play the alp horn. Nowadays, though, all those rustic little mountain cabins are equipped with CB radios.

We trudged up to my cousin's mountain valley cabin, right up in the clouds just a couple hundred feet below the peaks. After an exhausting climb up the steep, twisting cow trails, we found that my cousin's son and all the other young farmers go up on trail motor bikes.

We spent a day and night there, making cheese and butter, taking in the scenery and breathing mountain air.

We also made the obligatory visits to cemeteries in our two home towns, paying our respects to the relatives who had passed away since our last visits.

My German is virtually non-existent, and few of my Swiss relatives speak any French or English, so communication was via my mother and sister Thaïs.

All in all, it was a tranquil, unhurried visit. There's something soothing and reassuring about visiting the earth and houses of one's ancestors, trying to visualize them and imagining what they thought.

Inevitably, I found myself wondering what would have happened if my parents had elected to stay there and I had been born there.

The peculiar thing is that I get a sense of wholeness from it, but at the same time realize how different I, as a Canadian, am from them. We're the same, but at the same time, we're quite different.

The genes are the same, but the different environment and mentality has moulded a Montreal city boy rather than a peasant or small-town Swiss.

I'm happy it turned out the way it did. But my attachment to the land of my parents makes me feel I can enjoy the best of both worlds.

Nick, with his father, Severn, and brother Frank,
in front of the Sun Life Building.

A child's dashed hopes live on in recollections

[Monday, December 22, 1986]

AMONG MANY other things, Christmas is a time for memories.

It's one of those times of the year when invariably people look back and remember some Christmas past, recall an old family gathering or some circumstance.

Over the weekend, I had one of those flashbacks, when recollections of one Christmas about 30 or 35 years ago came rushing into my mind in such vivid detail it was like watching a movie in my head. We were at the Sun Youth Organization's annual food-basket collection and distribution event in its headquarters, the old Baron Byng High School building on St. Urbain Street.

Sid Stevens was showing us around, introducing people in the milling crowd of volunteers, clients and visitors. At one point, Stevens took me into an old classroom where they distribute children's Christmas gifts.

Several women and young girls were wrapping toys and other things and labelling them according to age and sex of would-be recipients.

Mothers walked in with a little form filled out for Boy, 6; or Girl, 9. And they'd walk out clutching gaily wrapped gifts.

Watching this scene, memories of my most painful Christmas came flashing into my mind.

On second thought, it wasn't really like a movie, because it came with all the pain and emotion I felt so many years ago. It was at a time when my family's fortunes were at one of their periodic low ebbs. We were broke, dead broke. And I was perhaps 10 or 11 years old.

It was a time, as I recall, when our family dinner usually consisted of a big stew, composed mostly of turnips, carrots and potatoes, with several marrow bones thrown in.

For long periods, marrow bones were the closest thing we got to meat. (To this day, I relish marrow, spread on bread with pepper and salt which, to my taste, is the greatest thing next to the nectar of the gods.)

At any rate, that year my mother informed me that Christmas had to be postponed for a while. She didn't explain, but I surmised it would have to wait until my father or someone managed to scrounge up a few dollars for whatever celebration we could muster.

I recall it was a couple of years after my older cousin Ottmar had callously told me there was no such thing as Santa Claus or Kris Kringle. That was an unhappy event, also.

But hope springs eternal and I kind of continued to believe, vaguely hoping Ottmar had made a mistake and there really was a Santa Claus.

We all went to midnight mass that Christmas. It was tradition in our family that we went to midnight mass and then came home and opened the presents.

Even though my mother had told me that part of Christmas—the gift-giving—was being postponed, I entertained great hopes that when we got home from mass, there'd still be a present or two in the house.

When we got home, I found a note from Santa Claus—written, I believe, in my brother's hand—saying that he couldn't make it for December 25, but that he'd try to be back for Little Christmas, which is what we called Epiphany, or January 6, the date the Three Wise Men visited the Christ child with gifts of gold, frankincense and myrrh.

That was it. Just a note.

I think it was the most bitter pill of my childhood. I remember sobbing and wailing. Surely it was the greatest disappointment any child could experience.

I guess I got over it after a while.

And at Little Christmas, Santa Claus did show up with a gift: a pair of cheese cutters, those funny little two-blade skates kids use to learn skating.

For some reason, I felt a strong aversion to those cheese cutters. In fact, I hated them. I suppose that's the reason I never did learn how to skate.

I don't know whether at that time organizations set up collections such as Sun Youth's and *The Gazette* Christmas Fund. Perhaps they did and my family felt too proud to avail themselves or whatever.

But thank heavens there are organizations that do these things today. It alleviates a bit of the pain for young kids who, because of the inescapable commercial activity around this time of year, must build up expectations— if only modest expectations.

A Christmas tradition passes to new hands

[Monday, December 29, 1986]

EVERY FAMILY has its own particular Christmas tradition.

In ours, Christmas meant turkey at my sister Terry's house in Pointe Claire. For maybe 30 years, we had all loaded up cars with packages and dogs and family members and made the trek out to join Terry, her husband, Jean-Paul, and their children. Jean-Paul would cook the turkey while the rest of us would get into heated arguments over politics and religion (being Catholic, we never discussed sex) or else we'd sit and catch up on what other family members had been up to since we had last seen them the previous Christmas.

You have to understand our family. We all have eccentricities, which is a polite way of saying many outsiders think we're a bit peculiar.

Terry is the oldest child in our family. (I'm the baby.) Most families have what they call a black sheep. But we always refer to Terry as the white sheep of the family.

I always loved those Christmases in Pointe Claire, because over the years they came to represent a point of solidity and family stability.

I guess that is why Christmas is such an important celebration for most families—because it centres on roots and tradition and thus offers a lot of meaning and comfort. But alas, Jean-Paul has retired and he and Terry have bought a second home in Florida where they now winter. No more Christmases in Pointe Claire.

And so, this year, it fell to me to prepare the Christmas turkey dinner. Like a lot of people, I had never cooked a turkey. At Christmas or Thanksgiving, someone else always did it.

How I was chosen to oversee the traditional dinner, I don't really know. But for the five days preceding the big family dinner, I received increasing numbers of phone calls and instructions from my mother—until on the final day it was averaging a call an hour.

"Did you get the potatoes? Are you sure the turkey is thawed properly? Do have enough chairs? What are you doing with the giblets? Make sure you get up in time to put the turkey in the oven." The last was good for at least five calls.

As per my mother's instructions, I went out and bought a 15-pounder and casually handled the task at hand while fielding all those calls.

The various members of the family and a couple of friends trickled in on Christmas Day, starting at noon. With my family, three members in one room is a lot of noise. Any more and it is cacophony. Throw in a couple of lunatic dogs and one cat and it is chaos.

My mother arrived with all sorts of sensible advice.

"You have to be practical," she said, "and use up all the heat energy."

She thinks if you have the oven on, it is a big waste to cook only one thing. So she handed me all sorts of stuff—stale bread to freshen up, extra containers of stuffing, a chuck roast, a slightly frozen cake and I don't know what else to fill the oven.

By the time she was through, the oven looked like one of those jam-packed refrigerators.

Anyhow, the whole thing turned out to be a huge success, if I do say so myself. The turkey was nothing short of perfect and that made up for the fact that the vegetables were all mushy. The whole thing is timing.

The dinner conversation was the usual eclectic shouting.

My mother told old stories about Swiss history. My sister Thaïs recounted how, after midnight mass and serving a reveillon for destitute people, she couldn't drive home in the freezing rain and how she took refuge for the night in a convent in Outremont.

My brother Frank told us details of his latest scheme to set up a gallium industry.

In the middle of dinner, my sister ordered all lights shut off, told everybody to shut up and played "Silent Night" in German on a ghetto-blaster she had brought along.

I was telling my nephews what a football star I was in high school. My sister told everyone how Frank lost his lower front teeth playing football for Royal Military College.

The dogs and cat begged for scraps.

My daughter asked whether other families' dinners were this noisy.

And when it was all over, I went out and joined Michael Sarrazin's family for dessert at the Assiette au Boeuf, a Polish-owned French restaurant with a Romanian gypsy orchestra that insists on playing Mexican music. In short, we had a very merry Christmas. Hope you did, too.

Lunch comes to a halt when my mother starts to yodel

[Wednesday, March 28, 1990]

THE RESTAURANT was still fairly crowded near the end of the lunch-hour rush Monday, when my mother appeared at the other end of the room, on her way back from "freshening up."

It was her 87th birthday, and she had insisted we take her to Better's, a sauerkraut, sausage and beer place on Stanley Street, because she read about the sauerkraut in a Bee MacGuire piece in *The Gazette*. She was walking slowly over toward us, cane in hand and a slight stoop in her now-shrinking form. Halfway across the room, she looked up at us and saw my daughter, my brother and me smiling.

Her face lit up, and she broke into a wonderfully bright smile that was framed by white hair and a sporty black beret.

Then she started yodelling. A high-pitched, hearty Swiss peasant yodel.

The other patrons stopped in mid fork-to-mouth, startled by the outburst. A waitress carrying a tray stopped in her tracks and stared.

My mother's yodel mixed in with her laughter.

I laughed with delight, while my daughter turned crimson to match her hair, victim of youth's embarrassment when attention is focused like that in public.

There she was, my 87-year-old mother, feeling happy and letting go in a spontaneous celebration of yodelling. She stood in the middle of the room, holding her arms high, the cane dangling incongruously, and she belted out.

As I looked at her smiling face, white hair and small stature, I remembered somebody trying to teach me as a kid to yodel by singing "little-old-lady" very fast.

It was perfect. Sheer joy.

My daughter is, of course, used to the eccentricities of the Auf der Maur half of the family.

Whenever we go on these family outings, I always sense the slight dread she feels that someone in my family—mother, sister or brother—

will do something that will make everybody stare at us. My brother choking to death at some joke, my mother breaking into a song celebrating some obscure Swiss military victory over Austrian tyrants, my sister delivering a very loud discourse on a visit to the Bronx in hope of seeing a promised apparition of the Virgin Mary.

No, we are not wallflowers.

Naturally, I get a kick out of these family get-togethers.

On Monday, we were actually celebrating my mother's, daughter's and my own birthday, all of which fall within a three-week span, my mother's being in the middle.

As my mother was yodelling, I looked at my daughter's face—blushing madly, but grinning broadly as she tried to hide her head under the table.

My mother is impervious to embarrassment. Is this a question of age?

Perhaps. After all, at a certain age you don't have to give two hoots about what anybody else thinks of you, and I suppose there's a sense of freedom and independence in that.

Younger people tend to be held hostage by their own minds, as they worry about their looks, their dress, their peers' attitudes, etc.

Youth, even the rebellious ones, tend to be pretty conventional, even when it comes to young punks dressing like all the other young punks or skinheads or whatever happens to be the convention this year.

I remember that as a kid, I was horrified if anybody took notice of me, if I did anything that would draw attention. I saw safety in anonymity, perhaps because I grew up in a time when cosmopolitan Europeans were frowned upon, when it seemed nobody wanted to have a funny name. And my parents spoke with accents.

I secretly wished my name was Brian O'Flaherty or something WASPish.

As a kid, you don't want to be different. You want to be accepted, be part of the gang, be like everybody else. That's what being cool is all about, I suppose.

That's why shortly after adolescence, I became a beatnik, said "Like man" all the time, tried to grow a beard, wore a black turtleneck and spouted poetry. Boy, was I cool and different, exactly like everybody I hung around with.

Anyhow, in that respect, my family isn't cool at all. My family's hot.

Quite mad, some would even say. So much so that we refer to my elder sister, the normal one, as "the white sheep of the family."

So as my 87-year-old mother stood there belting out the top 10 yodelling hits of Switzerland in celebration, I found it amusing to take my 18-year-old daughter by the elbow and say: "Hey! Loosen up. She's just having a good time."

It's a lot of fun when the old ladies manage to turn the tables.

(From left to right) the family dog, Ti-Loup, Nick's mother, Thaïs, Frank, Theresa (Terry), Nick's father, and Nick (centre).

Mama at 89: intimations of mortality, plus a sense of humour

[Wednesday, July 8, 1992]

IT'S AMAZING how, no matter how old we get, we always remain "Mama's boy." And she always manages to bring out the boy in us.

My mother is getting on in years, 89. Her hair is all white, she's shrinking, wears running shoes because of the arthritis and uses a cane to get by. Her hearing is failing, although she refuses to use the hearing aid the family got her because she claims she can't get the hang of the dials or adjustments or whatever.

Recently, she had a cataract operation on one eye but it didn't work and she can see only cloudy white out of it. She has to wear a black patch over the bad eye so she can see out the other one. She uses a magnifying glass to read, which she continues to do voraciously.

But I guess she is getting a sense of mortality because for the past several weeks she has been calling me to ask me to go to the bank with her to open a joint account. She wants to put a couple of thousand dollars in it so I can have it immediately when she dies.

The other day, I finally got around to it and went to pick her up at her house in Town of Mount Royal, where she lives with my brother and sister.

We walked slowly to the bank.

There they had a special line for old people, where they sort of play musical chairs until they get to the sit-down teller with a chair for the customer.

So we bumped along in these chairs until we got to the teller. My mother sat down, clutching her bankbook.

"And what can we do for you?" the teller asked pleasantly.

"My mother would like a wooden leg," I said.

"I beg your pardon," the teller said.

"A wooden peg leg," I said.

"What?" my mother said, craning her head so she could see me out of her unpatched eye.

"I'm sorry, I didn't get you," the teller said.

"And a parrot would be nice," I said. "A parrot for her left shoulder."

The teller seemed to have a hearing problem similar to my mother's, because, looking confused, she again said: "I beg your pardon, I didn't get you."

My mother, smiling, repeated: "What, what? What did you say?"

I leaned over and said loudly into her ear: "I told her you wanted a wooden peg leg and a parrot to go with your eye patch. Just like a pirate. Or banker, whatever."

My mother giggled.

The teller look alarmed. Customers in the regular lineup peered over. A bank official came over to ask what the problem was.

This conversation took less than a minute. When I ignored what I had said and went on to explain my mother's real business, there was a palpable sense of relief.

The teller and the bank official didn't say anything, but they seemed to think they must have misunderstood—although they eyed me leerily.

As we walked out of the bank, my mother nudged me and said: "That was funny."

The point is that at 89 my mother still has a keen sense of humour and delight. Which is why it will be years and years before I ever get to use that bank account.

The other day, I was recounting our bank adventure to my friend Peter Van Westrenen, who works for IATA (the International Air Transport Association), which means he's constantly travelling.

Last week, he popped into Rotterdam to see his mother for a brief visit on his way to a short meeting in Rome.

He had arrived at night and he sat up chatting with his 84-year-old mother, sipping geneva gin until early in the morning.

"She got kind of lubricated," Van Westrenen said, "so she told me: 'Don't get the wrong idea, I only do this when you visit'."

She retired to her room. Van Westrenen heard a loud crash and ran to investigate. At first, he couldn't get into the room because she was jammed against the door.

What had happened is that as his mother was getting into her flannel nightgown, she stepped on it from the inside, propelling herself into the door, her nose hitting the doorknob.

Her son picked her up and, ascertaining the damage was minimal, put her to bed. But her nose bled profusely and his suit, the only one he brought for the Rome meeting, was covered with blood.

The next morning his mother sported two black eyes and a slight hangover.

Van Westrenen rushed to the dry cleaners, telling the man it was an emergency and to do what he could to remove the fresh bloodstains. He had errands to do before catching a flight to Rome. His mother would be by in two hours to pick up the suit.

Then, realizing the cleaner would see his mother's black eyes and think he had beaten her up, he said: "The suit had better be ready on time because my mother has a bad temper. She's Mike Tyson's sparring partner."

Nick's Dad, Severn.

"Any day now" was my father's mantra

[Wednesday, May 7, 1997]

MY FATHER was a prospector and a mining promoter, a combination much in the news these days because of the Bre-X business.

He and my mother had come from Switzerland in 1929 because he was interested in geology and mining, and Canada was the place.

"The Alps are beautiful," he explained, "but there's nothing interesting there. Just granite."

They arrived a couple of months before the Wall Street crash and the start of the Depression.

"Swiss timing was not my forté," he'd confided to me years later.

And so through the Depression and into the '40s my family struggled, with my mother, I gather, mostly supporting the family through menial jobs.

My father spent much of his time slogging through the wilderness, up near Sault Ste. Marie, and then mainly in Charlevoix County, looking for the mother lode, just like those Bre-X guys.

My father had several mining companies, most notably Saguenay Mining and Smelting Co. (No Personal Liability, it said on the letterhead), and stake sites where I spent a fair amount of time during my youth.

The mining camp, which had a sawmill, a charcoal plant and other rudimentary facilities, looked for all the world like the crude mining camps I'd see in old photographs of the Yukon gold rush or in Western movies.

When I was a teenager, my father sent me out "diamond drilling," the exploration process used by Bre-X that we are becoming so familiar with.

I trudged through the blackfly-infested Quebec wilderness, seeing waterfalls that I imagined perhaps no other human had seen before, drilling core samples and packing them in wooden boxes, carrying everything in and out with one of my father's associates, Herbert Lulliwitz, a weird German who told me he was known as the Black Cossack on the Russian front.

But that was the thing about my father's "associates," they all seemed to be out of a Damon Runyon story, wonderful downtown characters who dreamed.

There was Frank Gagné, a Quebec City native who wore spats and always told me what a genius my father was.

I remember the excitement Mr. Gagné generated when he found Captain Kidd's treasure map and persuaded several investors to finance his expedition to dig up the treasure on an island off the Labrador coast.

My favorite was Alexander J. Roy, an opera-singing Western novel buff who looked just like Colonel Sanders. Much to my mother's chagrin, Mr. Roy was our boarder for a while, in addition to being "chief chemist" of my father's mining operations.

Once, he prepared a potion for Gros Bill, the old workhorse at the mining camp, to counteract what he diagnosed as a toothache. The potion knocked out Gros Bill, and when the horse woke up, it dashed into the lake and swam away. Took six days or so before it came back.

So when I was a kid, I grew up in a house full of rocks. Mineral samples from some previous Busang.

Through my high-school days we were poor, but my father assured me "any day now" the mining venture would pay off and we'd all be rich.

The problem was that J. Severn Auf der Maur's ore was "a very complex ore" and the "young, damn fool assayers couldn't understand it."

What was in it? As I understood it, it was a complex ore containing "rare metals" that included platinum, gold and silver, although on some days my father's associates would mention other stuff like feldspar or copper, or whatever seemed to be bigger in the Northern Miner that week.

The *Northern Miner* and the *New York Daily News* were my father's newspapers of preference.

The other big problem, as my father used to explain to me as we sat together in Toe Blake's tavern, was that "as everybody knows, the Quebec Mines Department is controlled by Masons."

Coming from central Europe as he did, he understood that the world's mineral wealth was controlled on the one hand by the British, with some tenuous connection to Zionist Communists, and on the other by American monopoly capitalists. But the central fact was that the whole conspiracy was administered worldwide by Protestant Masons, and what chance did a poor Swiss Catholic have?

This is the kind of stuff I listened to when I was a teenager in the

1950s and '60s, as my father would persuade my pals like Michael Sarrazin to sign papers renewing mining claims for him.

In reading about the Bre-X adventure in Indonesia, about their Filipino geologist de Guzman, the Dutchman Felderhof, I realized I met their equivalents years ago through my father.

Every now and again I get a phone call and someone asks: "Are you related to J.S. Auf der Maur? In 1955, I invested $4,000 in Saguenay Mining...."

And I remember sitting in Toe Blake's with my father and a man wearing a lumberjack shirt and big boots who was pleading and saying, "All I need is a grubstake."

And I remember thinking, I heard a line like that in a movie or read it in a comic book.

Then my father would say, "Maybe I can get you a grubstake."

The grubstakes were much smaller back then.

Nick (front) at the mining camp in Charlevoix county.

A fund-raising poster for Nick by Aislin.

Just a Pinch ...

Dr. Roger Tabah

I NEVER KNEW Nick Auf der Maur when he was healthy. Unlike most of his friends, I did not know Nick for a long time. I only knew him for the last year and a half of his life. During that time, I never was able to bring Nick really good news. Our dealings together were grim—but not always serious.

Even though I count myself among his friends, I shall always wonder why he never pinched my butt.

I am the cancer surgeon who was called by Nick's family doctor to see this man with a lump in his neck. The GP seemed worried about this patient and so I agreed to see him immediately. His doctor never got around to telling me his patient's name. I was surprised when the patient was none other than Nick Auf der Maur, the celebrated journalist, politician and one time revolutionary who now sported a Donald Duck tie. Everyone in Montreal knew who Nick was. One look at his tumour and I knew that there was a better than even chance that I was going to be a part of the last chapter of this man's life.

Nick never did care much for doctors and their poking and their needles and their X-rays. We made him squeamish. And because we made him squeamish he wanted as little to do with us as possible. He didn't want the details.

Often, as I droned on about tests and treatment, he would suddenly get up and pace as he did the night before his planned 10-hour surgery. This guy was a journalist. Wasn't he supposed to be asking a lot of deep probing questions? Instead, I reviewed the proposed operation with his family and friends.

I remember commenting that if this ever went to court, how was I to explain to the judge how I had obtained "informed" consent? Nick just wanted us to deal with the sordid mess so that he could get on with his business. He had a lifestyle to maintain and he did his best not to let a little cancer get in his way.

It didn't take me long to figure Nick out. Early on he established the ground rules. We were not to schedule any appointments before noon. Messages could be left for him with either Margo MacGillivray at Winnie's or Ziggy Eichenbaum at his pub.

He would quit smoking cold turkey but there was no way he would cut out the booze.

Okay, I thought. Once the radiation treatment got started, I reasoned, the resulting burning and ulceration in his mouth would force him away from the alcohol altogether. This was the first and last time I underestimated Nick.

To date, he's the only patient of mine who managed to keep on drinking throughout his radiation treatments. "How was this possible?" I asked. "Bailey's Irish Cream" was the reply. When he subsequently published his secret, he set medical care back about 10 years.

Someone once said that if Nick knew what was in store for him, he never would have opted for treatment. Bullshit!

Nick loved life and wanted to live. He had no regrets about his smoking and drinking but he knew that treatment was his only hope.

Nick exemplified the courage and dignity of the cancer patient. Throat cancer robs people of their ability to swallow, eat, breathe and communicate. The treatment is often disfiguring and debilitating and is offered without any guarantees for a cure. And yet most patients rise to the challenge because the alternative is a certain and miserable death.

Nick fought his disease with his own brand of humour and the grace, dignity and courage that we all have deep within. Even when things were grim, Nick would somehow lighten the mood with his wit and humour.

Because of his notoriety he was an inspiration to many who shared the hospital wards and cancer clinics. His example helped many others to successfully get through some awful times.

Nick led his life with the flair of an artist. Nick foresaw his death long before I. On the day before he died he thanked me for my help and promised that we would meet on the other side. Maybe then he'll pinch my butt.

Dr. Roger Tabah is a cancer specialist at the Montreal General Hospital.

FIGHTING CANCER

NICK AUF DER MAUR—1942—1998...

Confronting my mortality: On Christmas Eve,
I was told I have cancer

[Wednesday, January 15, 1997]

FOR ME, December was the cruelest month.

First, the roofers told me I had to get a new roof, about $4,500 worth.

Then two friends of mine got laid off from their jobs at different companies. Then, a week before Christmas, the new fiancé of an old friend left the bar where we were sitting—to clean up for a Christmas party—and went home to jump out of an 11th-floor window.

Then, on Christmas Eve, my doctors told me I have cancer.

I realize that, in the context of this column, these events look like odd bits of juxtaposition. But in the context of my life, which tends to go on one day at a time, they all seemed to fit in inexorably, as bad news followed bad.

Mind you, I don't really see how it would have made things much different if I had learned I had cancer after a long string of good news, like having won $10 million in a lottery, for instance. Probably, the cancer news would have depressed me just as much.

The funny thing is that, health-wise, I was feeling pretty chipper in December. Just a few weeks earlier, I had been given a clean bill of health from my new GP after my annual checkup.

Then, a week or so before Christmas, while in the shower, I felt a small lump in my neck, near the jawbone.

That was during a weekend, and uncharacteristically I called the doctor that Monday and asked for an appointment. Normally, I would have ignored the small swelling and waited weeks for it to go away before doing anything.

The doctor examined me late that Monday afternoon and immediately sent me to the Montreal General Hospital for a biopsy by Dr. Roger Tabah, one of the city's noted surgeons.

Both warned me it could be cancer, although there was a small chance it could be just a big infection of some sort. I preferred to believe the latter.

On that Wednesday, hospital doctors went on strike for the day and

Dr. Tabah called from the study session, asking me to meet him at his office after office hours for another biopsy.

On Christmas Eve, I met with him and Dr. Te Vuong, a radiation oncologist, for the verdict. It was a malignant tumour, squamous cell carcinoma, in the back of the left tonsil, near the larynx—well, to tell the truth, I can't quite remember all the details.

The major fact, that I had cancer, was enough for me to absorb, although I do remember asking myself why I was taking this so calmly, feeling not all that much more anxiety than if the doctor had told me I had to lose a tooth.

I supposed that my calmness was a normal reaction and that anxiety would come later. Oddly, I have yet to feel overcome by anxiety.

This, perhaps, has something to do with the strong level of support that I've received from friends and family, and my own attitude, which wavers from stoic fatalism to some inane confidence that this thing will pass without much ado.

I've been put through a variety of tests, including a CAT scan at 8 p.m. New Year's Eve, which somehow added to the surreal feelings I was having.

At the Christmas Eve meetings, the doctors outlined two options— surgery or radiation therapy.

Both had upsides and downsides, one being that surgery might lead to serious vocal disability. I didn't like the sound of that, so I followed their recommendation and chose radiation.

In a nutshell, they've told me what I have is treatable. The radiation therapy offers me a 50-50 chance of a cure.

It depends on the individual. They can't tell in advance how some tumours react to radiation, there being no test for that except the actual treatment. My tumour is about the size of an egg and must have started six months ago.

The therapy itself can be very debilitating. Some people manage it without too many side effects, while others have a hard time. Again, nobody can tell until the treatment starts.

The actual treatment will start in a few days.

Since I learned I have this cancer, friends have been calling up with news about others who have had it.

"Your buddy Freddy Langan at the CBC had the same thing," one would say. "He's completely recovered."

"Brett Butler of the Los Angeles Dodgers was diagnosed with the same thing at the beginning of last season," another would fax me. "He was back playing before the end of the season. Although he missed the last few weeks with a broken arm."

Another mentioned Solicitor-General Herb Gray, 65, who had cancer of the esophagus but is looking just fine after surgery last August. They say he didn't even miss a cabinet meeting.

So the anecdotal evidence collected by my friends is that everyone who has had this has fully recovered. Which leads me to worry that if I die, I will be the first person in history to die from it.

But seriously, the encouragement I've received has cheered me up as I'm forced to confront my own mortality. This I will think about in the coming weeks and perhaps share with you.

All in all, though, this is not the way I would have liked to start the new year. I'd have preferred a sprained ankle.

Kurt Cobain had a shotgun, and I had cigarettes

[Wednesday, January 29, 1997]

THE GIRL ON THE PHONE sounded sweet and sincere, expressing her sympathy.

Her mother had read two weeks ago in this column that I had cancer. The girl told me she had spoken to me once before, almost a year ago, when she called up to ask to speak to my daughter because she liked Melissa's band. The girl sounded as if she was perhaps 13 years old, and she presumed I remembered our last conversation. She sounded a bit nervous, so to be polite I pretended I remembered her. Frankly, I was really touched that she felt compelled to call me and express her sympathies.

We exchanged pleasantries for a minute or two, then she really threw me for a loop when she blurted out: "Do you think it has anything to do with Kurt Cobain's death?"

Well, I know people are into conspiracy theories again, and kids are into the X-Files, morbid things about death and stuff like that, but this was such a preposterous connection, so out of left field, that for once I felt at a loss for words.

Of course, I didn't want to insult her the way I would if an adult had asked me something similar, so I hemmed and hawed and stammered something about there being a world of difference between blue cheese and baseball.

And then, just as we were about to ring off our conversation something occurred to me.

"Yes, there is a connection, or at least something similar," I said.

"You see, Kurt had a smoking gun. I had smoking cigarettes."

And I told her, without being preachy, that I now realize my 30 years of smoking Gitanes were sort of suicidal.

"So why did you?" she asked.

That, of course, calls for a better answer than I am capable of at the moment, but it is a question that comes to mind fairly often these days.

One of the reasons I went public with my illness was that I thought it might help others in some small way, either a message about smoking or how to deal with cancer if you get it.

The smoking message I'm not sure of yet, because I keep trying to figure out some argument that would have been effective on somebody like me, who managed to ignore all the evidence and facts that are readily available.

Discouraging young people from smoking should be the top priority. Getting jaded old louts like me to stop smoking is another matter, one that sanctimonious, holier-than-thou evangelizing doesn't address. Au contraire, most often.

However, I do take some consolation in learning that, thanks to my (bad) example, at least two of my acquaintances are trying to give up smoking.

The other thing I think might be useful for readers is that getting cancer doesn't mean life is over.

It's been more than a month now since my throat cancer was diagnosed and 10 days since I started my twice-a-day radiation-therapy sessions. And frankly, I don't feel that bad at all, considering.

You must realize this isn't something unique, that you aren't singled out for some sort of woe-is-me treatment.

Every year, perhaps a couple of hundred thousand Canadians learn that they have cancer, and most of them survive for quite a time.

Feeling sorry for oneself or—just as bad—angry about it doesn't help in the slightest. In fact, it can only make things worse. I suppose I did consider getting mad at myself, but fortunately I'm so self-indulgent that I've already forgiven myself for what, I hope, is a permanently discarded smoking habit.

So I have managed a sense of equanimity about all this, and as a result physically I don't feel bad at all. Fatigued a bit, but even the side effects of radiation therapy haven't managed to bother me much. Mind, I'm only 10 days into a seven-week treatment.

Naturally, it helps when the medical team looking after you, like the one I have at the Montreal General, inspires a lot of confidence.

Maybe it's not as bad as it used to be only a few years ago, but in our society people seem to be afraid even of the word cancer, which is often whispered when somebody tells another person so-and-so has it.

Cancer isn't a gift or anything, but neither is any of the other diseases that afflict and disable us.

Ten days ago, a friend came in from Ontario to spend the weekend with me and cheer me up. He has full-blown AIDS and no chance. He's cheerful. So what can I be?

I look around the hospital and I see how many other people have things far worse than I have, and I realize that some of us are far too prone to whine and complain.

Something that has cheered me up immensely is the support and encouragement I've received from friends and strangers alike. In fact, sometimes I feel slightly embarrassed by the amount of attention from my friends and family, but that is something I think I can get over.

If you know someone, even just a little, who is facing some life-threatening battle, you have no idea how much a note, a prayer or even a joke can help out the spirit.

One last piece of advice: if you must have cancer and debilitating therapy, have it in January and February. Two great months to blow off.

Then comes spring, and all that it entails.

It's all a matter of taste: Right now, mine runs to roquefort and horseradish

[Sunday, June 8, 1997]

IT'S ODD what strikes people.

The most common query I get from people asking about my recent bout with cancer is about my taste buds.

One of the side effects of radiation therapy is that the taste buds are ruined.

All food ended up tasting bland, sort of like eating cardboard. So I began to appreciate different textures, and found, for example, my favourite was turnip.

It made for a completely different culinary appreciation.

Losing something you've always taken for granted gives you a new appreciation of many things. Fortunately, the taste-bud loss is only supposed to be temporary.

Like most people I suppose, I feel awkward when I meet somebody who's been sick and don't really know what to say. I don't want to pry or make the other person uncomfortable, so I usually mumble something.

Fortunately for others, I wrote about this taste-bud thing, so it gives everybody I meet a perfectly safe, even cheery opening gambit: "So how're the taste buds?"

Needless to say, I'm getting tired of answering that question, so here is my full report.

I couldn't taste a damn thing for months.

And then about two months ago, I was sitting in Else's, a little neighbourhood bar at the corner of de Bullion and Roy where I always go to read the Sunday papers, when Else sent me a shot of medicinal aquavit.

Else is Norwegian and aquavit is the national drink. Basically it is vodka flavoured with caraway seed. An amazing thing happened when I tossed back my shot of aquavit. I tasted the caraway.

It was the first distinct taste I had of anything since I lost my taste buds.

Naturally, I had another shot. This may explain why I go to Else's every

Sunday.

I thought that that caraway would be the precursor of a gradual return of all taste. But it was not so.

All foods remained more or less tasteless and bland.

And then a couple of weeks later, I had roast beef at Winnie's and in one mouthful I got a powerful sense of horseradish. I slathered more horseradish on the next bite, and yes the distinct taste of horseradish came through. I felt triumphant.

After that, I wasn't sure whether the taste buds were working or if the brain was remembering what certain things taste like. In any case, there was nothing to compare with the sensation of caraway or horseradish.

And then in Los Angeles recently, I ordered a cheese plate for breakfast, and bingo—I got a major taste of roquefort, that wonderful blue French cheese.

Again, I thought that this would presage a rapid return of my taste.

I have a growing sense of different things, but still, I'm not too sure.

The way it stands now, if I want to have an epicurean delight, I'd have to bring my own roquefort and horseradish and go to Else's for a shot of aquavit.

Otherwise, it looks like I'm going to get my taste buds back one taste at a time.

I was Auf der wall: Hallucinations followed surgery and I never got to Disney World

[Sunday, October 19, 1997]

WELL, HERE I AM back "live," or at least "semi-live," as opposed to column re-runs, as it has been for the past two months.

When we were interrupted, I was going into hospital for major surgery for throat cancer.

Originally, we thought radiation treatment last winter and spring had eliminated it, but the squamous cell carcinoma recurred this summer. So I checked into the Montreal General Hospital for an operation, performed by Dr. Roger Tabah, that was to last about 14 hours.

The operation was apparently successful, but it has taken a physical and mental toll.

For one thing, there were the hallucinations.

I'm not sure when I woke following the operation, perhaps a day later. But when I awoke, I rapidly became quite agitated, convinced the hospital authorities were conniving against me.

I couldn't talk, but when I had my first visitor I scribbled on a piece of paper: "They're trying to cheat me out of my trip to Disney World."

I was convinced when I was wheeled out of the operating room that a TV camera was there, and I said: "I'm going to Disney World."

Now, here I was in the intensive-care unit, with tubes coming out of my nose and arms, and the trip to Florida wasn't forthcoming.

In my mind, I was supposed to be on a plane to Florida.

Well, the trauma and, I suppose the drugs, made the first couple of weeks of my hospital stay rather bizarre.

For one thing, I suffered sleep deprivation, never managing much more than a couple of hours a night, despite drugs.

That's when I learned the truth of Einstein's theory of relativity and that time is not constant. The sleepless hours between midnight and 6 a.m. in a hospital ward are excruciatingly slow, and take much, much longer to get through than the hours between noon and 6 p.m.

Then I developed bronchial pneumonia and anemia, my sinuses went kaplooey and who knows what else.

In the middle of the night, I'd get these delusions and get out of bed, ripping the tubes out of my nose in the process.

One night, I was convinced I was in the storage room of a cantina in Guatemala. I crept close to the wall to hear what they were saying in the cantina.

In reality, I suppose I was listening in on the nurses' and orderlies' station. I was puzzled by the strangeness of their Spanish.

Another night in the ICU, I got out of bed in the middle of the night convinced I was in the bowels of a ship docked on the Danube at Bratislava, Slovakia.

The ship was supposed to be a floating movie studio, but that wasn't true; the people running it had some nefarious scheme. So I surreptitiously wandered about the hospital-ship to investigate. Literally, I sneaked about looking into rooms and broom closets, getting massively confused.

I remember looking out the eighth-floor window, and wondering how they managed to disguise the Danube waters to make them look like a parking lot.

Every morning, the doctors and residents would troop into the ICU or my room (I got bounced back and forth) and they'd be confronted by these tubes they'd have to reinsert, while I made feeble written explanations about the situation in Guatemala or Slovakia.

I particularly hated the process of inserting the tube up the nose— "You've got more tubes than London," a visitor remarked. But every night I kept ripping them out.

Reality finally set in when I was confronted by a Czech soldier made out of those chocolate medallions that look like gold coins.

I don't know what this full-size Czech chocolate soldier was trying to do, but even in my feverish state it dawned on me that this was absurd and didn't really exist. (Had it been a Swiss chocolate soldier, maybe I might have accepted it, who knows.)

Closing my eyes and dismissing the Czech phantom seemed to bring an end to my nightly demons and ushered in something akin to normalcy, although every now and then a psychiatrist would show up and ask me if I knew what year it was and where I was.

Well, now I can laugh at it, of course. But even back then, I think that in the back of my mind there was a mischievousness that told me that some day I'd laugh about my predicament.

And then, just the day before yesterday, I happened to be leafing through the September issue of *Harper's* magazine and I saw this piece by Saul Bellow, the author and Nobel laureate for literature.

In it, Bellow recounts his own hallucinations, quite different from mine, while in an intensive-care unit.

"I know only that the oddity of my hallucinatory surroundings was in a way liberating," he wrote. "And I wonder sometimes whether at the threshold of death I may not have been entertaining myself lightheartedly, positively enjoying these preposterous delusions—fictions that did not have to be invented."

I don't know whether that's exactly the way I'd put it.

For one thing, I never felt on the threshold of anything. But it does resonate.

So now, tired of feeling like an invalid, and while my convalescence continues, it's good to be back in the column business.

Heartfelt thanks to all of you who sent messages or prayers and to whom I haven't been able to respond. Merci sincerely.

Discovery of brain tumour latest trial in a tough year, but I'm tough, too

[Sunday, December 28, 1997]

A YEAR AGO, on Christmas Eve, my doctor informed me I had throat cancer.

A few days ago, just before Christmas, my doctor told me I have a brain tumour.

Jeez, the thought formed in my mind, what do I get next year? Leprosy?

Yes, 1997 was a bad year for me, bad to the extent that just as I thought I had this cancer thing beat, along comes a brain tumour.

That's the bad news.

The good news is that tomorrow I go into the hospital for something called "radio surgery" or "radiation surgery"—my memory is a bit confused—that promises to fix the problem in one shot. So maybe 1997 can be redeemed after all.

My latest problem manifested itself a little over two weeks ago, when I woke up and found there was something wrong with my vision.

At first, I thought I simply couldn't wipe the sleep out of my eyes. But after a couple of days, I realized I had double-vision.

It didn't strike me as a huge problem, because I could see quite well if I closed my left eye. But if I went out on the downtown streets at night, there would be far too many lights, with everything looking like a crazy kaleidoscope. I couldn't distinguish if cars were coming or going.

So I tell my surgeon, Roger Tabah, who sends me to see ophthalmologist Robert Lewendowski—who I went to school with, as it turns out. He in turn sends me to a neuro-ophthalmologist, who conducts a CT scan that reveals a small tumour. Two centimetres at its widest, it is located behind my sinuses and bridge of my nose at the base of my brain—right in the middle of my head.

Now I'm no brain surgeon, but I can figure out that this tumour is in a delicate spot, rather inaccessible to any physical probing.

Tabah tells me it is "rather unusual," and that he's never come across one in that location.

So enter Luis Souhami, a radiologist at the Montreal General Hospital who is, I'm informed, a "world leader" in the highly sophisticated field of radio surgery.

Put in layman's terms, which are the only ones I can sit still for, tomorrow they are going to outfit me with some kind of space helmet. There are needles involved and my head is frozen. And then with the help of magnetic resonators and 3-D graphic computers, they line up an extremely high dose of radiation. In a flash, they nuke the tumour and blow it up.

Souhami tells me its a one-shot operation with no side-effects, and that I should be out of the hospital by 5:30 p.m.

"In time for happy hour?" I asked him.

He looked a little dubious, then said: "Oh yeah. Sure. I suppose."

"Doctor's orders," I'll be able to tell the barmaid afterward. "I just had brain surgery, so make it a double."

Just joking, of course. But you suspect, nonetheless. Naturally, I don't really mean to be flippant about a brain tumour. It is grave.

But I don't intend to allow it to get me down—just as I stood up to the bad news of last year, the throat cancer and lengthy radiation treatment. Then there was the recurrence of the cancer, followed by radical surgery, from which I have now recovered.

Last year, I wrote about the cancer forcing me to confront my own mortality. In these circumstances, you are left no option.

But that doesn't mean sitting around feeling miserable and sorry for yourself.

Sure, I go through a lot of introspection. When I lie down for a nap or for the night, waiting for sleep to claim me, thoughts race through my head. I sometimes sense the damp, humid presence of death.

But my morale is such that I am not intimidated.

This is partly because I've had an exceptionally good time in my life, did just about everything I wanted. I don't in any way feel cheated.

And in my lonely thoughts in the dark, I realize that despite a lifetime of private, critical self-assessment, I've not been too selfish. Life has not been a self-centred odyssey. I know some might contest that, but it doesn't matter, because it's how I feel that counts.

And so, following this logic, to give in to morbidity, to constantly fret about my health, to let worry consume me, would be an awful act of self-centredness.

The two people most important to me in my life are my 94-year-old mother and my 25-year-old daughter. The incredibly strong sense of connection—I might not see them all the time, but their presence is always in my feelings—and the reciprocal love we have, sustain me.

To give in to despair would be to let them down.

Yes, it has been a tough year. But, as trite as it sounds, I'm tough, too. I will to live and to continue laughing.

Brainstorming: How top-notch team attacked my tumour

[Wednesday, December 31, 1997]

ON MONDAY MORNING, the commotion downstairs brought me fully awake.

My head was throbbing (brain tumours tend to cause headaches) as I heard my sister, Thaïs, lining up my daughter, Melissa, and my cleaning lady, Winsome Shaw, to pose for photos. As we left down the front stairs, Thaïs was shouting at Melissa and Winsome, telling them where to stand for more photos. As I got into Thaïs's van, my mother was praying loudly in Swiss German. And so we set off for the Montreal General Hospital and my brain surgery.

First thing, Dr. Luis Souhami, a McGill professor and associate director of the radiology department at the General, took me into a room to fit my head with a sturdy frame.

The frame was needed to hold my head rigid and attach a box to it, so they could scan my brain with millimetre precision.

Trouble is, they have to bolt the thing to my head. Needles I hate, but if I have to have them, I prefer a fleshy part of the body, like my bum. Not in the skull, where there is mostly bone.

I managed to survive Dr. Souhami's freezing of the four corners of my head without fainting. Then he affixed the frame, screwing the bolts into my head, the noise of the turning bolts making me writhe.

Melissa accompanied me to the magnetic resonance imaging machine, where the patient is slipped into a long tube that whirs and conks as detailed mapping is done of the internal head workings (brain included).

"This is so high-tech," Melissa said. "What did they do before?"

"They died," I answered.

The MRI took about a half-hour, after which Dr. Souhami said he and his group of experts, including physicists, would have to work for four or five hours on computers to calibrate their proton- and/or photon-beam machine for what is called stereotactic radiosurgery, the refined technique of which was developed at McGill.

So we had a few hours to kill. Melissa and I giggled at how ludicrous the aluminum frame looked on me.

"It looks like a medieval torture device," she suggested.

I tried putting my hat on. It looked even more ludicrous.

So, not being able to resist a laugh, I suggested we head to Winnie's for lunch. (For me it was turkey soup put through a blender.)

At first at Winnie's, the weird headgear was greeted with silence, people knowing I was due for brain-tumour treatment that day.

But soon they lightened up: "Look, a tête carrée!" or "Excuse me, we've had complaints you are interfering with the TV reception."

"How could you sit here enjoying soup and a beer while radiologists and doctors and physicists are slaving away preparing your treatment right through lunch hour?" Irwin Steinberg asked me.

"Yeah," I replied, "but I'm the brain of the operation."

Ziggy Eichenbaum drove me back to the hospital, where we met Brian McKenna.

We were informed that the irregular shape of my brain tumour was prolonging the calculations. I promised them that next time I'd produce a perfectly round one.

So we sat and waited.

Soon, the waiting room was vacant and the department shut down.

Dr. Souhami then took us into the computer room where they were working. We were astounded.

The technology, with 3-D computer graphics showing my tumour cut into millimetre slices from every possible angle, was naturally impressive.

But it was the people there who impressed us most.

There were three physicists—Spanish-born Conrado Pia, Portuguese-born Horatio Patrocino, and Ervin Podgorsak.

Dr. Souhami is Brazilian-born (as is his wife, who showed up to pick him up after work and ended up waiting for 3½ hours while I went through the procedure). His associate in radiology was Mitchell Liu, Vietnamese-born, I think, making it a wonderfully perfect Montreal medical team.

It turns out that when this form of stereotactic radiosurgery was developed at McGill, Pia and Podgorsak played major roles.

Pia came from Spain to work in Saskatchewan as a nuclear engineer, then worked for a time as a systems analyst at Canadian National before coming to McGill, where in the last 10 years he married his talents in nuclear sciences and computers, working with clinical medical specialists, and spent 17,000 hours developing the computer-generated surgery I was to receive.

The bulk of the computer work was done on his own time.

The McGill team is a pioneer in this technique, which has spread to other medical centres. I was shown a list of 68 medical papers produced by the team.

And they were all working overtime, after having spent their whole lunch hour on the problem, and into the night with no overtime pay.

The Regie de l'Assurance Maladie doesn't recognize the treatment, which has a high success rate.

So Dr. Souhami, for example, got paid $150 for his efforts on my behalf.

Most of this information we had to pry out of them because, after all, they were preoccupied with doing their jobs and we were pestering them.

Finally I was strapped onto a platform gurney, which could be manipulated by computer in all directions, under a huge radiation-beam machine that could also move back and forth and turn 360 degrees. They don't have anything like this at La Ronde, I thought.

When I was bolted in, and as the team left the room, Dr. Souhami placed a small Canadian flag in my hand.

"We'll be watching you from TV screens," he explained.

"If you experience any difficulty, have trouble swallowing or anything, wave the flag and we'll come running."

The whole procedure took two long hours.

There were seven people in the control room, all highly trained specialists from around the world.

And they were working long hours, using their skills to save my life while I clutched the Canadian flag they gave me.

And next week they will save somebody else's life, perhaps a truck-driver or an insurance executive or a welfare mother.

This procedure is obviously expensive, and not only in terms of equipment. It is also manpower-intensive. I mean, three physicists for a whole day, to say nothing of regular hospital staff?

In the United States, they would share a $30,000 fee for this operation.

These are dedicated people, whose talent measures up to the best in the world.

Lying there in the operating room, while my head throbbed in the vise grip of that frame, I thought about how those people could put so much time, energy and imagination into helping somebody who is, after all, a stranger.

I felt immensely grateful and proud of my city and its talented people.

I thought of other things, too, of course, like how dry my mouth was.

After we all said goodbye, I went to Ziggy's bar for a late happy hour.

And Ziggy went around the corner and got me the Ben & Jerry's milkshake I had been dreaming of. I went to bed with a mammoth headache, but feeling elated nonetheless.

In six weeks, we'll know whether it was totally successful.

Celebrating the birthday of Ziggy Eichenbaum (left)
at Ziggy's Pub, April 24, 1997.

From the friends I've never met

OVER THE PAST YEAR, I've received many hundreds of letters and messages of good will.

These notes, cards and letters have had a salutary effect on my spirits, and make it easier for me to carry on my efforts to fight off my cancers. One thing they have done, though, is make me feel rather guilty for not having answered them personally. Not that I ever was terribly good with correspondence, but lassitude has been one of the major effects of the therapy-illness-treatment-recovery cycle I go through. My apologies for not answering, but my thanks for your kind words.

I sit there in my living room or office and stare at the piles of letters scattered around the house, picking one up at random and rereading it for energy.

Here's a sampler:

Dear Mr. A:

I have always enjoyed reading your column, but the most recent ones on your illness and brain tumour I followed with interest because my husband has been operated on three times for a brain tumour that "just won't go away."

He has been left paralyzed. I just want to mention that there are a lot of good and kind people in the world, and one should not look at the few bad apples.

The last few weeks, we have gone shopping for Christmas and Hanukkah presents, and I've encountered so many people willing to open and hold doors, lend a hand and even accompany my husband to the public washrooms, where, of course, I could not enter. When we thanked these strangers, they always smiled and wished us a good day and a good holiday.

These are the simple things in life that, I must admit, we always took for granted. How can I express our thanks? Maybe by drawing people's attention to how much it means to us. Thank you all you good Samaritans.

Keep giving people encouragement, Mr. A.

B.K.

* * *

Dear Mr. A:

This morning (in November) I rushed to my mother's room because she was shrieking and yelling. I thought she was having a fit, because she had just recently arrived home to recuperate from serious surgery.

But to my surprise, she was laughing and crying at the same time, while pointing to your column about the hallucinations you had when you went in for surgery.

My mother suffered similar hallucinations, but never told anybody, fearing they would think she was crazy. She kept it a bottled-up secret.

Now, she was laughing and crying, saying, "I'm not crazy after all. Or least least only as crazy as Nick."

You have no idea how much that helped her. She thought she was all alone.

J.D.T.

* * *

Dear Mr. A:

Two years ago, I had a quadruple-bypass heart surgery at the Royal Vic. Everything you are describing in your column could have been written by me, if I could express myself. I never talked to anyone about it, because I was sure nobody would believe me, and most likely they'd think I was crazy. My daughter was called by the hospital twice at 4 a.m. because I was raving and trying to tear off bandages and tubes. Anyone near me with a needle was coming to kill me; everything I touched burst into flames. I was afraid I had a scar on my mental faculties.

I want to thank you from all my heart, for writing about things that matter to the everyday living of people like me.

Suddenly, I feel relieved if I know that people like you or Mr. Saul Bellow had the same terrifying experiences and let us know about it.

I am not the only one.

G.T. and family

* * *

Dear Mr. A:

Your forthright discussions of your illness and treatments are heartening to those of us who are also undergoing rigorous and often horrible treatment of life-threatening illnesses. In my case, it's breast cancer. Like you, I have tried to use humour and openness to mitigate the unpleasant (to put it mildly) side effects and results of chemo and surgery. Currently both lopsided and bald, I share your faith in contemporary medicine and look to the future with hope.

F.H.

Old Tappan, N.J.

* * *

Dear Mr. A:

Last spring, I was diagnosed with cancer. I'm sure normally I would have been devastated and gone into a tailspin.

But I had been reading your column, and how you'd had the courage to take it on up front. I followed your example. Now my doctors think I'm in full remission and recovery. Thanks for the example.

A.S.

Ville d'Anjou

* * *

Dear Mr. A:

I have long admired your spirit and integrity and always enjoy your articles. Your generosity of spirit and your courage have made you a friend, even though we have not met. You are part of my mental landscape, one of the people I care about. As one of your unknown friends, I wish you well in this new year, and hope to read your essays for many more years.

M.E.K.
Kirkland

* * *

Dear Readers:

I can't thank you enough for the sympathy, encouragement and, dare I say, love that I have felt from the community at large. Merci, mille fois merci.

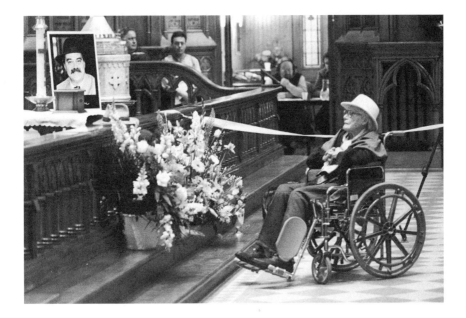

Saint Patrick's Basilica, April 13, 1998

I would like to gratefully compare this collection of my son Nick's columns to a bouquet of herbs and flowers whose petals reflect the glory of hope and divine love that was present in Saint Patrick's Basilica on Easter Monday.

It has been said that our souls turn into stars absorbing the eternal light of God in different degrees.

Theresia Auf der Maur-Schaelin

Afterword

Melissa Auf der Maur's Eulogy
for Her Father

[Saint Patrick's Basilica, April 13, 1998]

This is the eulogy I gave for Nick at his funeral. I can't think of a better way to express my feelings in print. Thank you all for helping the Nick Fund.

BONJOUR, Thank you for being here today, Merci d'être avec nous aujourd'hui. Nous sommes ici pour Nick. Nick was the son of a special woman, my grandmother, who's here with us today. She was always proud when she felt that Nick was helping other people, and Nick did that here in Montreal.

He was a passionate Montrealer, a Swiss, a Canadian, a great friend to so many—an entertainer, a writer, a bum pincher, a politician, a brother, a celebrator, a peace disturber, a ranter, an explorer, a private man, a downtowner, an initiator. He loved to argue and enlighten people, he was a believer, a fighter, a proud person, a teacher, a historian, a little boy, a young man, a dying man, and such an enthusiastic and loving father. He loved me and I love him. He was so brave and I am so lucky to be his daughter and to have been with him until the end.

He was someone who inspired people to go that extra mile for things he believed in, for this city, and for him—and we all rose to the occasion in this last year of his life. I'd like to thank those people beyond his family, who were there for him at all times in the difficult months leading up to his death.

Thank you Michelle and Catherine Sarrazin, Ziggy Eichenbaum, Stephen Phizicky and Brian McKenna, Dr. Roger Tabah and the staff at the

Montreal General.

Thanks to all of the Montrealers who sent him all those letters, good wishes and prayers, it cheered him up enormously.

Thank you for all being here today to celebrate my father's life, and most of all I want to thank my father for his irreplaceable love and inspiration. He's no longer with me here, but when I told him I was scared of missing him he told me he'd be around.... I feel it and I believe him.

Merci à tout le monde, Adieu, Nick, and I love you.

(London, 1983)